0500

Letters from a
WW II Combat Infantryman

0500

Letters from a
WW II Combat Infantryman

Editor: Keith Gilbertson

VERDI GILBERTSON

authorHOUSE®

AuthorHouse™
1663 Liberty Drive
Bloomington, IN 47403
www.authorhouse.com
Phone: 1 (800) 839-8640

Published by AuthorHouse 11/06/2015

ISBN: 978-1-5049-5932-2 (sc)
ISBN: 978-1-5049-5930-8 (hc)
ISBN: 978-1-5049-5931-5 (e)

Library of Congress Control Number: 2015918195

Print information available on the last page.

CONTENTS

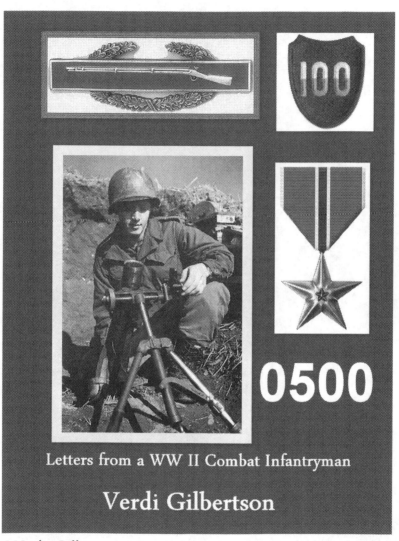

Letters from a WW II Combat Infantryman

Verdi Gilbertson

PFC Verdie Gilbertson posing with his mortar in France March 14th, 1944
Combat Infantry Badge earned in France January, 1944.
Bronze Star earned for meritorious service in ground combat
in France and Germany
100th Infantry Division insignia

DEDICATION

To my family at home who wrote me many letters, always prayed for me and read my letters when I was so far away from home. This is how my parents often signed their letters to me.

May God Bless and Keep his Protecting Hand over you and bring you safely home soon.

Dad

Our prayers are and we know yours are too that God keeps his protecting hand over you and brings you safely across and coming back home again.

Love, Mother

"I was so awfully glad to get your letter this morning. Mail is more important than food I think. *"From a letter I sent November 20, 1944*

To my Fox Company infantry buddies who served with me and helped me make it through many difficult days while we were together in combat.

ACKNOWLEDGEMENTS

Two primary book sources were used for photos and details of battlefield movements included in this book. While I own these books I am also very grateful to the George G Marshall Foundation which archives World War II materials and makes them available on their webpage to the public and researchers. www.marshallfoundation.org/

From the George G Marshall Foundation web page "What We Do"

"The non-profit, nonpartisan, independent Marshall Foundation is the one place where the values that shaped and motivated Marshall are kept alive. As a unique resource, the Foundation perpetuates Marshall's legacy as the person who "won the war and won the peace," his leadership qualities and exemplary character through educational programs and facilities such as a world-class archives, a research library and a museum that offer a wide range of resources and materials for use by members, the general public, amateur historians, scholars and students of all ages."

Photos from "The Story of the Century"
Photographs
100th DIVISION PRO U. S. SIGNAL CORPS
COPYRIGHT 1946 BY THE CENTURY
ASSOCIATION 100TH INFANTRY DIVISION
"The membership of the 100th Infantry Division Association regretfully approved the dissolution of the Association, to be effective on December 31, 2012."

Cover and inside cover of "The Story of the Century"
which I bought when I returned home in 1946

Photos from: *The 399th in Action, With the 100th Division*

Inside cover of 399th *in Action*
"Photo credits largely to 163rd Signal Photo Company. Artwork
and Planning by Willi Yogt, Stuttgart Printed by Stuttgarter
Yereinsbuchdruckerei Ltd., Stuttgart, Germany, 1945"

Thanks to my sister Clarice for taking many family photos of
the Gilbertson brothers in uniform. Thanks to my buddies who took

photos after the war when I traveled to Paris and London. Thanks to my platoon members who took photos with me posing with buddies. Thanks to my mom and dad for saving all my letters and photos I sent home. Thanks to my family for always being interested to hear my stories. Thanks to the readers of our first two books, *Verdi* and *Gilbertson: An American Family Adventure.*

Thanks to my son Keith for reading all my letters, listening to my stories and compiling this book. We hope you enjoy it and learn from it.

To view more photos, maps and Bill Mauldin cartoons visit www.0500vg.blogspot.com

A Very Rare Opportunity

From the editor

As my dad and I were compiling this book we often said to each other something like this, "You and I taking part in a very rare opportunity together." Here we were seventy years after World War II ended and were talking about it and writing about it. The man telling the stories was a combat infantryman on the front lines who fought the Germans for over 175 days in France and Germany. At the end of the war in May 1945 only 30 out of 184 men in Fox Company who left the states with him and landed in Marseilles, France in October 1944 were still around to talk about it. In 2015 Verdi is one of an increasingly small group of soldiers who are still alive and well.

We added up just what all it took to put this book together and realized it needed several very rare ingredients. First we needed these 60 letters that were sent from the front lines in Germany and France after being written in foxholes, civilians' homes and abandoned buildings. Next they had to be lovingly saved by his parent's. They needed to be stored carefully so they could rediscovered in the attic of Verdie's home place in 2014. Next we needed Verdi who was WW II combat infantry man with a prodigious memory for details to talk about the war and the letters. At age 92 he is willing to enthusiastically share his "war stories," some of which are difficult for any combat infantryman to tell even 70 years after they occurred.

Next we needed a son who is interested in every story his dad tells and also had the talents to ask questions, listen and record Verdi's recollections. Then he needed to type his dad's memories into a manuscript. Then this son needed to have the experience to organize it all together with words and photos that were ready to publish in a book?

Very few World War II veterans have been willing to tell war stories and only a precious few who are still alive have the detailed memories of Verdi. Many of the stories he has told over the years are backed up by the letters he sent home so many years ago. Yes, this collection of letters is very rare some 70 years after the end of World War. We are so thankful that as father and son we are sharing them with those that interested in this story of Verdi Gilbertson, a World War II combat infantry man.

While working on this book I've heard people say to me many times, "My dad never talked about the war". Thanks Dad for telling many humorous stories about it but also sharing several that make us all understand with certainty that war is always something to be thought about carefully and avoided.

Why the Gilbertson boys all served their country in the military

Roy and Earl joined up soon after Pearl Harbor. The oldest son Roy wrote telling home Verdie to "stay out of it." The next brother Earl thought Verdie should get a farm deferment. Verdie wrote to his younger brother on Jan 20, 1945. "Whatever you do Curtis, don't get into anything military. A uniform may look good now, but there is no glory in it." The younger brothers did not take their older brother's advice.

What was it that made all four Gilbertson boys put on military uniforms and serve? Was it patriotism? Was it a sense of adventure? Was it the feeling of doing the right thing? When we ask Verdie, he leans more towards the third choice but acknowledges the other two played a part in the decision process. At the time, brothers, relatives, friends, neighbors and classmates were all serving their country in the military. Verdie says he felt like the right thing to do was to join them all and be a part of the war effort.

INTRODUCTION

Many times I've thought of writing a book about my time in World War II with the United States Army fighting the Germans. The title, "0500," seems just right because that was always the time that we were getting something started. (*Military time is written as 0500 meaning 5 am*). We it said aloud as "O, five hundred." In this book we have included all of the complete letters I sent home from November 1944 to December 1945. Some of the war stories from our first two books are included and in addition we have added several more stories that these letters have helped me to recall. In order to give readers a chronological history of where our unit was located, reports from several 100th Division historical sources have been inserted between these letters.

All of the letters written from the front lines while fighting in France and Germany in the long months from November1944 to May 1945 were saved by my parents and stored in their attic. It was almost seventy years later when I had the chance to read them again. It was very surprising to me that my letters still existed. Reading the letters brought to mind many more memories and details of my nights and days serving with Fox Company, 2nd Battalion, 399th Regiment, of the 100th Division.

CHAPTER ONE

Dreaded words… "Jumping off at 0500 tomorrow".

Word came up that F Company was going on reserve for the next three days. Oh, that was great news to hear. We were moved back a few miles and given good food with hot chow and everybody was happy. We hadn't been there too long when here came a runner with a message. Our platoon leader Lt. Nicholson was sitting right there with us. The message was, "Platoon leaders meeting." Oh no, we knew what that meant.

Bam, it got quiet. We waited and pretty soon Lt. Nicholson came back and said, "All right you guys, every one of you write home. We are jumping off at 0500 tomorrow." These were the most dreaded words in the infantry, "Jumping off." That meant we had an objective of attacking a German position. There wasn't much sleep that night. Everybody was thinking about what might be happening in the early morning

For some members of the platoon this may be their last letter. We had the highest casualty rate when we attacked a German position. What do you write home in case this happens to be your last letter? You can imagine that everyone was thinking the same thing. It was kind of hard to know what to write in the letter.

What I'm going to do is write a normal letter, a fairly positive letter. You didn't want to imply that this could be the last letter. You wouldn't say that. No matter what, you wouldn't say that. Maybe I'll write the same as I always write and keep it as positive as possible. I was thinking about when my family got this letter. You can imagine… What did they expect to read?

Report at 0500

When we cleared a German village and the Germans had pulled back, the Captain said, "Find yourself a place to sleep and report at 0500." He usually gave us an incentive saying, "If you clear the village you can sleep inside tonight." The Krauts probably wanted to stay in the same places we did but many times we had a "meeting" together and convinced them to leave.

Still shake my head

We scattered and found a good place to sleep. This town in France had been cleared and we were going to be there the rest of the night. It was pouring rain. Sometimes the villages had been evacuated but this time there was a Frenchman who said, "You come in and stay with us." We ate supper by the table with the man and wife and we slept in the house until five the next morning. I still shake my head when hearing 0500…. O five hundred.

Military = Civilian	Military = Civilian
0001 = 12:01 am	1300 = 1:00 pm
0100 = 1:00 am	1400 = 2:00 pm
0200 = 2:00 am	1500 = 3:00 pm
0300 = 3:00 am	1600 = 4:00 pm
0400 = 4:00 am	1700 = 5:00 pm
0500 = 5:00 am	1800 = 6:00 pm
0600 = 6:00 am	1900 = 7:00 pm
0700 = 7:00 am	2000 = 8:00 pm
0800 = 8:00 am	2100 = 9:00 pm
0900 = 9:00 am	2200 = 10:00 pm
1000 = 10:00 am	2300 = 11:00 pm
1100 = 11:00 am	2400 = 12 Midnight
1200 = Noon	

Military Time Chart

At home just before the war

In the spring of 1938 I graduated from District Fifty Four. Mary Ann Goulson, Verdie Ellingson, and Verdie Gilbertson were the top three achievers in our class all the way from the first through eighth grades. In the fall of 1938 I went to Morris, Minnesota for an agricultural program and we had other high school classes in Math and Science. After a few months I changed my mind and went back home to go to Milan High School. Now I was back with my whole country school class from district Fifty Four.

It was quite a change as we joined with kids from all the other country schools. We had a huge ninth grade class of thirty students. From there on all the way up to my graduation in 1942, I rode the bus for about an hour each morning to Milan High School. We got on the bus at seven in the morning and got home about five thirty in the afternoon.

Sometimes during lunch we could go to downtown Milan. When some of us I went into the drugstore to buy, "Popular Aviation". There was only one copy in there at a time but a new one always seemed to be waiting for me the next month. It was an interesting magazine to take back to school for something to read. At least one time I got caught by the teacher when reading it during a study period. The teacher walked behind us and spotted me sneaking it into my textbook to read. She kind of smiled but didn't say anything. She closed the Aviation magazine and pointed to the text book. She was nice enough about it but I knew I should be reading the book instead of about airplanes. Airplanes were more interesting to me.

During high school I took all the math and science courses possible knowing I needed these to pass a written exam to get into the Army Air Corps. After graduation I went to the Minneapolis recruiting station to apply to for flight training in the Army Air Corps.

In my junior year 1940, a speaker came to Milan High School. He told the class what was going on in Germany and how they were working toward a pure Aryan race. He called it a "super race." It didn't seem then like I would ever be doing anything in Germany. It was the farthest thing from my mind.

3

December 7, 1941

December 7, 1941: I didn't realize that morning when the Empire of Japan bombed Pearl Harbor what a profound affect it would have on my life and that of our entire family. We woke up early on a Sunday morning and were getting ready to go to church. While listening to the radio, we heard that Japan had bombed a bunch of American ships in Pearl Harbor.

When we got to church all the people were talking about it. Some folks were saying, "Ya, well, that little country of Japan, that will only take about a month to finish them. Ya, with a country as powerful as the United States….." What little we knew at the time. Soon our family was very involved and by the end of the long wars in Japan and Germany, four Gilbertson brothers from our family were in Army and Marine uniforms.

The first week after the attack by Japan the lines to enlist were blocks long at the recruiting stations. Young men were angry that Japan had the audacity to sneak in to Pearl Harbor so many were volunteering to join the fight. We were still thinking, "How did Japan even dare to attack?" But we knew the handwriting was on the wall. We knew Germany had been building up their military and the United States had started building our forces to show the Japanese and Germans our strength.

I was a senior at Milan High School and had turned eighteen in September 1941. The Army had starting drafting almost a year before Pearl Harbor and my oldest brother Roy had enlisted in the Marines before he'd be drafted. My brother Earl joined the Army before I graduated from Milan. I had already made up my mind earlier that I was going to join the Army Air Corps whether or not there was a war. My dream was to be an airline pilot. I knew I could finish high school and graduate in May. I didn't have to make any decisions about the Army until June of 1942.

"Audacity of Hope"

In early June, right after my graduation, I drove 130 miles to the Army Air Corps recruiting office in Minneapolis, Minnesota. I was kind of walking around and wondering if I really dared try to try getting in. The only thing that could be done was to throw me out the door. Why not give it a try, and see what happens? I went in the office, walked up to the desk and said, "I would like to enlist the flight training program of the aviation cadets," The recruiter asked me, "How old are you?" I told him, "Eighteen" Then he asked me, "Do you have two years of college?" He knew very well that I didn't have it.

He said, "The requirement for the Air Corps is two years of college and twenty years of age." "It says or its equivalent doesn't it?" I said. He asked me, "Do you think you have the equivalent of two years of college?", "Yes, I think I do" I said. Then he asked me, "Why do you think you have two years equivalent?" "After taking all the math and science I could in high school that should be equivalent of college." I said. We both knew each other was bluffing, I was just going to see what might happen. He sat there and was thinking. "You know," he said, "I'd just like to know if you could actually pass the written test. You come back this afternoon. The test takes four hours.", "Okay I'll be back." I said.

After lunch I went back to the office. All the other guys waiting were older than me. There weren't any other eighteen year olds. We sat down at the desks and he gave us all a big booklet. "Okay you have four hours." he said. The first part was math and science. "Jeepers, this isn't so dog gone hard. I can pass this." At Milan High School I had taken geometry, physics and higher algebra. The first part in Math was easy.

Then there were the word meanings. "Now this was trouble," We had never had many vocabulary words study at Milan High so I had to do a quite a bit of guessing. I went over it again and again. There was nothing else to do so taking up the whole four hours was my best bet. Picking up more and more as I went over it was my only hope. Even missing out on a big share might be okay if I made up the difference in the math part.

"Okay, times up," the recruiter said. "If I pass this test will you call it the equivalent?" I asked. He didn't know what to say. He hesitated and said, "I think so." He didn't really have an answer because he had never run into it before. "I am anxious to see if I passed," "If you wait, I will go over it now." He said, "Ya, I'll wait." I said. After a while he came back said "I'm sorry to say you missed by one point." Well, when thinking about it later on, I should have asked him to go over it again."

Right now in 2015, the guy might have been lying and I really did pass it. The recruiter probably didn't know what to do with an eighteen year old kid. How far could I have pushed it? You can't get into a controversy with the Army and I really didn't have a foot to stand on. You'd think at the time when recruits were really needed, a way could have been figured out to squeeze out one more point for me. I did not qualify with the age and college requirements but gave it a try. You could call that the "audacity of hope"

After this experience I needed to make a decision and volunteering for the draft seemed to be the best plan. With me joining the Army my family now had three boys in the military and the only ones left to help plow the fields at home were my brothers, fourteen year old Curtis and twelve year old Lyle.

You didn't enlist in the Army but were given a choice of which branch of service you wanted to join when you were drafted. My choice was to join the Army Air Corps. By that time the requirements had been changed to being a high school graduate and eighteen years of age. The written test did not have to be taken again because it was in my records.

Maybe I really did pass the test in Minneapolis a few months earlier. We had to take our flight physicals at Camp Campbell, Kentucky and waited for several days to get it. The doctor who gave me my physical said, "Oh, you will be flying in six weeks." Well read on and you will see what happened to his plan for me. There were my plans and the Army's plans. These were two different tracks that didn't always coincide.

My Military posts from 1943 to March 1946

Fort Snelling, Minnesota March 5, 1943
Volunteered for the draft in Montevideo and had my exams at Fort Snelling, near Minneapolis and was sworn in to the Army. Application to join the Army Air Corps. Qualified during my exams.
Camp Campbell, Kentucky Arrived by train in March 1943, took basic training and then was supposed to be transferred to the cadet program. 20th Armored Division, Company C, 100th Armored Recon Battalion basic Training, Motorcycle school,
Fort Knox, Kentucky Armored Force Radio School 20th Company August 23, 1943
Camp Campbell Kentucky transferred back December 11, 1943 Radio Operator Company A 220th Armored Engineer Battalion.
Campbell Army Air Field, Kentucky 26, February 1944, waiting to be transferred to Sheppard Field

Sheppard Field, Wichita Falls, Texas 16 March 1944
Aviation Cadet Training
Camp Gruber, Muskogee, Oklahoma April *15 1944,* 42ⁿᵈ
Rainbow Division Infantry, Basic training Rifle Company
Rifleman
Fort Bragg, North Carolina May *15 1944* 100ᵗʰ Infantry Division
399ᵗʰ Rifle Company F 30 caliber Machine gun squad, 60mm
mortar squad, Advanced Infantry Training
Camp Kilmer POE, New Jersey arrived September 1944,
Embarked for ETO October 6ᵗʰ, 1944
Marseilles, France arrived October 20ᵗʰ, 1944

Wanting to be an Army Air Corps Pilot

A transfer to the Air Corps in thirteen weeks seemed likely but the Army had a little different plan. It wasn't until February 21, 1944 until when this order was sent:
From Aviation Cadet Examining Board

By the command of Major General Collins.
Special Orders)
Number 29)
1. Each of the following EM(Enlisted Men) having been found qualified for apmt as Aviation Cadet is trfd to AC unassigned, effective 26, February 1944

Rank Name
Pvt Verdie H. Gilbertson
Pvt H

When this order came I had finally got my wish but had to wait at Campbell Airfield for a couple of weeks until we received orders from Army Service Forces.

Fort Hayes, Columbus, Ohio
This time the order was dated 10 March 1944
Special orders
No 60

Each of the following named EM (Enlisted man) is relieved from attached orgn No 3 to arrive Sheppard Field 16 March 1944.

Pvt Verdie H Gilbertson, 37552245
My name was the first one on the list followed by 45 more new aviation cadets.

In aviation cadet training wearing a summer uniform. This was a photo sent home to my parents in 1944.

Sheppard Field, Wichita Falls Texas
March 16 to April 15 1944

We started going to classes as soon as we got to Sheppard Field. The field was full of airplanes and the barracks weren't too far from the airport. We studied air force navigation and had basic air crew training. After this we were scheduled to go on to preflight.

About all we did was look at the airplanes but we didn't get to fly any of them yet. The training we needed before flying was scheduled to take us two or three months. One day in early April an order came from General Arnold, the Commanding General of Army Air Forces,

Washington, DC. We had a big meeting with all the cadets and were handed a copy of the telegram from the general.

<u>This was the Telegram:</u>
29 March 1944
"AFBMP 6122 You will return to the ground and service forces all enlisted men who have volunteered from these sources and have been found fully qualified for training as pilots, bombardiers and navigators but who have not yet entered pre-flight school. This action is necessary as the result of a critical and immediate need for young vigorous and well trained men with leadership qualifications to meet the <u>urgent need of the ground and service forces</u>. It is essential that every one of these soldiers be made available for pending operations in view of the accumulated shortages that have developed since last July in selective service. It is with profound regret that I consent to drop from the AAF team these spirited young men who have aspired to join our combat crews which are gaining for us the superiority in the air in every theater of warfare. It is however the very success of the AAF teams now in combat which makes this shift of fighting power wise and proper. <u>We must present a balanced front to our enemies</u>. The AAF team has succeeded better than we dared hope for when our quotas were set and now it permits a reduction in our training rate. We shall of course continue to train combat crew in as close a ratio as possible to our exact needs. I am sure that these men will understand that in a program of such magnitude there will be times when the number of men who qualify in any particular period will exceed the training quota for that period. While it is my duty to regard this matter in a practical light it is my desire that you hand each of these men affected a copy of this message explaining the reason for his being obliged to forego this TNG. Will you also convey to each man my personal appreciation and thanks for his interest in the AAF and wish him good luck and good hunting in the branch to which he returns? I am confident that these fine American soldiers who want to do the <u>greatest possible damage to the enemy</u> will prefer the opportunity for earlier engagement to the alternative of waiting for training with the AAF at some later date.

General Arnold

The order said preflight but even men who were already flying airplanes were transferred to infantry units. Pilots became infantry men. One out of sixteen soldiers in the army was infantry and the rest was support. To the infantry the other soldiers were known as, "rear echelon."

Now for sure my dream to become a pilot was not going to happen as I was being transferred to a new unit. *Ground and service forces* turned out to be the infantry and a few months later I was on a troop ship to France with the 100th Infantry Division.

Camp Gruber Oklahoma April 15-May 15 1944

42nd Infantry Rainbow Division, 220 2nd regiment unit company G. This division was famous from World War I when General Douglas Macarthur was the division commander. Now in 1944 it was an infantry training division and this is where my first infantry basic began. The 42nd Rainbow was very strict in discipline. With my assignment to company G, I now knew that I was really in the Army. We were told, "When you salute an officer you say, "Good Morning sir or Good afternoon sir," depending on the time of day. If we knew he was a southern officer we were expected to say "Good evening sir" if it was after lunch. How we could tell if he was a southern officer, we weren't told. There was a special Rainbow salute where we had to tilt our head back we brought our saluting hand up. We lined up in front of a full length mirror and practiced the "Rainbow Salute." A month later a shipping list was tacked to the bulletin board sending me to Fort Bragg. It was a very welcome change to leave Camp Gruber and the 42nd Rainbow Division. They later went overseas.

1. Fort Bragg, North Carolina May 17, 1944

Company F 399th infantry regiment
100th (Century) Division

We received advanced infantry training at Fort Bragg, North Carolina. Our company commander told the four who came from the Army Air Corps, "I know you are disappointed about this assignment to the infantry because you wanted wings but there is nothing we can do about that." We were told men with leadership ability were needed and the first thing the company commander did was offer us a chance to go to Officer's Candidate School (OCS) at Fort Benning, Georgia. In three months we could be a second lieutenants if we passed or didn't get washed out. At the time I was in no mood to do any more volunteering. Being a private soldier in the Army and doing whatever I was told to do sounded better and hopefully the war would end soon.

My first assignment was with the machine gun squad so I trained on a machine gun for a few weeks. My squad leader was Ambrose Duncan, a full blooded Indian from California and he bunked next to me. Later for some reason I was assigned to mortar training but don't remember why. It was the same platoon of about thirty two men. There was one section each of machine guns and mortars. So the rest of the time was spent in training until we got ready to ship overseas. We were scheduled to go to Europe but we didn't know where.

Before we went overseas, I got a furlough in July and went back to our farm in Minnesota for a few short days. My two brothers Roy and Earl were already in the South Pacific. Roy was in the 2nd Marines Division with a tank unit and Earl was in the 96th Army Infantry Division. My parents had a lot to worry about with three of overseas in combat but they just had to accept it. Nothing could be done about it.

My mother and dad were probably very concerned with all three of us in combat but were typical Norwegians who don't say much. The feelings were there but our parents weren't too apt to reveal their true emotions. After furlough it was time to go back to Fort Bragg.

Camp Kilmer, NJ October 1944

This was a staging area with physical exams to see if we were fit for duty overseas. It took a while before we boarded the ship to Europe and during the waiting time I got a pass to New York City. It was the first time I ever had been in such a big city. In my little book I wrote. "Had a swell time seeing Broadway, Times Square, Astor Bar and a lot of tall buildings."

John Delewski, who we had trained with at Fort Bragg, had a broken arm before he ever joined the Army. His arm had a little bend but he had passed his physical to get into the Army. Before we left Camp Kilmer in New Jersey we had to get another physical to see if we were fit enough to fight. The medical guys spotted Delewski's bent arm and told him that he couldn't go overseas. He put up such a resistance saying that he wanted to go along with his unit. The officers listened to him talk and then decided to let him go. He could still do what the rest of us could. He could have stayed stateside but didn't want to leave the unit. That would have been a perfect way for Delewski to sit the war out in the states. We were glad he was with us in the mortar section during our days in combat.

We got plenty of shots at Camp Kilmer before we went into combat. These shots must have been good for something. I don't know what all of them were for but mine worked very well. While in the infantry I kept pretty healthy out in the cold, rainy and snowy weather while always looking for something to eat.

We embarked to Europe for combat from New York City on 6 October, 1944.

Here is some background details to show readers how Verdi arrived at the front lines.

Marseilles, France   *20 October, 1944*
Atlantic Crossing, Destination ETO European Theater of Operations.

We spent two weeks on the USAT George Washington on our way to France
US Navy photo # NH 85263 from the collections
of the US Navy Historical Center

Landing in France

The ship we boarded for Europe was the *USAT George Washington*. It had been built in 1908 as a German luxury liner and was in New York harbor when World War I started. The Americans kept it and never gave it back to Germany. Now we were in World War II and it was being used as a troop ship. The huge ship was crowded as there were over 7,000 troops aboard. We had bunks and troop compartments that folded down and were held up by chains. There was not much room as we were practically touching each other noses.

There were plenty of seasick soldiers but I got by pretty good without getting sick during the two week trip across the Atlantic Ocean. One night we had a real bad storm and were maybe only few days out of North Africa and still in the Atlantic. Our ship was damaged in the rudder steering mechanisms so we were left behind. We got up in the morning and when we looked around we didn't see another ship in sight. The water was very calm with no destroyers around us and we began to worry about submarines. In a way we were probably fortunate because the German subs had followed the convoy. Otherwise we would have been sitting ducks. There were about 150 ships in the convoy.

The *USAT George Washington* was in built in1908 in Germany and was seized by the United States on 6 April 1917. It was used as a troopship carrying 100,000 troops to and from France. In January 1944 the *USAT George Washington* began regular service to England and the Mediterranean Theatre of Operations, landing in Liverpool, Southampton and Le Havre. The ship was occasionally sent to Marseilles, France where we landed in October 1944.

Mediterranean Sea

The Germans were very active in the Mediterranean. Our ship went through the Straits of Gibraltar and into the Mediterranean Sea. The whole convoy went through the straits and that is where the Germans had sunk some US cargo ships when they had tried to enter. We came through the strait at night so we didn't see any ships get sunk. In the dark we were pretty safe and the danger was less when we got closer to the coast of France because we had our airplanes patrolling for enemy submarines and planes.

Landing in France

We landed right in the harbor at Marseille, France and climbed down over the side of the ship on cargo nets and into the landing craft. The harbor was full of sunken ships and docks that had been bombed and shelled. It was a complete mess. Our LCI landing craft carrying about 25-30 men went in between the sunken ships and masts and was a rough ride to shore. Finally we landed on the beach, the ramp was dropped in the front and we went onshore to join the war.

The Germans started pulling back as we were coming so we didn't hit anything right away as their units were retreating. We spent a few days in a staging area and then we hiked right past a lot of big residential buildings. In my book I wrote, "A rough city." Marseille was one of the biggest cities in Europe. We didn't have much time to write letters as we were catching up with the German Army. Their winter defense was to be set up in the foothills of the Vosges Mountains. Here was where the Krauts were making their last stand to keep American soldiers from advancing towards the Rhine River in Germany.

The First Day in France

The first night we were brought in trucks up to a little village. The church bell rang continuously all night. It was tolling and tolling. I didn't know why it was being rung and we never saw the bell ringers. Maybe when the bell rang it was for protection. We never knew but it still stuck in my mind. Maybe some people in that town had been lost in the fighting, I didn't know. It was pitch dark and something like this could have easily been made into a movie. It was really weird. It didn't even seem like it was real. "How come I happened to end up here?" Maybe I was in a state of denial. I said to myself "I don't believe this." Some things really stuck with me. Maybe it was because this was right at the beginning of the fighting. We could hear the small arms and artillery fire all night especially machine guns. "I know we are going to get involved in this mess shortly." I thought to myself.

From the Story of the Century

"On this first day no one tried to start a fight. The Century men wanted a few precious hours to adjust minds and bodies to realities of front line combat." From the, *Story of the Century*. The Century Association 100th Infantry Division, Copyright 1946

While reading this, I remember the meeting we had that first day in France. Our platoon leader got us all together and gave us a pep talk. The average age of the men in our company was 19 years, so this was who was listening to our platoon leader. He didn't know what was going to happen but he said, "If we all look after each other and work together and we all have a better chance of getting through this." We got together with thirty two of us in a big tent. Our platoon leader Lt. Charles Nicholson, tried to get us prepared and he stressed working together as a unit. He told us to look after each other. He had no more idea of combat than we did but he had to try get us prepared for war.

This was a psychological transformation that was going on that morning in the foothills of the Vosges Mountains before my first combat experience. Now we were committed to combat and it continued from November 1944 to May 1945. It was early in the first morning when one of our guys, machine gun squad leader Ambrose Duncan, got hit. He was wounded and didn't make it through the first day. The medics picked him up and he was angry that he wouldn't be able to stay with the platoon.

We were all intact at the first meeting but it didn't last long. It was a matter of an hour or two when the reality really hit. Before the first month of fighting was over half of the thirty two members of my platoon had been captured by the Krauts.

Some other words from *The Story of the Century* which mean a lot to me when thinking back on my first day of combat in November 1944 at the beginning of the Vosges campaign in the foothills. *"1 November, the day of our date with destiny, a change comes over man at such a time. A change as miraculous as the transformation of a pumpkin into a gilded coach with results even more inspiring. For here was the miracle of the fellowship of man come true. There is neither time nor inclination to give thought to a man's past or position in society when life is at stake. Foxholes are considerably more important."* I relate to this when remembering the meeting we had on that first day before we jumped off at 0500.

Editor's note: from 1946 to 2015 many stories have been told by Verdie about his time with the Century Division in Germany and France. Over a period of a few years I have typed these stories while Verdie told them to me. My dad kept saying "We are walking across France and Germany." We got a little tired but it was an enjoyable walk with no shells going off anywhere near us. As Verdie says, "World War Two vets are getting so old that we are starting to believe all of the old stories ourselves."

I have always believed my dad's stories ever since he started telling them when I was in college. The stories are nearly the same each time but seem to get even more interesting to listen as both of us grow older. If he were making them up he wouldn't be so consistent. There might be some holes in his details. Like he says before most stories "I may have told you this before but…" I don't ever remember anyone saying, "Oh no, not that one again."

We keep asking him to tell them over and over and he is happy to oblige us. We usually end up laughing each time when he talks about meeting civilians in France and Germany. Our family is very happy that Dad's, Grandpa's and Great Grandpa's stories are now written and available for your enjoyment and education. The many letters he wrote while in combat serve to back up so many of the stories he has told over the years. They have been a valuable addition to refresh his memory enabling Verdi to tell even more day to day infantry in action stories that are included in his third book.

Epinal, France: Foothills of the Vosges Mountains

We caught up with the Germans here. They had strict orders that no enemy troops were to advance through the Vosges Mountains in southern France. On the way up to the battle front we saw the wreckage of the German 9th Army which had tried to hold the American Army off and were unsuccessful. There were hundreds of our 6x6 Army trucks carrying troops with half a platoon in each one. On the front of the trucks was a 50 caliber machine gun to protect us in case of German planes strafing. We each took turns manning the machine guns as we traveled to up to the front. Now we were on both sides of the German Army and behind them so the Krauts were in bad shape. It was unbelievable.

100th Division report: The attack jumped off, 12 November, the Division driving against the German winter line in the Vosges Mountains. The Division took Bertrichamps and Clairupt, pierced the German line, and seized Raon L'Etape and St. Blaise.

The Unit I spent most of my time with in France and Germany
Company F (Fox)
2nd Battalion
399th Infantry Regiment
100th Infantry Division known as Century Division

My Unit

100th Infantry Division included three regiments with a total of about 9,000 infantrymen plus all the support units that added up to 12,000- 20,000 men depending on how many supporting units we had. The Regimental Combat Team (RCT) was made up of artillery, tanks, signal corps, quartermasters and others.

399th Infantry Regiment three battalions 3,000 men each
2nd Battalion four companies about 700 men each
Company F four platoons full strength 184 soldiers
Platoons 32-48 soldiers
Squad 8 to 12 men. Mortar 8, Machine gun 8, Rifle 12

CHAPTER TWO

Letters from the Front Lines

Envelopes from letters to Ma, Pa, and my brothers, Lyle and Curtis

Letters found in the attic

Until March of 2014, we had no idea that the war time letters I had written to my parents from France and Germany had been saved and kept in the attic of my home place. My sister-in-law Ruby and her daughters were clearing out the attic as Ruby was preparing to move into town. She married my brother Lyle in 1952 and had lived in our home place ever since then. While moving everything around, Ruby found a box containing over sixty letters I had written while sitting in foxholes and in civilians' homes while in the war zone. My folks had saved the letters that all four of their sons had written home while in the service during the war. Now some of the stories I have been telling for almost seventy years were there on paper as I had written in during 1944 and 1945.

Keith and I sat down in our comfortable living room chairs for about three or four hours and quickly read most of the letters, some to ourselves and others aloud to each other. My first thoughts were, "Well, there is not much news here." As Keith was reading each letter, he excitedly told me a few times, "Wow Dad, these letters are a treasure—a history of an American infantry man and need to be shared with your children, grandchildren, great grandchildren and future generations. People who study World War Two history will also be interested. They are a priceless archive of a soldier attempting to keep his parents as emotionally comfortable as possible while he was in the war zone of France and Germany."

Many times I had written home saying, "Don't worry about me, I am perfectly okay." If my mom and dad only knew what was really going on they would have had plenty of reasons to worry. We couldn't really tell many details because of censorship and the fact that the Army read all of our letters before sending them home. Each envelope has a *"Passed by Army Examiner"* stamp on the lower left corner with a signature of the person who read it.*

What would be the point to complain or tell my parents any bad news? The folks had enough to worry about with the farm and three boys in the war: Roy, Earl and me, with Curtis getting ready to go as soon as he had the chance.

My parents may have read about the 7th Army in the newspaper. That was what was going through my mind, so I felt best when writing positive news. My philosophy was, "Why not just say the good things?" This helped me feel good and I hoped it made my family feel better about their son who was in combat across the ocean.

In almost every letter there were questions that I asked my family. "How are you doing? How is the farm work going? What is weather like?" *Editor's note: From the words he wrote in his many letters we can see that Dad was continually thinking of his family and asking, "how are **you** doing?" even during his roughest days and nights.*

19

There were probably more important things going on in my life at the time than wondering how the crops were doing and how the animals were getting along at home. It helped me feel better when wondering about what everyone was doing. My family was always busy working and asking questions about our farm gave us something to talk about. Letters were like talking with my family. It was my way of keeping contact when thinking about home. Visualizing what was going on back on the farm was helpful and I didn't have much inclination to tell what we were doing in France and Germany.

We couldn't say much because of censorship and there wasn't any point of telling things like: we took an objective today, there were casualties, it was cold today, or my feet got wet. That wouldn't make me feel any better and it wouldn't make my family feel any better so why even say it? Writing about something more positive seemed the best choice. That helped my morale and I hoped it helped their morale too. My parents saw enough in the papers and heard enough on the radio about graphic stuff so they didn't need to read anything more about that from me.

> * *Most of us knew our letters were being read and censored by our platoon leaders. This was verified in 2015 when I looked at the signatures written over* Passed by Army Examiner *on the envelopes. Lt. Nicholson, Lt. Emery, Lt. Snyder and Lt. Sisca were some of the platoon leaders who signed off on my letters. It'd be very surprising if they really read each letter. Maybe they did but it would have been very hard to find the time to do this. What real secrets did we have to tell our parents? Maybe the officers looked to see if we wrote strategy, troop locations or about low morale and just skimmed over the rest of what we wrote. There are no signs of any words crossed out or cut out in any of my letters.*

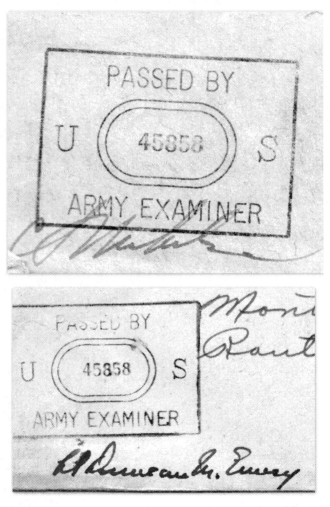

Army Examiner Stamps and signatures from our platoon leaders

My family who sent me many, many welcomed letters and also read all the letters that were sent home from France and Germany in 1944 and 1945. L to R, Earl (home on leave) Lyle holding Shep's ears, Mom, Dad, Clarice, Vernice, Curtis and Mildred. Roy was with the Marines in the Pacific.

My brothers and parents after the war. L-R, Verdie, Roy, Mom, Dad, Curtis, Earl. Two Army soldiers and two Marines.

A letter from my Mother

We have this letter from my mom because I wrote to her on the back of a letter she had sent to me. At the time it was the only stationery I could find. This is very precious to me and tells how Ma and Pa always kept us in their prayers and hearts. This meant everything to us. We were not able to keep letters we got from home while in combat because we could not carry them around during the fighting.

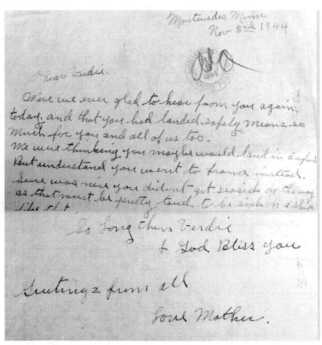

Part of my mother's letter of November 3, 1944

Our prayers are that God keeps his protecting hand over you.

Dear Verdie,   *November 3rd, 1944*
                                          Montevideo, Minnesota

Were we ever glad to hear from you again today and that you had landed safely means so much for you and all of us too. We were thinking that maybe you would land in England but understand that you went to France instead. It sure was nice that you didn't get seasick on the way as that must be pretty tough to be sick on a ship like that.

How many days were you on the water? Maybe you can't tell us that. I bet it is strange to step off the ship on the other side of the big waters. Our prayers are and we know yours are too that God keeps his protecting hand over you and brings you safely across and coming back home again. It is going to be a great wonderful day when all our loved ones return and there is peace all over the world again. It can't come too soon.

We were so happy to hear from Earl again after waiting six long weeks to hear from him. He can't say where he is but that he is all right is the main thing. We are worried that he is in the Philippine Islands someplace and that is a pretty bad place now. We had a letter from Roy today too. He is still on Saipan and was all right which means so much to us all. Roy said he was waiting to hear from you again so you if you have time write him again soon.

We have had a nice Indian summer here for a long time now but I think it's due for a cold spell now as it is blowing from the northwest tonight. It's pretty cold out now but we haven't had any snow yet and I hope we don't have any for at least another month.

Say Verdie, if there is anything you want, you have to request because we can't send anything other than Christmas packages without a request from you. We will be glad to send anything you want, just let us know. *(Notice in later letters, Verdie requests several items including, candy, rubberized gloves, wool socks, the newspaper, cookies, hunting knife…)* Verdie, I know you would like to get the *Montevideo American* but you have to request that too. You better do that soon and we will subscribe for you so you will get it more regular.

Curtis is working for Alvig and Lowell picking corn and they still have about two weeks left. Curtis is still taking flying lessons. I don't know how many hours he has. He will have to write and tell you about that I guess. The plane has been out here a couple of times. It's kind of interesting to watch them too.

We hope you have good eats there and get a nice Thanksgiving dinner too. Wish I could send you pheasants and lefse like I did last year but I guess that's out of the question now. Hope and pray you boys are all home when next Thanksgiving comes around. Then it's going be a real Thanksgiving Day. May God grant this to us very soon. We are all the same as ever.

Hope this finds you feeling fine and we hope to hear from you again soon. I am enclosing a picture of Earl and the boys that were home on furlough at the same time. It was taken at Ellingsons. They all look real good.

So long then Verdie and God bless you. Greetings from all

Love, Mother

Set Record in French Advance

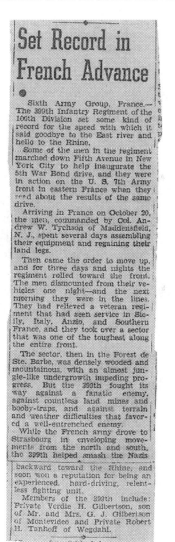

Set Record in French Advance

Sixth Army Group, France.— The 399th Infantry Regiment of the 100th Division set some kind of record for the speed with which it said goodbye to the East river and hello to the Rhine.

Some of the men in the regiment marched down Fifth Avenue in New York City to help inaugurate the 5th War Bond drive, and they were in action on the U. S. 7th Army front in eastern France when they read about the results of the same drive.

Arriving in France on October 20, the men, commanded by Col. Andrew W. Tychson of Maddensfield, N. J., spent several days assembling their equipment and regaining their land legs.

Then came the order to move up, and for three days and nights the regiment rolled toward the front. The men dismounted from their vehicles one night—and the next morning they were in the lines. They had relieved a veteran regiment that had seen service in Sicily, Italy, Anzio, and Southern France, and they took over a sector that was one of the toughest along the entire front.

The sector, then in the Forest de Ste. Barbe, was densely wooded and mountainous, with an almost jungle-like undergrowth impeding progress. But the 399th fought its way against a fanatic enemy, against countless land mines and booby-traps, and against terrain and weather difficulties that favored a well-entrenched enemy.

While the French army drove to Strasbourg in enveloping movements from the north and south, the 399th helped smash the Nazis backward toward the Rhine, and soon won a reputation for being an experienced, hard-driving, relentless fighting unit.

Members of the 399th include: Private Verdie H. Gilbertson, son of Mr. and Mrs. G. J. Gilbertson of Montevideo and Private Robert H. Tanhoff of Wegdahl.

December 1944: An article that was put in my hometown newspaper,
the Montevideo American, about our 399th Regiment. My parents sent
this story and the guys in our unit really enjoyed reading it.

Sixth Army Group, France

The 399th Infantry Regiment of the 100th Division set some kind of record for the speed with which it said goodbye to the East River and hello to the Rhine. Some of the men in the regiment marched down Fifth Avenue in New York City to help Inaugurate the 5th War Bond drive, and were in action on the US 7th Army front in eastern France when they read about the results of the same drive.

Arriving in France on October 20, the men spent several days assembling their equipment and regaining their land legs.

Then came the order to move up and for three days and three nights the regiment rolled toward the front. The men dismounted from their vehicles one night —and the next morning were in the lines. They had relieved a veteran regiment that had seen service in Sicily, Italy, and Southern France and then took over a sector that was one of the toughest along the entire front.

The sector in the Forest de Ste. Barbe, was densely wooded with an almost jungle-like undergrowth impeding progress. But the 399th fought against a fanatic enemy against countless land mines and booby-traps, and against terrain and weather difficulties that favored a well-entrenched enemy.

While the French Army drove to Strasbourg in enveloping movements from the north and south the 399th helped smash the Nazis backward toward the Rhine, and soon won a reputation for being an experienced, hard driving, relentless fighting unit.

Members of the 399th include **PFC Verdie Gilbertson**, son of Gerhard and Selma Gilbertson of RR 5, Montevideo, Minnesota.

100th Division enters the Vosges Mountains Campaign

Arriving in Marseilles on October 20th, the Division test-fired its weapons and moved by truck convoy over 500 miles to the front near Baccarat, France. As the 399th Infantry Regimental Combat Team began its relief of elements of the 45th Division on the southwest bank of the Meurthe River, the Century Division fired its first shot at the enemy. "At 1711 hours on 1 November, Battery B of the 925th Field Artillery Battalion fired its first registration round into the gathering gloom of a mountain nightfall." The 100th Infantry Division had entered the Vosges Mountains campaign. www.100thww2.org/overview/overview.html

Chapter Three

"Baptism of Fire"

When we were first committed in early November to a combat situation in the Vosges Mountains we moved up to a position and we had a French officer that guided Fox Company up there. We didn't have any experience yet and were having trouble navigating in the mountains and making the right connections. The French officer knew the area well. So when we got to the position we dug in and set up all the gun placements. It was getting close to dark and we were digging in for the night. We had no sooner finished when word was sent down to the platoons to get ready to move out. "Moving out already? We just finished digging in." Okay... that's what we did. The new position was about 200 yards away to our right flank. In a matter of minutes the Krauts laid down an artillery barrage you wouldn't believe in our original position.

They had probably spotted us when we were moving in and waited until they thought we were settled in to let us have it. They really laid the artillery into the area we had just left. Well, we thought, moving to a new place sure saved a lot of us!

So we dug in again and set up our gun positions. It was cold and it started raining with a mix of snow. Our foxholes started filling up with cold water. Beehive and I had dug in together but we spotted a big tall evergreen tree that was good for shelter from the cold driving rain so we got underneath it. It was dark so we figured the Krauts wouldn't be moving at night. We weren't going to sit in the foxhole in the water. We stayed under there wearing our raincoats.

Shortly the Krauts figured out our new position and started laying in artillery again. The first barrage landed in our area. Beehive automatically ran towards the hole which was close by. He jumped right in and there was a big splash. I came in right behind him and slid on my hind end because it was so muddy from the rain. The water came up over my boots and I crouched down as low as I could without laying down. Maybe as I crouched the Krauts might quit firing and pretty soon they did let up.

We waited a little as the firing stopped and then got out of our hole. Beehive was wet all over and my feet were wet because the water in the hole came over the top of my boots. Well, what do you do when this happens in cold rainy weather?? Beehive and I sat down close together under the big evergreen tree. Then we pulled open our raincoats and buckled them together so we were both inside in the same area. We figured our body warmth helped the one who got the wettest. By only crouching in the hole my top part above the waist was fairly dry so I was okay and Beehive could get warmer and dry.

The rest of the night was quiet as we sat there together under the evergreen tree trying to get warmer and drier. It was still cold and it is the coldest night I can ever remember in my life. The next morning it got light and it was pretty quiet with no shelling. We went around to some of the other holes where some of our platoon had been laying in the water all night. We pulled out a guy who had almost turned blue. Two of us put his arms around our shoulders and started walking him around to see if we could get some movement in him. Of course he was still wet. We kept on walking him until finally he started to move a little. That was probably what is now is called hypothermia. We had never heard of that back in 1944. Our platoon member survived this and stayed with the company. There was no way to get dried out quickly. The only thing that worked was your body heat if you could keep moving.

That was our first experience, the first night we spent on line. That was our "Baptism of Fire," and it was a true wet baptism. This was the same night one of our guys got wounded and I was laying next to the medic and helping out some. We held our position and the next day we had an objective of taking an observation post the Krauts had in a church tower in a small village. We moved out and no one said, well you guys are wet and tired so we will rest for a day or two.

Editor's note about *Up Front* by Bill Mauldin

Not long after he returned home from the war in 1946, Verdi purchased Bill Mauldin's book, "Up Front." It is Mauldin's collection of wartime cartoons that appeared in issues of "Stars and Stripes" during the war in 1944 and 1945. Along with the cartoons are Mauldin's comments and stories about the background for them while he served as an infantryman in Italy and France. He wrote, "I draw pictures for and about the dogfaces (*infantrymen*) because I know what their life is like and I understand their gripes." p 5.

It wasn't until the 1970's when I was in college that I recall my dad telling the stories you are reading in his book. What I remember is looking at the cartoons in *Up Front* and many photos in a five set collection of World War II history books my dad owned. We didn't talk about them but I got a flavor of what a combat infantryman may have gone through from the perspective of Mauldin's characters, Joe and Willie.

After collecting Verdi's stories for this book, we paged through *Up Front* again and selected four cartoons that mirror very closely the experiences my dad talks about. *Baptism of Fire* recalls a story of Verdie, crouching in a wet foxhole while hoping to keep as dry as possible. *Occupation in Germany* talks about becoming experts on the types of European soil in France and Germany. *They Stole our Chickens* tells the story of infantrymen finding some chickens to eat. The civilian stories tell about kids looking for food from soldiers and Mauldin's cartoon, *The Prince and the Pauper,* dramatically captures the relationship of an American soldier and a hungry child. *From one of my dad's letters* "There are some German kids here that meet up by the garbage cans after every meal and eat the garbage we throw away. There's always a line of children begging for anything we have left over in our mess kits." We did not get permission to publish the cartoons in this book but you can view them @ www.0500vg.blogspot.com

Many more of Mauldin's cartoons cause Verdi to smile and nod his head in agreement as he recognizes how they truly capture the day to day experiences of men who spent many difficult and trying nights and days serving in the wartime infantry. A few words from Mauldin that mean a lot to me now are: "The surest way to become a pacifist is to join the infantry" (p. 14). "They are so damned sick and tired of having their noses rubbed in a stinking war that their only ambition will be to forget it." (p. 10). Mauldin helps me realize why my dad never talked much about the war until many years later. I also understand why he was so against the war in Vietnam and any other wars since then. He tells me now that he just "dreaded the thought" that his two sons or any other sons would have to fight in any war like he did.

This is part of a letter I wrote to my brother Curtis on Nov, 11, 1945

A year ago tomorrow is a day I'll never forget. That was the first time we attacked the Krauts. We got them off the hill and when we got up there our own artillery started shelling us and then the Kraut artillery started in too. We hadn't even dug in but it didn't take long to get a hole dug.

A gopher has nothing on me.

Dear Mom and all of you,
    Monday November 20 1944 somewhere in France *(Raon L'Etape)*＊

I spose you are all wondering why I am writing on the back of your stationary. Well you see I am all out of stationary and I can't get any here. I hope you will send me some when you can. I would really appreciate it if you would send me some candy and best of all cookies. And say could you get some of those rubberized canvas gloves. I really could use them and some wool socks. Leather gloves with liners would be nice too. I hope you don't think I am asking for too much. *(I was requesting what I wanted just like my mother told me to do.)* I know it is hard to get back there so if you can't that's okay. I am not suffering so don't worry about me.

    I was so awfully glad to get your letter this morning. Mail is more important than food I think. I can't expect too much mail because I don't get a chance to write very often now but keep writing as much as you can anyway and tell everybody else that too. I'll answer as much as I possibly can. I haven't heard from Verdie Ellingson since I was home so if you see him ask him to write will you? I will try to answer Clarice, Mildred and Vernice as soon as I can. Tell them I'm getting their letters regularly. I appreciate so much that they write even if I can't answer them. I am getting your letters regular too.

Say Mom, it's about Christmas time and I can't get Christmas cards to send home so I am asking you to do my Christmas shopping for me. Will you buy a gift for you and Dad and the whole family and Verdie E and Orton too? I wish you would take the whole $50 I sent home and spend it all for gifts for you all back home. It will make me feel better if you would. Don't be afraid to spend the $50 because I'll be sending some more home soon. It won't be much of a gift for everyone but I hope it will help some. You can buy what you feel best yourself. I hope this terrible war is over soon so I can do my own Christmas shopping again.

You should see the super deluxe foxhole I have. I am sitting in it right now. Some of the foxholes I've had have even had running water. Pretty nice eh? A gopher has nothing on me. In fact he better be a fast digger if he ever expects to catch up with me. When I get back home I'll have to dig me a hole in the woods so I will feel at home. To tell the truth a foxhole is a pretty welcome thing to crawl into up here. Things do get a little rough up here sometimes but I guess that is to be expected. I am perfectly okay though so don't worry.

You should see these poor French people, when us doughboys come into a town they practically go nuts with joy. I feel sorry for them though. They have had a pretty hard time of it. Most of them have left the towns and as soon as their homes are liberated they start coming back with carts and some or most of their belongings on their backs. The kids in the towns beg for chewing gum or candy as soon as they see a Yank. I gave away all the gum I had one day and there must have been about twenty kids following behind. The people stand along the streets waving, hollering and waving flags.

Nope, I will have to close for this time. Oh yes, we had church services yesterday. It seems kind of strange to go to services here but I'm so glad we can have them once in a while. *(Church was not in a building. It was out in the woods someplace when the chaplain came up.)* It helps so much when we can turn to God for comfort. I read my New Testament** nearly every day and it helps so much. It isn't very often we can have services up here.

31

I hope to get to a rest area soon so I can catch up on my writing. So long for now and God Bless you all. Tell everybody Hi.

Love,
Verdie

Locations added for this book. We were not allowed to write about where we were other than France or Germany, The list of towns and the days we were there is from a record kept by S/Sgt Bill Rogers that was included in a book by fellow 399ᵗʰ soldier Hal Bingham MD. He called it Son of Bitche *to commemorate the 100ᵗʰ Division being the first army in history to conquer the fortifications in the Vosges Mountains near the town of Bitche, France.*

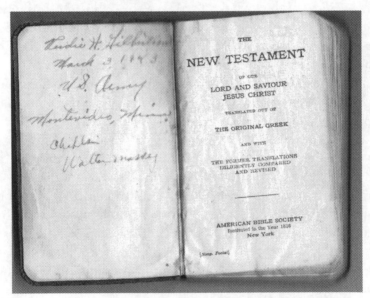

**During basic training at Camp Campbell, Kentucky, the chaplain gave each of us a New Testament that he had signed. I carried it in the left pocket of my field jacket during my whole time in combat. This is one of the few things I kept with me, along with the spent "lucky bullet" that ricocheted from a 30 caliber machine gun on the firing range and ended up in the pocket of my work uniform.*

Going into French Towns

Somehow many of the French villagers got a hold of small American flags and waved them as we came into their towns. What I remember most is the kids following us. Some were looking for candy and many of them were asking in French "cigaretten pour Pa, Pa." We didn't know if the kids were smoking the cigarettes themselves or giving them to Pa, Pa. Maybe their dads had to find their own cigarettes. The adults were talking to us but most of the time I couldn't understand them.

One night we came into a village and it was raining and cold out and miserable weather. It seemed like in France the people always lived upstairs. The people invited us to stay in their house to keep dry out of the rain. The commander said "find yourself a place if the civilians invite you in, and report here at 0500 in the morning." It was getting dark so we found a place and slept on the floor. We took our stuff and tried to dry it off by the stove. Other times in some of the villages we'd stay in the barn in the hayloft.

The table was set for all of us and we ate with the French family. We gave them whatever we had in our K rations, which was just a little packet of hard candy, four cigarettes, a pack of hard crackers and a little tin of canned meat. The Army called it pork luncheon meat. It was finely ground and packed real hard into the can. We shared some of our rations and the family gave us some of their food. There wasn't any real coffee, just ersatz coffee, like a substitute for coffee. It was like chicory and it wasn't real good but we drank it.

We stayed there overnight in the house. At 0500 it was still raining when we formed out in the street in front of the French villager's homes. We had an objective that morning.

Safety in One

This was before Lemberg and we were all pretty green. We had an objective to take the small French village of Pintervald.

It seems like it was always dark and foggy in France. One night we rode on tanks into town and this time it was dark and rainy. We all got separated and I couldn't find Simmons or any of the others from my platoon. We had gotten split up bad in the dark and rain but we couldn't start looking around and hollering for somebody, "Hey, where are you? Hey, I'm over here." This was called SNAFU (Situation normal, all fouled up). In a little while I found our squad leader who had crawled into one of the tanks to keep dry.

It was nice to find a nice dry place so I decided to look into a cellar and there was Clyde Simmons together with a bunch of civilians. Some of our platoon finally got together and set our machine gun between the banisters on the front porch to be ready for any action. Another guy went into the cellar and found a wine barrel, so he grabbed a bucket and filled it. The guys sat around the table and dipped their canteen cups into the bucket of wine. We were sure glad to get out of the miserable weather. We never saw our leaders around that night. The infantry was trained to do whatever we were supposed to do even when we were separated from our squad leader. We were able to act on our own.

The streets were narrow, it was very dark, and the Krauts were on the other side of the street. We couldn't see them but we could hear them and they could hear us. Nobody could see much of anything because of the darkness and rainy weather. We couldn't figure out what the Krauts were doing but we heard them moving during the night. They were walking up and down the cobblestone streets with their hob nailed boots. It was dark and we didn't know what was going on because it rained all night. We were sweating it out because we were so close together; just across the street from each other. We lit some candles and waited but we couldn't just lay down and sleep. We had been trained together and we didn't need any orders on a night like this. We knew we should sit tight. We all wondered just how was this going to turn out.

We found out in the morning that the Krauts had been moving out during the night. They must have decided it was best to leave in the dark. Early in the morning we sent out a patrol to see what was going on. "Beehive" and I were walking down the street. "I'm walking right down the middle. The Krauts won't give their position away for American soldiers," I said. We never heard anything and didn't see anyone. The noise that we heard in the early morning was the Germans leaving the buildings during the night.

That was one day we didn't have any confrontation with the Germans. It wouldn't have made any difference if we tried to sneak down the street. There was no sense in the Krauts getting only two of us when it was obvious there were many more of us. In this case there was "safety in one" rather than in numbers. No one went after a single soldier. This would never be shown in a movie about the war. We didn't know what the Krauts were thinking but we kind of guessed and this time we were right. They must have thought the Americans wouldn't start anything in this weather.

The Krauts were a lot like us just wanting to get in out of the rain and cold like we did. German Soldiers wanted to get home too just like American soldiers did. I doubted the Krauts were any more patriotic than we were and I took that for granted.

A vow I made to myself

Sometimes, when laying in a foxhole with the noise of combat all around, I made a vow: "If I ever make it home again I will never complain."

Rumors

The rumor from the beginning of combat was that we were going to commit for ten days and then be pulled back. We were thinking, "How could anyone get through even ten days?" I remember counting those ten days and then seven months later the 100th division had been in 185 days of uninterrupted ground combat. On April 25th of 1945 I wrote to my family that I had put in about 170 days on the front.

For the first few days it seemed like the food just stuck in your chest as it only went part ways down. We'd be hungry but the food just didn't seem to go down. This didn't last long though as pretty soon we ate everything in sight because we were so active all the time. Maybe ten days was the point when we could make a psychological transition to cope with the dangers of ground combat.

Somethings that pops up in the files of my mind

The first ten days in combat were definitely a time for psychological adjustment. My experience of seeing wounded men and what happened after a firefight was well within these ten days. A combat medic from our unit was working on a wounded guy after an artillery barrage. The guy was hollering, "Medic, medic!" That was the first thing we heard when I happened to be lying on top of the ground next to our medic. One guy was hit by shrapnel very close in front of us as the Krauts were firing 88s in there. He was half dazed and walking out in a circle in front of us. We were laying flat with the rest of the guys and he was the only one out in the open. The medic didn't want to go out there to help because he'd be too exposed to enemy fire. He wanted the wounded guy to get under the trees. He kept hollering at him, "Come over here, come over here!!"

Finally the wounded guy came into the woods and went down onto the ground. The medic rolled him over because he had been hit in the back. The medic said to me "Give me your trench knife." When I handed it to him, he got the knife under the wounded man's jacket and pulled it open so his whole back was exposed. He quickly gave him a shot of morphine. Pretty soon the guy passed out as the medic kept telling him, "You'll be okay, it is a million dollar wound. You will be okay." He started patching him up to stop the bleeding. The medic did everything he could to try to save him. Not much longer the litter bearers picked the wounded man up to bring him back to a battalion aid station. It was hard for the medics to work on the soldiers in the open. I just hope this wounded guy got through it. That was my first experience of being so close to a wounded fellow soldier and something I still remember to this day.

We were going to see the same thing so many times over again that we somehow got adjusted to it but I don't really know how. We saw men who got direct hits from machine guns. These images are in my file and still pop up every so often. Then there were guys who got direct hits from a mortar shells or artillery that you can't hardly describe.

Sometimes in the winter we got to a place where the GRS (Graves Registration Service) hadn't picked up the bodies or "stiffs" yet. It didn't seem right to call the bodies "stiffs" but that was just how infantry men talked. Maybe it was like whistling in the dark. We put names on things we didn't really want to think about or talk about. For some reason or other we didn't use the names of buddies who had lost their lives.

The image of a glove on a hand sticking out of the snow still comes to my mind. Sometimes it might be a Kraut but we knew it was an American when we saw a khaki colored GI glove. Sometimes in a defense position we'd see this for a few days until the GRS came up to get the casualties. We never went to see who it was that was frozen solid in the drifting snow. We left them alone. That is what bothered me. There was nothing we could do for them.

Another image that was heavy on my mind was a town when a soldier was laying by the edge of a street of cobblestones. It was a miserable day in this town and we could see a faint little pink trail running in the water near him. It was a rainy cold day. These are just a few images that keep coming up now when I am thinking about it again. This opens up the files in my mind and then they disappear again. It has been said that war for an infantry man never ends. The active war ended but the psychological war never ends.

When you think of the price that was paid in World War II to have freedom in the United States, I hope everyone appreciates our country and what it stands for. The privileges we have of going to the voting booth to choose our leaders should never be taken for granted.

Chapter Four

Is this real?

One night in November, the only survivor from the machine gun section and I set up a gun position on a forward slope of a long ridge. We had lost our whole machine gun section except this guy so I was moved from mortars to machine guns. We dug in our 30 caliber machine gun and piled dirt high enough around the gun and us so we could just barely see over the top of our hole. There was a deep draw or valley and on the other side were evergreen trees.

It was misty and foggy early the next morning as we stood there looking across the valley. It was just getting daylight around 0500. The fog was hanging in the trees and a few branches came into view. As we were watching, we said to each other, "This doesn't even look real. It seems like we are in a movie." We asked each other, "Do you think this is real or is it just something that is happening to someone else?" It was a strange feeling with many emotions but, yes, it definitely was reality. The reality hit shortly thereafter when we heard loudly and clearly from the Kraut machine gun that was positioned across the draw from us and pointing in our direction. We sure woke up from our wondering about whether all of this was real.

This happened during the first ten days that we were committed in France.

Who is your brother?

Not long ago, while listening to Father Paul Timmerman's Sunday sermon at St. Joseph's Church in Montevideo, another story from my time in the war popped into my mind. I don't hear well enough to hear the whole sermon but I heard this question which is often asked of all of us. "Who is your brother?'

There was a German soldier who was wounded during one of our battles in France. Our medics of course always took care of our own wounded Americans first and then if there was time, sometimes our medics took care of wounded German soldiers. One instance that sticks in my mind was one of my first experiences in this long war. As we were walking back from some fighting, there was a young German soldier who had been wounded badly and he was laying right in the road. It was starting to get dark and the German was down and away from where our company was gathered. The medic had finished with our own casualties and now here he was all by himself with this German soldier. I decided to walk over and sit with him to give him some company. The German soldier was a nice looking young guy about my age. He wasn't able to talk anymore and he was most likely in a coma. Our medic was working very hard to bandage him up and trying to save him.

While looking at the German soldier, I kept thinking about what we had learned at home and from the Bible, "Now just who is your brother? Is an enemy soldier also your brother?" Our medic worked so hard trying to keep the young enemy soldier alive. There he was getting frustrated because he was running out of skills to keep him alive. He called out to an officer, "Isn't there some way we can get a Jeep to get him out of here? The officer said, "I don't know what we can do." The medic kept trying very hard to save this wounded German soldier. The officer said, "You are just going to have to let him die," and then he turned around and walked off. The soldier didn't last the night.

He had a family some place. His family felt as bad as any American family that had lost a son. This was an actual experience where I found out and witnessed the kindness of an American medic to his German enemy. This pops up in my mind every once in a while when hearing the sermon or the question, "Who is your brother?" I don't know if anyone besides the three of us, the medic, me, and the platoon leader ever knew about this. The medic was alone over there and he needed some company. He could have just as well said to himself, "What do I care about him, he is the enemy?" The realization came to me then that infantry men did have a sense of compassion in time of war.

That sermon brought me right back to this time in the war. This was one time that our own medic must have asked the question, "Who is my brother?" He could have said: forget it, he is just the enemy. He answered the question as the scripture tells us. There were most likely German medics who asked themselves the same question and decided that an American enemy soldier was indeed their brother. I didn't know about an example from the German side until I met up with a buddy at a 100th Division reunion forty years after the war. He told me about what happened when one of my platoon members was wounded and captured by the Germans while another was also captured at the same time but was not wounded. He said that a German medic had treated the wounds of our buddy.

Woody letting the Krauts know how he felt about them

Douglas "Woody" Woodard

First you dig a hole to get into and then you dig sideways for your head so you can stick it in under the dirt. Then you dig sideways so you can lay on your side and not be exposed to shrapnel from tree bursts. I can still see Woodard just like I took a picture of him that day in our foxhole. He was laying on his side across from me. The shelling was so dang bad that it was almost unreal. The dirt was falling down all over us while Woodard swore steadily and had cuss words that I had never heard before or since that day. He swore a steady stream. "You dirty rotten, #$^*&!* Krauts."

He kept going on through the whole time we were in the artillery barrage. It was amazing how he could think of all the words but it just streamed from him. About the only words that can be repeated are "you dirty rotten…" It wasn't fit for civilized people to hear and with all the artillery we were probably the only two that heard "Woody" yelling.

We always kept digging under the ground as fast as we could so we were covered from the barrage and we laid sideways from each other. I still laugh a lot when telling this story and wonder how a guy could cuss that steady without even taking a breath. Times like this come back in my mind when thinking about those times in foxholes. Douglas Woodard…We all called him "Woody."

We have so much to be thankful for even if the war is still going on

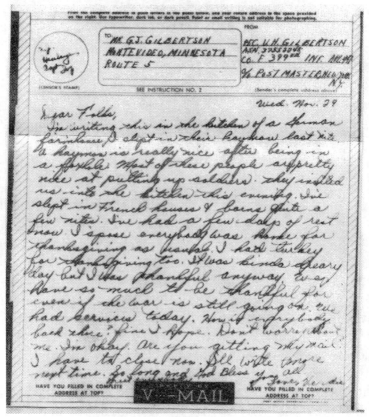

The only V-Mail letter we found. The rest of my letters were sent with 6 cent Air Mail stamps

Dear Folks,   *Wednesday, November 29, 1944 France (Pintervald)*

    I am writing this in the kitchen of a French farmhouse. I slept in their hay mow last night. A haymow is really nice after being in a foxhole. Most of the people are pretty nice at putting up soldiers. They invited us in to the kitchen this evening. I've slept in French houses and barns quite a few nites. I've had a few days of rest now. I suppose everybody was home for Thanksgiving as usual. I had turkey for Thanksgiving too. It was kind of a dreary day but I was thankful anyway. We have so much to be thankful for even if the war is still going on. We had services today. How is everybody back there? Fine I hope. Don't worry about me. I am okay.

So long and God Bless you,
Love, Verdie

A map of some of the locations in the Vosges that were taken by the 100th Division From The Story of the Century

That will be a wonderful day when the guns are silent again

Dear Folks,   *Saturday, Dec. 2 France*

    I am having a little rest now so I'll scribble a few lines. How are you all coming along back there in good old Minnesota? I suppose you have quite a bit of snow by now. You won't have such a hard time getting down to the highway now that you have that nice big road. I'm sure glad that they finally got it made.

I spose you're all preparing for Christmas by now. I sure wish I could be there with you. I hope and pray we are all back together by next Christmas and I feel sure we will too. I spose the kids are busy practicing for the Christmas program in Church. I got a hold of three Christmas cards and that's all I could get. But then I am depending on you to do my Christmas shopping for me. I received Dad's letter yesterday and thanks a million. I also got a letter from Verdie Ellingson. I wrote to Clarice, Mildred and Vernice so I hope they get there soon. I didn't have anything but V-mail stationery so it might take a while before they get there. I'll try to write to Earl and Roy as soon as I can. We have such a hard time getting stationery.

Yes, it was kind of strange stepping off the boat after being on the water for so long, but boy am I going to be glad when I get on that boat again and head for the good old USA. That will be a wonderful day when the guns are silent again. I have been staying in a house and barn for quite a while now. It's so nice compared to a fox hole. The people over here are so different from our people. They wear wooden shoes, nearly all of them. They use oxen to pull their plows and wagons, it's very seldom you see a horse. I've even seen them use one horse and one ox on the plow as a team. The farmers live in a village and the fields are scattered around. The house and barn are together in one house.

I am glad you got a good corn crop. How are the prices now?

Yes, I certainly heard about the election. Of course there wasn't much doubt Roosevelt would get it again. About 90 percent of the soldiers around here are for Roosevelt. I didn't vote this time because I wasn't quite 21 when we were supposed to send in for ballots. I guess I could have voted anyway but then figured I'd wait until next time.

I met a fellow from Appleton over here. His name is Harvey Stensrud. It sure is nice to meet someone from back there.

How are you coming with your flying Curtis? How many hours have you got now? It's pretty nice when you can use the alfalfa field isn't it? Golly I would sure like to fly again. I saw a dogfight over here one day.

I could get a truckload of souvenirs over here, German helmets, rifles and junk but I don't think I want anything to remind me of this dirty fighting over here. I'll try to bring some souvenirs though. I sure wish I had a camera so I could get a few snapshots.

Say, I sent $25 home the other day so you can expect it. There is nothing to buy over here so I don't need any money. I am glad you got my allotment. Those $30 checks are supposed to come every month so I hope you get them all.

Nope, I guess I have to close now. I hope this finds you all in the best of health and spirits. Greet everyone for me because I don't get much chance to write. So long and God Bless you all.

Love,
Verdie

Sat. Dec. 2
France

Dear Folks,

I'm having a little rest now so I'll scribble a few lines.

How are you all coming along back there in good ol' Minn? I spose you have quite a bit of snow by now you won't have such a hard time getting down to the hi way now that you have that nice big road. I'm sure glad that they finally got it made.

I spose you're all preparing for Christmas by now. I sure wish I could be there with you. I hope & pray we are all back together by next Christmas. I feel sure we will too. And I spose the kids are busy practising for the Christmas program in church. I got hold of 3 Christmas cards and that's all I could get. But then I'm depending on you to do my Christmas shopping for me.

I recieved Dad's letter yesterday, thanks a million and I also got

a letter from Verdie E. I wrote to
Clarice, Mildred & Vernice so I hope
it gets there soon. I didn't have
anything but V mail stationery so it
might take awhile before they
get them. I'll try & write to Darl
& Roy as soon as I can. You
see I have such a hard time
getting stationery.

Yes it was kinda strange stepping
off the boat after being on the
water for so long. But Boy, am
I going to be glad when I
get on that boat again & head
for the good old U.S.A. That
will be a wonderful day when
the guns are silent again.

I have been staying in a house
& barns for quite a while now.
Its so nice compared to a fox hole.
The people over here are so different
from our people. They wear wooden
shoes nearly all of them. They use
oxen to pull their plows & wagons.
Its very seldom you see a horse.
I've even seen them use one horse
& one ox on the plow as a team.
The farmers live in a village & then
the fields are scattered round. They
always have the house & barn together
in one house.

I'm glad you got a good corn crop.
How are the hog prices now?

Yes, I certainly heard about the election.
Of course there wasn't much doubt
that Roosvelt would get in again.
I think about 90% of the soldiers
over here are for Roosvelt. I didn't
vote this time 'cause I wasn't quite
21 when we were sposed to send in for
ballots. I guess I could have voted
anyway but then I figured I'd wait
until next time.

I met a fellow from Appleton
over here the other day. His
name is Harvey Stensrud. It
sure is nice to meet someone
from back there.

How are you coming with
your flying Curtis? How many
hours have you got now? Its
pretty nice when you can use
the alfalfa field isn't it? Golly I
sure would like to fly again. I
saw a dogfight over here one
day.

I could get a truckload of
souvenirs over here, German helmets
& rifles & junk but I don't think

I want anything to remind me of this dirty fighting. I'll try & bring home some souvenirs tho. I sure wish I had a camera so I could take some snapshots.

Say, I sent 15 home the other day so you can expect it. There is nothing to buy here so I don't hardly need any money. I'm glad you got my allotment. Those 30 bucks are supposed to come every month so I hope you get them all.

Phyl was telling me about the nice gift she got from your folks. Did you get to go to Hazel Run that time?

Hon, I guess I have to close now. I hope this finds you all in the best of health & spirits. Greet everybody from me because I don't get much chance to write. So long & God Bless you all.

Love,
Verdie

<u>From Century Division Reports</u>: In December, the Division went on the offensive in the vicinity of Bitche. Wingen and Lemberg were occupied in fierce fighting, 6-10 December and Reyersweiler fell. **Story of Century p 75**

December 3, The 398th, the 399th Inf. took over the area around Schalbach, Veckersviller, and Sieviller

The enemy which the 399th Inf. faced on the gray and rainy anniversary of Pearl Harbor was not merely entrenched on all the commanding ground near Lemberg; he also manned concrete pillboxes at the junction of the road running north from St. Louis to the Lemberg-Enchenberg road, on the hill at the east edge of Lemberg. At the western base of Hill 345, on the north side of the Lemberg-Mouterhouse road, he had anti-tank guns covering all routes of approach. 20mm. anti-aircraft guns, used as anti-tank guns mounted on armored vehicles, had been dug in to serve as pillboxes P78-79

In its third day of attack, 8 December, the 399thInf. Began to succeed on the Lemberg sector. The2nd Battalion, moving up from reserve in Goetzenbruck, was committed to an end run to flank the German strongpoints on Hill 345, that hill in the curve of the Lemberg-Mouterhouse highway which had stopped the 3rd Battalion for two days.

Along the railroad and high ground northeast of Lemberg, Co. F had two platoons dug in north of the railroad and to the west of a bridge spanning a railroad gorge. Except for one squad of the 3rd Platoon, the remainder of the company was south of the railroad on ground between two steep ravines. The wild terrain, the deep gorge of the railroad, and the thick woods, limited vision and made contact difficult to maintain. The enemy did not attack during the night, though a flak-wagon—a half-track vehicle armed with a 20-mm. anti-aircraft gun—did approach the 1st Platoon, withdrawing on sighting the E Co. men.

Early in the morning of 9 December, however, the enemy attacked from two sides with two flak-wagons

Tanks and TDs lined up along the main street of Lemberg preparatory to moving forward in the drive against Bitche supported by infantry armed with automatic weapons.

Having the advantage of terrain and fire-power, the Krauts forced the 1st Platoon into their foxholes and then overran the positions, firing into them at pointblank range. The 2nd Platoon, unable to come to their *comrade's rescue, with their own right flank exposed, circled back to the south side of the railroad and joined the rest of the company in regrouping.*

The combined fire of Cos. F and G finally stopped the attack, and late in the afternoon, with Co. F holding on the right flank. **The Story of the Century p 78**

Mopping up in a town in France
Army Signal Corps photo from **The Story of the Century**

Chapter Five

The Story of Lemberg

We jumped off Dec 7, 1944 at 0500. The objective for our battalion, the 399th infantry with three rifle companies, was to "cut a railroad and a highway" that was running close together near the city of Lemberg. The Krauts were using that for a supply route. Our commanders wanted the infantry to take that road and stop the German supply lines. The tactics of the German infantry, which were the same as ours, were to have secondary lines. The Krauts were on the defense and we were attacking. The first thing that happened when we jumped off was to hit their initial line of resistance. The Krauts' positions were so hidden we couldn't see them. You could probably walk right up there not spot anybody because of the camouflage.

There wasn't anybody standing up in the open so there was no one to be seen. We laid down on the ground and the weather was really nice that day as we were waiting for coordination between the units. We were on the forward slope of a hill waiting for the next move and taking a rest.

This was a downslope toward the Krauts' positions. This was really a bad situation as we were very close to the German positions. We started getting nervous whenever we were in this kind of spot. We weren't dug in and were vulnerable to mortar and artillery shells. We were just waiting to move and looking for a place to go to get some protection from enemy artillery. For some reason our squad happened to be the first one there. Our company was spread out so we were probably closest to the enemy.

There was a little cut in a side hill beyond a little swampy area with a road going across it that I kept eyeing. If something happened I was going to head for that place. It was about 200-300 yards away and was cut out like someone had dug out gravel and there were some trees around it. It looked like a perfect defense position. I wasn't looking at it thinking there was a German gun emplacement there but because I figured if the artillery started, we'd head for that as place as fast as we could.

Some of the others guys were looking at it too. We were getting kind of nervous since we were exposed while lying on the forward slope. There was a narrow dirt road that was part water and part truck tracks. That was only way we could cross. We waited and waited and then all of a sudden we started getting artillery. A Kraut was sitting up there watching us. We took off running as hard as we could for the position we had been eyeing. It happened there was a machine gun there and the Kraut was looking right down the barrel at us from 200 yards. We couldn't see him. As soon as we started running, he opened up right away and covered that road. It was like a trap. You couldn't have found a better position to set up a machine gun. The Kraut gunner had been watching us in range all the time we were laying there and was so well camouflaged that we couldn't spot him.

I just made to the road when he started firing and the dirt was flying all over. You couldn't stop or turn back. I made it to the cut and got right underneath him as he was right over my head shooting at most of the other guys in my squad. If I had jumped up, I could have almost grabbed the barrel of his machine gun. He might have been three feet over my head. He was right smack above me on the bank. The Kraut kept firing but I didn't have any grenades that could have been thrown over my shoulder into his camouflaged foxhole.

Our squad was most likely fortunate that we were the closest to the German position. He started firing as soon as we started across but we got underneath his field of fire because he couldn't lower his machine gun. Maybe when we jumped up he didn't get started firing right away. We made it close enough to the German machine gunner to avoid his fire. Some of our company farther back were there a little later and got much of the full blast, but took off going on both sides to stay out of range to avoid the firing. It must have worked for them to just slog through the swamp. Others came up behind running and fortunately the machine gunners finally ran out of ammunition.

There were most likely two Krauts in there but one of them must have took off. The guys circled around and ran behind the other Kraut who had to give up of course. He was on his hands and knees, petrified and begging for his life. He figured it was the end for him. The guys were so dang mad at this Kraut gunner but someone finally stepped in and he was let up. As far as I know we took him prisoner. If he talked, maybe some information could be gained.

One of our guys stayed back with the wounded men until the medics came so he didn't get in on the major part of the Lemberg battle. The rest of us kept right on going towards the main objective. I can see this place even now just like I have a slide of it.

That was the first German position. Then we went a little further to their main line which had an SS unit protecting it. When a company "goes in," they spearhead -meaning one company goes in a "V" and the other company protects the flank so the enemy cannot get around them. It was F Company that was spearheading this time. We came in first and E and G were on our sides. Well, the Krauts held both E Company and G Company back. So F Company got up on the point and the Krauts got behind us. The artillery was really powerful because the Krauts were strongly protecting that place.

When we approached the railroad tracks, the first rifle platoon and the machine gun section of our fourth platoon moved across the tracks. My mortar section stayed back with the riflemen and the rest of the company because we couldn't fire mortar shells through the trees that covered this area. If we fired into the branches the shells exploded right over our heads. It was a bad situation. We could have raised a lot of heck in there if hadn't been for the tree cover.

The railroad track was in a gully with a foot bridge going across it. We crossed the bridge and dug in on the other side of the tracks. The Krauts' armored vehicles came up and pinned the machine gun section in their holes. Because of the strength of the German force, the first platoon and the machine gun section got orders to pull back over the tracks towards the rest of the company. Well, the machine gun section had been pinned in the holes by the armored vehicles. There wasn't any choice. One guy from our machine gun section got out and the rest were captured. Sixteen men from my platoon were taken prisoner by the Germans but not all from F Company made it to a prison camp.

It's hard to know why, but some were shot and not taken all the way to the camps.

When the first platoon pulled back over the tracks there wasn't time to dig in and of course took they brunt of the fire. The rest of us were trapped and the Germans held E and G Company back. We were just plain overpowered. Some of us got into sort of a gully and it was very rough terrain with a lot of trees. We dug in and the Krauts knew we were in there. Maybe their thinking was, "We aren't going to send our infantry in there because we don't want to pay the price or maybe our heavy artillery will get the Americans."

We were well dug in at that point so we got through that. We weren't getting air support because the weather was so bad. Tanks weren't able to get in through the heavily wooded area to support us. We didn't know why we weren't getting any artillery support when we were trapped in there for a of couple days. The enemy didn't try to come in this pocket. While sitting in there for a long time just waiting and waiting, I swore up and down, "I am not giving up to them... no way."

After about two days in there we were running short of supplies, stuff to eat and everything else. The company commander had been on the field phone for days asking for support but we weren't getting anything. He kept telling them, "We need support, we need support." Finally, the artillery from each side that could reach the position started laying it on the Krauts' position something terrific. Everything in range zeroed in on that spot. The artillery blew a hole in there for us and the Krauts had to back off. We finally got across the tracks. Captain Huberger told us, "We held our objective." After this, Fox Company was put in reserve for a few days.

From : *399th in Action* page 62

"In the woods to the east of Lemberg, Fox Company pushed across the fortified railroad. Captain Newton Huberger sent out a call for flank support, tank, anti-tank guns; he got nothing. Alert to the tremendous danger of their exposed position, Lt. Caspar Breckinridge, Sgts. Schillberger and White kept every foxhole awake and alert during the night. At 0500 of December 9th the first of four hit-and-run flak attacks struck when a 20 mm wagon rumbled up to the foxholes. There were two more scouting attacks with three flak guns and a light tank and when no anti-tank or tank fire challenged them they grew bolder. The 1st platoon put up a valiant

fight but were virtually wiped out. Sgt Snyder charged to destroy a burp gunner who had Lt. Duncan Emery pinned and some of the second platoon escaped. Fifty five men were hit before Fox Company finally drove the attack to the flanks."

"Gilbertson, take a man with you."

Everybody was a little worked up while we were trapped by the Krauts. Lt Nicholson said to me, "Gilbertson, take a man with you, go up on the ridge, dig in and see what's going on." I kind of looked at him and said to myself, "Who should really be doing that? Should it be a PFC like me, a squad leader or even the platoon leader?" Well it was a direct order and I couldn't say anything. You never said, "No, I am not going to do that." You never said anything like that. It just wasn't done.

There was no hesitation before asking, "Beehive, do you want to go?" "Yep, Yep," he said. So we went up the ridge. When we got there we laid down flat looking around to see if we could spot any Krauts. We were very careful and picked out an escape route like any animal did.

A little clump of trees with some rocks piled around it looked like a good place to get behind if something happened. We carried one short handled spade to use for digging in. We looked all around and didn't see any Krauts. We both stood up on the ridge which you should never do. Beehive was right next to me and I had the spade. Just when I put the spade in the ground to start digging, all of a sudden a tank opened upon us. We hadn't seen them because their position was camouflaged so well. We were right smack in front of the Kraut tanks.

The shells hit the trees over our heads. Beehive did a backwards somersault and rolled down the hill as I quickly dove behind that little pile of rocks. I was still there laying flat as the 20 millimeter tank fire was hitting the trees around us. While laying there flat on the ground, I slid backwards to make it below the brow of the hill. Then we were okay. How the fire missed us is beyond me because we must have stood up right in front of the Kraut tanks.

I thought a lot about Beehive. You know that could have almost been my fault if he had been hit. Why did the platoon leader choose me? He probably knew my name better than anyone else in the platoon. Whenever anything was going on it seems he said, "Gilbertson." Going up there to see what was going on should have been his responsibility. Not mine. We weren't in a normal situation so we kind of excused some guys. Everyone was pretty worked up and just because he was the platoon leader didn't mean he always made the right decisions.

I still think about my decision of choosing "Beehive" to go along with me. What could have been...? When you talk about "Beehive" Everhart, he was the kind of guy you could always depend on. As long as he had a wad of *Beechnut* tobacco in his mouth, he was in good shape.

We got back to the platoon and abandoned the idea of moving to someplace else. You just couldn't go up on that ridge. The Krauts had us covered so there was no way we were going to sneak out of there. We were pinned down and it looked like we were going to have to stay right there for a while. Some people might call this a "near miss" but that wasn't anything infantry guys ever talked about. That's just part of it all. None of us said, "I had a near miss today."

What was the difference if it was fifty feet or one foot? That didn't have a thing to do with it as long as it missed you. When we were sitting around together I never heard anybody say, "Boy, I had a close call today." I guess we figured if it didn't happen, why even talk about it? It was just something that might have happened. We probably shouldn't even put it in the book because we didn't get hit.

In the book, "When the Odds were Even," Keith E Bonn wrote about the Vosges Mountain campaign of 1944. Bonn examined the morning reports from 7-10 December 1944 for a battle in Lemberg, France. He reported **Company F of the 399**[th] *Battalion and 100*[th] *division of 184 at full strength was met with well over 100 percent casualties during the course of November1944 to May 1945. This includes many replacements. "Although the 399*[th] *had succeeded in seizing Lemberg and opening the way for the 398*[th] *Infantry to pass thorough toward Reyersville and Bitche, operations such as these could not be sustained for long, as casualties in some of the 399*[th]*'s line were staggering.* **Company F lost 50 men out of 179,** *company B lost 44 men out of 164. The German delay slowed the American advance to two or three kilometers per day average."*

After the Lemberg battle December 11, 1944

When we left Fort Bragg, North Carolina our company strength was 184. When we finished this battle in Lemberg, I recall there were 63 of us that walked out of there along the railroad tracks. We were never at full strength after the first month in combat. We were walking very slowly while strung out along the tracks. We started moving back and then another company took over our positions. So that's what happened in the gap of the 3rd and 13th of December between my letters home. We didn't have any chance to write letters. We were just trying to hang on.

That was one instance when we had casualties and had not moved on before the GRS (Graves Registration Service) came. It was their job was to pick up casualties. When we moved across the tracks that morning Company F were still there when the GRS came and picked up the guys we lost. We hated to be there when the GRS picked them up. Since it was kind of early on in December, these guys were the ones we had known from our training days at Fort Bragg.

This was one of the few days when we were still as there the GRS guys came up. For some reason if you moved out of there when they came… well. Most of the time we had moved on but that time we hadn't. It was probably one of the worst times of all. These were guys who we had trained with, fought with and knew very well.

That was one time when the Krauts captured our guys and some never got as far as the prison camp. Some SS Krauts took prisoners but some didn't. Why I don't know. SS guys wouldn't always take prisoners but sometimes they did.

The mortar and machine gunners were usually together. I may have been captured had I not been transferred from the machine guns to mortars. Lodato was one of the machine gunners that got captured that day. I met up with him at a 100th Division reunion and he told us about that day. "The Germans lined us up against the wall and I thought that was it," he said, "I gave up because I figured it was over. The SS took a few prisoners but for some reason didn't take all of us."

The guys in Fox Company were so outraged that some said "That will be the last Kraut prisoners we take alive, period. Never!" Our guys were so worked up that they were just wild. The company commander, Captain Huberger, was very upset too but he told us "You don't want to lower yourself to the level of those people by doing the same stuff the Krauts do."

During the Lemberg battle we hadn't been able to get food and water supplies because we had been trapped for a long time. As we were dug in, we kept shrinking our rations down. As soon as we got out of there we were put in reserve. The company was ineffective because of the tremendous loss of soldiers and the fatigue from battle. We hiked back three miles from the front and got in line for some good food. The cooks had hot chow for us in the village. When the hot chow came up I was never so hungry in my life. We were warned to take our time and eat because we might get sick if we ate too fast.

The cooks had been keeping the chow warm while waiting for us. I still remember just what we had to eat. It was pancakes and big slabs of Spam. It came from Hormel and the slabs were plenty thick and more were more concentrated than the little chunks we got in our tins. We were so dog gone hungry and our stomachs had shrunk from eating K-rations all the time. I knew better but ate way too much. That was about the sickest I ever was in my life waking up stiff and hardly able to get up. My stomach hurt something terrific but I made it up just enough to get outside. That was the end of the pancakes and Spam. The cooks could have reminded us to hold back but probably figured we knew not to eat too fast and too much. That was the only time in over a year that I ever got sick while I was in France and Germany.

Verdi's note: The letter below was written in France after the three day long battle of Lemberg. The letter mentions receiving a letter on December 11ᵗʰ which was the day after we moved back to Goetzenbruck, France to regroup. Our unit was pretty beat up after being pinned down in a draw by the Germans for almost three days. We slept on the floor in a house which felt much better than sleeping in a foxhole.

All we can do is pray to God that this terrible fighting will end soon.

Dear Dad,   *Wednesday, December 13, 1944 France (Goetzenbruck)*

I received your letter the day before yesterday and thanks a million; I wait so much for mail. How are all of you coming along back there? I suppose you are walking around in snow. I'm perfectly okay. I'm in a house again right now. I am not going to say what I am doing because as you know I can't say much. Don't worry about me though.

I am so sorry to hear that Earl is in the Philippines. So, he has seen action too. All we can do is pray to God that this terrible fighting will end soon. The war over here should be over soon. I don't hear much news so you know much more about the war situation than I do. It seems funny that I am right here where it is happening but I still can't get much news.

By the way, this is German stationery I am writing on. I don't like to stoop so low as to write on Kraut paper but I couldn't find any other paper.

(Once in a while we'd go through the Krauts' packs and find a can of sardines, which we never got in our rations. We thought it was a treat to get sardines and a type of hard bread called "knackabread." It's possible there might be stationery too. It was sometimes a problem to get paper to write on)

I am glad to hear you got your old jobs back at the church.

(Pa had been a custodian for many years at Mandt Lutheran Church. Most likely I had a letter from him that said there had been a yearly meeting where it was decided he should be the custodian for another year. The money was really good in those times. He got 25 dollars a year for taking care of the church and the grounds.)

Mandt Church wouldn't seem the same if you weren't taking care of it. I've wished so many times I could be up there helping you sweep on Sunday morning. I'm not kidding either. We are so lucky we are living in a country like the good old U.S. where we are free and the churches are free. You know it really hurts when we read about people striking in the factories. Some of the people should spend 15 minutes at the front and I don't think there would be any more strikes. This war is so foolish anyway. Us guys are really getting a wonderful backing anyway so we shouldn't complain.

(The people in the United States were working in the factories and the farmers were in the fields and shipping food overseas. The people were behind us and we knew that. Everybody was working hard back at home, whatever their job was. They believed in our cause, that what we were doing was right. The people were buying war bonds and supporting us. That could be called backing too.)

It seems funny to think that Christmas is only eleven days off. I feel sure that we will all be back together by next Christmas. I suppose you are all sitting by the stove nearly all day now. I bet you have quite a bit of milking with seven fresh cows. I wish I could be helping you. Is Curtis still picking corn? I suppose you and Lyle have do all the milking then but I suppose corn picking is all finished now. The farmers over here have had to hide in the cellar too much lately to get any work done.

Well I better crawl in my sack now. A doughboy has quite a long day ahead of him you know.

Here's hoping this finds you all happy and well and may God bless you all.

Love, Verdie

We feel the true meaning of Christmas

Dear Mom,   *Friday December 15 France (Lemberg)*

I'm in a house again right now. There is a fire going in the stove so I am nice and comfortable. You must have quite a bit of snow now. I spose you've had few snowstorms. I bet you're glad you've got the new road now.

Well only ten more shopping day until Christmas. I bet everything is plenty scarce and hard to get. That's what everybody is saying. We had church services the other day and we sang some Christmas carols. It made me homesick. I imagine you will have the program in church pretty soon now. It won't seem much like Christmas here but we feel the true meaning of Christmas so much anyway and that is the main thing. I wish I could get hold of a few Christmas cards at least. I got only three sent.

Have you heard from Earl lately? I expect the war over here should be over soon now and that will be a wonderful day. The Japs are going back plenty steady too. There's only a little over two weeks left of 44. I hope and pray that 45 will get the world settled down to peace again.

Say, would you send me the addresses of some of the boys over here that I know? Maybe I could run across some of them. I met another fellow I went to radio school with back in the states.

How are Abner and Sam coming along now? Greet them from me will you?

Nope I have to close again now and I'll write again as
soon as I can. So long for now. God Bless you all.

Love, Verdie

Eat some lutefisk and lefse for me

Dear Folks,   *Monday December 18 France (Lemberg)*

I'm still staying in a house so I have it pretty nice now for a while. The chow has been good too so you don't have to worry any about me. Well a week from today is Christmas. I've been counting the days anyway even if it will be like any other day over here. I suppose you're going to have the usual family reunion on Christmas Eve and of course you will have lutefisk and lefse. Boy what I wouldn't give to be with you. We'll make up for it next year though. I suppose you are having a Christmas tree. It wouldn't seem like Christmas without one.

I hear that there are 25 foot snow drifts in South Dakota. Maybe you have just as much by now. I imagine you read in the newspapers just about where I am. I've seen some towns. I saw Saarburg and Raon L' Etape and a lot of small villages of course. Everybody has high hopes that the war over here will be over in 44 and I hope and pray it is.

How are you coming with your flying Curtis? Have you soloed yet? I spose you have to use skis on the Cub now. Say, can you send some snapshots of you and the Cub and everybody? I really like to get snapshots of all of you and the snow and everything but I spose you can't get much film now.

How's school Lyle? I hope you'll go to high school next year. You'll never be sorry you did. That must have been quite a basket social you had in school I bet it was a lot of fun.

Say, I sent $ 25 home last payday. Have you gotten it yet? I sent it through this personal transfer account. Have you gotten any more of my class E allotments? Have you heard from Earl or Roy lately? I wrote to both Earl and Roy a few days ago and Mildred, Clarice and Vernice too.

I have to tell you about the wells the French have here. They have these old fashioned ones where you drop the bucket in and crank it up with a cable on a log. I often wonder what these people would think if they saw our modern America.

Nope, I am running out of paper so I will have to close for now. Eat some lutefisk and lefse for me too will you? I'm enclosing some French money. That's what I got paid off in. One Franc is worth 2 cents.

So long and God Bless you,
Love, Verdie

<u>Century Division report</u>: *20 December. With the outbreak of the Von Rundstedt offensive, the Division was ordered to halt the attack and to hold defensive positions, south of Bitche, as part of the Seventh Army mission during the Bulge battle.*

Cold nights in the Vosges Mountains

After the long days we were ready to sleep for the night. It was tough to find a good place to lay down. Sometimes we got into an area where the ground was frozen or we may have to move out right away in the morning. We each carried a half tarp and blanket rolled up in it. We laid down and put the shelter half over us. Some of the platoon took turns on patrol. We never got to sleep all night. Even when we were in holes we got under a heavy pine tree or put the shelter half over the hole and laid down on the ground. Sometimes overnight it snowed and you when you woke up you could see humps of snow covering the sleeping soldiers. Four inches of fresh snow was good insulation and kept us warmer.

On cold nights when our feet got real cold we rubbed our feet and often times we rubbed each other's feet. We only had one extra pair of socks. We carried the extra pair hitched around our waists and sometimes the socks were wet. We slept with all of our clothes on including our boots. We couldn't build a fire to dry out or cook because the Krauts could see the smoke and that would be suicide.

When we got into a village that was cleared we might get into a barn or go inside a house. That was part of our defense. Then we could have a fire and warm up. We fired up the wood stove and got dried out. We looked for a kettle and cut off some potatoes to throw in there. The civilians had evacuated or sometimes hid in their cellars right below us. Just imagine these poor petrified civilians hiding right below us. They didn't know if we were Krauts or Americans.

One time we were sitting at a table in a French civilian's home and there was a trap door under it. We hadn't looked down there yet and then the door opened a little. A Frenchman looked up and asked us, Boche? Which is what they called the Krauts. We said, "Nix Boche, Americans." He shut the trap door and didn't come out while we there. We thought, he can stay down there he isn't bothering us. We were along the Germany/ French border so we really didn't know if he was French or German.

Now this seems like I might be lying. We were getting out in to more open country still in France and we had tank support. The tanks stopped right outside of town and we got off and walked down the street on the edge of town looking at houses. We could smell something cooking and it smelled like potatoes. We soon found where it came from so walked into the house. We had to light matches to see where we were going and there on the table was a pot of warm potatoes. There were three or four of us and we stood right there and ate the potatoes out of the kettle. I'm sure the people who lived in this house had gone down into their cellar to hide from us. We were hungry and by gosh the potatoes really tasted good.

When we got into the next village the captain said, "Find yourself a place to sleep and report at 0500." We scattered and found a good place to sleep. The town had been cleared and we were going to be there the rest of the night and it was pouring rain. This night when we found a house the Frenchman said, "You come in and stay with us." We ate supper by the table with the man and wife. We slept in the house until five the next morning. I still shake my head at hearing 0500. O five hundred.

I sure could go for some of your lutefisk and lefse and potato soup now.

Dear Mom,   Thursday Dec 21 France *(Lemberg)*
I received your very welcome letter yesterday. Thanks a lot. I got quite a bit of mail yesterday. I got two Christmas cards one from Tobiasons and one from Mrs. L Rear. Thank them for me when you see them, will you? And wish them a Merry Christmas and Happy New Year. I wish I had more cards so I could send to more people back home. I got a letter from Roy. He sounds like he has it pretty good now. I hope he can stay there.

Well today is the shortest day of the year. The days sure are short. Time goes so fast that pretty soon we will be looking for spring again. Only three days left until Christmas. I am hoping to be in a house for Christmas. The fellows said the other day that we would have a Christmas tree if we are in a house. I don't know what we will decorate it with but it would be fun to have anyway.

You asked me to request things so now I will be requesting all the time, "tsk, tsk." I really would like a box of homemade cookies and if you could send me some candy, a jar of jam or peanut butter. I would really like that and peanuts too.

I'm getting so many good clothes now that you don't have to worry about me. I hope you got my request for gloves. I sure could use a pair of lined leather gloves.

How does the war look from that side of the pond? I guess you read plenty about it in the newspapers. All I can say is that I hope and pray that it ends soon and we have peace on earth and good will toward man again. I can't see why the Krauts keep fighting anyway.

So Roy sent home a Jap rifle. I bet that is interesting. I've had plenty chances to pick up German rifles and machine pistols in the woods but it isn't convenient to take any of them along. I woke up one morning and I had had been sleeping on a German machine pistol all night. I felt like I was laying on something but I didn't feel like moving. I will try and send some souvenirs home or wait and take them home with me. Yes, I've seen a lot of interesting things but I've seen a lot of things that aren't so nice too. The sight of a battlefield isn't so nice and the Germans have sure annihilated these little villages. I haven't had it so bad so don't worry.

Gee Mom, I sure could go for some of your lutefisk and lefse and potato soup now. I get plenty to eat but there is nothing like home cooking. I'll make up for it when I got home though. Have you gotten any more snow? You'll have a nice white Christmas then won't you?

Nope, it's time for chow now so I better scram. I will write again as soon as I can. May
God bless you all.

A very Merry and Blessed Christmas to you all,
Love, Verdie

December 22 *When the division had completed its adjustment to its new lines on 22 December, these were the sectors held: The 2nd Battalion of the 399th, holding the right flank, was in defensive positions facing east from just above the Lemberg-Mouterhouse road north to the hill called le Kreutzberg across the Lemberg Bitche railroad, and then north along a line of hills just west of that railroad to the Lemberg-Bitche highway.* **The Story of the Century p 79**

Chow for an Infantry Man

Chow for us was usually where ever we happened to be. I may have used the phrase, "it's time for chow now" to give my family the idea that I was eating with a bunch of us in the mess hall just like in basic training back in the states. We didn't really need to go to any other place to have chow because it all came in a little box that wasn't much bigger than a Cracker Jack box. Why not make write a letter thinking of what the folks are going to read? I knew it wasn't easy for my parents. Why not make them feel as best as I could? What would be the purpose of saying I was sitting in a foxhole hole eating a chunk of cheese, some crackers, some hard chocolate and a round piece of hard finely ground meat? And say it was either raining or snowing.

We usually ate our K-rations whenever we had time after we dug in for the night. When we were in defense positions it was pretty much to each their own. It was hit and miss most of the time. Sometimes I carried a piece of cheese in my pocket and took a chunk out of it while we were moving.

Supper rations most often were eaten after dark. It was one can of pork luncheon meat that was finely ground. It came in a round can and was packed hard so you could grab it and chew pieces of it. The solid chocolate bar had a warning on it. "Do not eat the whole bar at once and then drink water." There was a lot of nutrition in the chocolate bar as we chewed little pieces.

Eating rations while under fire.

We were in defense positions and dug in on the backward slope of the hill so we had some protection. The back side gave us cover from small arms fire. We were there for a few days so we had even covered our holes with some logs to protect us from shrapnel from artillery bursts. We went out of our holes sometimes and three or four guys sat together to eat our rations. There was a Kraut machine gun position that was within range of us. Their guns were raised up and fired high and the rounds dropped down at a fairly sharp angle. We called it "plunging fire." It arced up and then came in behind the hill where we were eating. It wasn't very effective so it was more like harassment. The Krauts were hoping the shells dropped into our area and sometimes they did.

One day four of us were sitting on a fallen log and it was pretty quiet around us. All of a sudden the Krauts opened up and the plunging rounds were dropping into our area. The shells happened to get in our range. Pretty soon we saw dirt and leaves flying all over the place. We said, "The heck with it. Let's go into our holes," but one of the guys said, "The heck with them, I am just going to sit here and finish my rations." Every once in a while the dirt and leaves were flying around him. The other three of us were in our holes. The firing very wasn't effective but he could have gotten hit while he was eating under fire. I guess our guy was just tired of eating rations in a fox hole.

Replacements and plunging fire

The ground was frozen but you could still see the dirt and leaves fly when the rounds hit. It was pretty cold on this bright moonlit night and you good see pretty well in the woods. A couple of replacements were brought up to join our platoon. A few of us were standing when the new guys got there. It was pretty light even real late at night. We must have made some noise so the guy bringing the replacements heard us. Of course the replacements were petrified coming up there at night. You can imagine how the new men felt- just think about it. The experienced guys partnered up with the new guy in a foxhole and gave them instructions to get in and stay there for the night.

Just then a Kraut who had probably heard us too decided to let go with a burst of plunging fire. This is gunfire directed from an elevated position in order to fall on an enemy from above. It was shot up high and it dropped right smack in the area where we were standing. It was mostly for harassment. It wasn't a bit funny but we were experienced and just stood there. The minute the shells landed the two replacements hit the dirt and layed there as flat as possible. This is what we had all learned during our infantry training. That was the only burst that was fired that night and nobody was hit but can you imagine this kind of start for a replacement coming late at night? This was orientation for real. No more practice. This was a place where we stayed for two or three days and the Krauts kept harassing us with plunging fire.

Sleeping Barrages ... Getting a night's sleep

105 mm Howitzers
From The Story of the Century

It got to a point where a company of infantry men was so sleep deprived that we were not very effective in battle. Some nights the artillery laid down what were called "sleeping barrages." Before it started the artillery let the infantry know when the shelling was to start. It sounds crazy, but when the artillery went over us for most of the night, we could get some much needed sleep. With all the heavy artillery landing, the enemy wouldn't be moving so we did not have to stand on an outpost. We could get a pretty good night's sleep during all the artillery noise.

One night I was in the foxhole with "Beehive" and we were both sleeping. Any other time one of us had to be awake and listening. We knew it should be reasonably safe that night because our artillery unit was firing sleeping barrages. Early in the morning the artillery suddenly stopped and right away we woke up. "Beehive" looked around and said to me, "The artillery stopped, do you suppose the war is over?" That meant it was time to get up when the heavy artillery quit firing. Maybe the artillery men needed to get some sleep after being up all night helping us.

Huge search lights that were mounted on trailers and made for spotting airplanes at night could shine way up in the sky over 20,000 feet. Sometimes when there was an overcast night and clouds were low, the lights were turned on, and reflected off of the clouds. It was really weird. It lit up the whole unit almost like daylight. It suddenly went from pitch dark to bright light. This was done it while we were dug in. This way we could spot any movement. Sometimes the lights were left on for hours.

Another weird thing from the artillery was the big eighty-one mortars behind us quite a ways. Flares with a parachute were fired in front of us. It was absolutely pitch dark and then we heard a loud, Pow! And then the flares went off. This lit up the sky like someone had turned on the lights. It was weird to go from pitch dark to the lights going on. It lasted for about ten minutes as the parachutes slowed down the flares. We never knew when the artillery unit was going to fire one. The Krauts never fired anything like that in our direction.

Oh Holy Night

This night made the winter a little shorter

Every time I hear "Oh Holy Night" on Christmas Eve I think of a little French village in the Vosges Mountains back in 1944. It was the first time I had ever heard this song. It was a beautiful song to me after we had listened to and felt the roar of artillery while we were clearing the Vosges Mountains. Our platoon leader asked for two volunteers to go to a Christmas service that night. Most of the men wanted to stay put and hold their positions in the snow but two of us decided to go back to the service.

Clyde Simmons and I hiked back a couple of miles from the front to a village where we had a nice Christmas service in a little building. The next day it was still pretty quiet so we decorated a small pine tree with pieces of foil that had been dropped from bombers to foul up the radar. We gathered tin foil and yellow foil that the Germans had dropped and hung it on the tree. The ground was piled high with snow.

GREETINGS . . . .

TO ROY, EARL AND VERDIE GILBERTSON

Through the good will of The Montevideo American we are hereby sending to you, Roy, Earl and Verdie Gilbertson, our best wishes for a Merry Christmas and a happy New Year, that we hope will again bring peace and good will toward all mankind.

God bless you all.

MR. AND MRS. GERHARD J. GILBERTSON, Curtis and Lyle

A note my family put in the Montevideo American. It was always nice to know people back home were thinking of us.

"The Yanks don't take no monkey business from anybody."

Dear Folks,   *Tuesday December 26 France (outside Lemberg)*

Well how did you celebrate over Christmas? I imagine you had the usual family reunion and of course you had lutefisk and lefse. I did my celebrating out in the woods in a pup tent. (*I may have been making the part about a pup tent up to make it sound better than it really was that night*). I had a pleasant Christmas though. Christmas Eve here was the same as any other night up here of course. I sure did think of you folks back home. I had it all figured out when you would be eating lutefisk and lefse and sitting around the Christmas tree. I was homesick but so was everybody else. A couple of us went out in the woods and got a Christmas tree and set it up. Of course we couldn't decorate it. On Christmas day we had services in a little village so I hiked in for that. It was a very good sermon. For Christmas dinner they brought in turkey, mashed potatoes, string beans, cranberry sauce, pie, nuts and candy and boy did I eat.

I got packages from Clarice and Eleanor Weckhorst and one from the Luther League. Golly, they really were swell. I got so many nice things from Clarice and Eleanor. Clarice sent some homemade candy. The package from the Luther League was also very nice. They sent the Monte American and some magazines and candy. I appreciate it all very much. I wish there was something I could do to express my thanks. I hope everybody realizes how much things like this mean to us doughboys over here. I got a quite a few Christmas cards too. I am going to try and write to everyone if I possibly can.

I'm in a house today and the woman who lives here used to live in Minnesota. Her brothers are in Dakota now and she speaks good English which is rare over here. Today we got six candy bars, a cigar and two cans of beer *(2014, I recall it was Ruppert Beer)* and some peanuts. I never cared much for beer but it tasted good now.

No doubt you had a white Christmas this year. Did you go to many Christmas programs?

I guess Christmas this year was just like the chaplain said in his sermon. It isn't a Merry Christmas and there's no peace but we feel the true meaning of Christmas so much anyway. We are so thankful that our almighty God is ever present to protect us no matter what may come.

Well what do you think of the war? It looks like the Krauts are making a last effort. Don't worry, they won't get far. The Yanks don't take no monkey business from anybody.

How's the Chevy percolating? Are the tires holding out pretty good? I got a letter from Verdie Ellingson and he said that Clarence Jerve is coming home and Marvin and Orville Jerve too. He was saying that Marvin is in pretty bad shape. I hope he comes out okay. It's too bad we have people like Japs and Germans. They'll suffer plenty for it though.

Have you heard from Earl lately? I hope he isn't having it too bad. I had a letter from Roy and I'm glad he is still in the same place. The plaster is falling down from the ceiling in here so I think I better put my steel helmet on. I just finished using it as a wash basin.

I'm sitting by the window writing and I wish you could see some of these civilians. You would get a big kick out of them. They go clomping down the street in their wooden shoes. I don't think they've changed much in the last hundred years.

Tues eve. Here I am again. I just came back from chow and I received your very welcome Christmas package so I thought I'd write a few more lines before I mail this. Thanks for everything in the Christmas packages. I started in on it already, the candy is so very good and I can really use the socks and handkerchiefs. And I'm so glad you included the candles because most of the time that is the only light we have. I am so glad you sent the cough drops too. I can make use of everything in the packages so very much. You don't know how much I appreciate it so thank you so much again. I also received Mildred's package at the same time and that is so very nice too. I am really eating now. I will be filled up for a long time. Those Christmas packages make me so happy. It makes it seem so much more like Christmas.

Nope it's soon time for chow so this will have to be all for now.

Thanks so much for everything, I appreciated your very nice card and thanks again. Goodnite.

Here's hoping this finds you all well and happy and may God Bless you all.

Love, Verdie
Tell Shep hi.

Locations

During darkness of 28 December, the division put "Plan Tennessee" into action. This was an attempt to achieve a defense in depth on a front so long that our lines were spread dangerously thin. Strategy called for each regiment to have two battalions on line and one in reserve. Every day of our defensive operations, each regiment was to dispatch a patrol of at least platoon strength, in daylight or dark, to gain information or take prisoners.

The 2nd Battalion of the 399th, taking over from the 3rd Battalion 398th, left its defenses facing eastward along the Lemberg-Bitche highway and came into line next to the 1st Battalion 399th Inf. in position north of Legeret Farm. From "The Story of the Century"

CHAPTER SIX

"Now don't start worrying anymore about me"

Dear Mom,   Saturday December 30, 1944 France (near *Enchenberg*)

I received your letter this morning and I was so glad to get it. Thanks for the envelopes, stationary and stamps. I can sure make use of that. I got some more Christmas cards today from Vernice, Clarice and Aldora Goulson.

How is the weather back there now? Have you gotten any more snow? I sure wish I could be back there with you shoveling snow. I've seen a lot of new places since I've been in the Army but there's no place that can compare with Minnesota.

It sounds like Earl has been through quite a bit. I've been waiting to hear from him. They've taken over all of Lyte now haven't they so I hope he won't have to see any more action.

I'm still staying in a building. I've had it pretty nice now for a long time. Yes Mom, I've seen quite a bit of action. Of course it isn't pleasant, but there's nothing we can do except hope and pray this war ends soon. Now don't start worrying anymore about me because I've got it nice now. It was pretty rough for a while though. I expect to see this war over any day now. It won't be long before it is though. Only one more day left of 1944. Time sure flies.

Did Mildred and Vernice get their big Christmas presents yet? I am waiting to hear. I suppose Lyle is having his Christmas vacation now. I bet he can hardly wait for school to start again.

I heard about President Roosevelt's speech and he said the boys will be home by next Christmas. That really will be a wonderful day when everybody can be back with their loved ones again. it won't be long till that day either, I feel sure of that. By the way that letter I got from you today was mailed December 1ˢᵗ in case you like to know.

Thanks a lot for doing my Christmas shopping for me. It makes me feel much better. I will be home so I can do my own shopping next year.

Well I have to close now it is time to eat. Here's hoping this finds you well and happy and may God bless you all.

Love, Verdie

On outpost

We were sent out at night to look and listen for any Kraut activities. Two of us stood back to back and continuously rotated turning around and around. We'd be someplace in the woods in front of the company. We pretty much stayed in one place but if it was bright moonlight we got in the shadow of the trees. We slowly turned together and by moving we kept our feet warmer. We were back to back all the time listening and watching for the enemy.

"Beehive" usually chewed tobacco and he spit it out in the snow as we rotated. I always kidded him that it looked like a bunch of turkeys had been sitting up in the trees. We were usually out there for two or three hours at a time. Our platoon leader made the roster of who was on outpost together. When two came in, two other guys went out to replace them. We took turns and knew who the next to go was. After a short rest it was time to go out to our post again. It was usually eight guys taking their turn and we all got back together in the morning before light. Most of the time we stood and just listened for any movement coming from the Krauts. Usually we didn't hear or see anything. The Krauts were most likely doing the same thing as us but we didn't run in to any of them in the woods at night.

One night we weren't just listening, we were looking to catch some of the enemy on their outposts so we could question a prisoner for any information that may help us. Lt. Emery was leading the patrol and it was snowing when he came across two Krauts laying in a foxhole. He jumped in there with his 45 caliber pistol and took them back for questioning.

A SOLDIERS STORY

*The rifleman fights without promise of either reward or relief.
Behind every river there is another hill - and behind that hill,
another river.
After weeks or months in the line only a wound can offer him
the comfort of safety, shelter and bed.
Those who are left to fight, fight on, evading death but
knowing that with each day of evasion they have exhausted
one more chance for survival. Sooner or later, unless victory
comes, this chase must end either on the litter or in the grave.*

General Of The Army

Omar N. Bradley

A *Soldier's Story* by General Omar Bradley

**My letter from January 3, 1945 right after
the New Year's barrage of NordWind**

Dear Dad,

Wednesday
Jan. 3, 1945 evening

Happy New Year to you all! I'm a little late as usual but you know what a lazy boy is like. How did you celebrate New Years? I imagine things were pretty quiet. New Year sure came in with a bang here too. I think we all saw the new year in too. I think we all celebrated by saying a prayer to God that this year will be a peaceful year.

I received your letter the other day & today I got moms, mailed Dec. 23. Thanks a million. And I got a very nice box from Phyl today with plenty of stationery & candy. I was so glad to get it.

Oh I have to tell you. I got the combat infantryman's badge the other day. I'm sure proud of that. To get it you have to see action under small arms fire like rifles & machine guns, and also artillery fire. I feel that I've earned it too 'cause I've been on the front lines for 63 days now. I didn't do anything heroic to get it tho. I also got a $10 a month raise with it so I get $74.80 a month now. The badge is something the infantrymen get when mine seen action. Maybe you've seen pictures of them. It has a silver rifle on a blue background with a wreath around it. I'm planning to send it to either you folks or Phyl to keep for me. I never get a chance to dress up under fire so I don't think it's any use to keep it over here.

I'm glad to hear that you're all okay. I'm just fine. I've got it pretty nice now so don't worry a bit about me. I get a chance to stay in a building once in awhile & that really helps. I've gotten so many good clothes too now. I've got a fur lined overcoat & wool lined pants. I've also got shoes that look just like those hunting pacs. I'm really waiting for those gloves, & sure you sent tho. I realize how hard it is to get rubberized gloves so don't worry about that. It isn't raining now so I don't suffer any.

Well we had a white New Years anyway not much tho. Have you had any more snow? I heard that it was 18° below in Minn. now so _____ ___ ____ it's been kinda cold ____, I'm in the 7th Army so you know about where I am.

Can you send me Dan's address? If I know what outfit he's in I might be able to run into him sometime.

I haven't heard from Carl yet. I'm waiting to hear from him. I imagine he's seen plenty.

I sure hope that you & Mr. Brown get a chance to go fishing together. Say, I was going to ask you how you two get along on politics.*

There's a couple of cows in one of these barns in this village so I was kinda figuring on going out & milking tonite. I'm hungry for milk. I think the farmer moved out today. I think he milked tonite so I'll have to wait awhile till some more milk has come in (ha ha). S'pose I'll get kicked but it's worth the chance.

I have one more letter (of course) to write tonite so I better close now. I'll tell you next time whether I got the milk or not. So long & may God bless you all. Goodnite.

Tell Skip Hi

Love,
Verdie

Minnesota Farm Boy in France/ New Year's came in with a bang (ha, ha)

Dear Dad,   *Wednesday January 3rd, 1945 France (Hottveiler)*

Happy New Year to all of you. I'm a little late as usual but you know what a doughboy is like. How did you celebrate New Year's? I imagine things were pretty quiet. The New Year came in with a bang here. (ha, ha) *(*See story below about the bang coming from Operation Nord Wind).* I saw the New Year in too. We all celebrated by saying a prayer to God that this year will be a peaceful year.

I received your letter the other day and got Mom's mailed December 23rd. Thanks a million. Oh, I have to tell you I got the combat infantry badge the other day. I'm kinda proud of that. To get it you have to see action under small arms fire like rifles and machine guns and also artillery fire. I feel that I've earned it too because I've been on the front lines for 63 days now. I didn't do anything heroic to earn it though. I also get a $10 a month raise so I get $74.80 a month now. The badge is something us infantrymen get when we've seen action. Maybe you have seen pictures of them. It has a silver rifle on a blue background with a wreath around it. I am planning on sending it to you to keep for me. I never get a chance to dress up over here so I don't think it's any use to keep it over here.

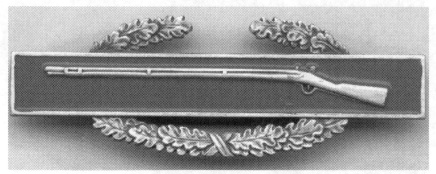

My combat infantry badge earned in France

I am glad to hear you are okay. I am just fine. I've got it pretty nice now so don't worry a bit about me. I get a chance to stay in a building once in a while and that really helps. I've gotten so many good clothes too now. I've got a fur lined overcoat and wool lined pants. I've also got shoes that look just like those hunting packs. I'm really waiting for those gloves and socks you sent though. I realize how hard it is for you to get rubberized gloves so don't worry about that. It isn't raining now so I don't suffer any.

Well, we had white New Years anyway. Not much though. I heard that it was 18 below in Minn. It's been kinda cold here. I am in the 7ᵗʰ Army so you know about where I am.

There are a couple of cows in one of these barns so I was kind of figuring on going out and milking tonight. I'm hungry for milk. The farmer moved out today. He milked the cows tonight so we will have to wait awhile until some more milk has come in. (ha ha) I supposed I'll get kicked but it's worth the chance.

I have more letters to write tonight so I better close now. I will tell you next time whether I got the milk or not.

So long, and May God Bless You all. Good nite.
Love Verdi

Tell Shep Hi *(I never forgot Shep, our family dog)*

For award of the Combat Infantry Badge a Soldier must meet the following three requirements:

1. *Be an infantryman satisfactorily performing infantry duties.*
2. *Be assigned to an infantry unit during such time as the unit is engaged in active ground combat.*
3. *Actively engage the enemy in ground combat.*

www.army.mil/symbols/CombatBadges/infantry

*Operation NordWind

On New Year's Eve 1944 I was on outpost and Lt Nicholson told me to wake him up right before midnight so we could bring in the New Year with a little sip each from his liquor ration. We were staying in some old French barracks the Krauts had been using. Well, I woke him up a little before midnight and just then, at the stroke of midnight, we heard the loudest sounds of the war. We thought the world was ending. The Krauts must have all been keeping their eyes on their watches because at exactly midnight December 31, 1944, they let loose with their entire artillery arsenal. This was no time for us to share in the liquor ration as we all scattered to group up for another fight.

We met up with the 17th SS Panzer Grenadier Division. In English this meant "armored tank supported infantry." This unit broke our lines and we had to pull back and join together in a building to regroup.

NordWind

We got the report about our position telling us that we were surrounded by the enemy. We were given a compass heading and told to head out by twos and threes and try to get to a half mile gap about two or three miles through the woods. We left immediately with our mortars and machine guns and headed back towards the gap we had been told about. There were more than three in our group and Captain Huberger was with us. There weren't many others around as the rest of the company was moving out as fast they we could. We managed to get to that half mile gap by staying in a heavily wooded ravine. We finally came to a clearing and found one of our artillery positions. The artillery men had already left but the artillery pieces were standing in the open field with ammunition stacked next to them. We just passed it by and kept going back. Our artillery was usually five miles behind us and when we got to their positions none of the artillery were still there. The tanks were gone too. The infantry is always the last to leave. This was the first time I had even seen any artillery up close.

The artillery men must have jumped in the trucks in a hurry and hadn't done anything with the artillery because the ammunition was still sitting there. After a while we met up with the rest of our company and formed up again. The Krauts closed the gap somewhere thinking we were pinched off but somehow we got away. Their plan called for trapping the whole 100th Division. We regrouped at least five or six miles back from where we started.

In a couple of days our unit counter attacked and drove the Krauts back out of the area taken from us when we made our strategic withdrawal. We got back to the positions we had left in such a big hurry. On our way back we found our artillery again and one of the fellows in our company knew how to use it. He lowered the 105mm howitzer barrel piece and fired point blank into the Kraut positions. We were able to drive the Krauts back.

We were up against the 17th SS Panzer Grenadier Division that had tanks and infantry. Our officers told us later that that we were outnumbered six to one by the three German divisions that had encircled us. We didn't know at the time that the German plan was to encircle us but we found out later that their objective was to annihilate the 100th Division.

The Panzer Division was well equipped, but after the 399th regrouped, we held the Krauts from coming any further back. We dug in and held our ground. There were three days of what the reports called, "ferocious fighting" and I can verify that from personal experience. While we were fighting we didn't really know how many days it took so I get the time details from historical division reports.

After this with a lot of moving and fighting everyone in the division was pretty well worn out so we went into a defensive position. There are many stories to tell about each battle and each person certainly had different experiences about how he got out of the trap that was planned by the 17th SS Grenadier division.

After the Krauts had closed in the gap, we set up outposts to see if there were any patrols we could spot at night. Two of us were assigned to an outpost and it was a trail that came through the woods where we figured the German tanks may be moving. Engineers had wired huge trees with *prima cord*.* You could set off the explosive and the tree would come down. It was set with a fuse and all you needed to do was pull the fuse and take off and that was enough to drop the tree. Our division wanted to set up roadblocks so two of us were assigned to go back in the woods quite a long ways where the Krauts might be moving tanks. Someone who knew where this location was took us in there and left. We stood there at night and waited and waited.

We were told, "If a tank comes through there, just blow the tree and head out." We waited and waited and there were no tanks. It was quiet and we didn't see or hear anything out there. We began to wonder when we were going to get relieved. "Jeepers, how long are we gonna be out here? Did our relief forget about us?"

We were supposed to be there a couple of hours and here we had spent the biggest part of the night and it was soon daylight. Finally we were watching around and there was a big fallen tree that we hung around for some protection. We figured, if someone doesn't come to

81

relieve us soon, we are going to dig under the tree and just stay here… period.

Pretty soon we could see a guy coming up from behind us. There was snow on the ground and he was dodging from one tree to next; zigzagging. We watched and figured he might be coming to relieve us. It was moonlight but you couldn't tell if it was an enemy or one of us. As we watched, he went through the shadows and kept zigzagging behind trees. He got close to us and he had the password. It was an officer but he wasn't our platoon leader. He was a 2nd lieutenant. He was all shook up and told us, "Come on, come on, get the hell out of here now! Follow me." We took off running right away towards his jeep. He had brought it up quite a ways to get close to us. We jumped in the jeep and headed off for our own area as fast as we could go.

This officer that we didn't even know told us that our unit had sent out a patrol to relieve us but upon their return said they couldn't find us. I don't think those guys even went out as far as we were posted. They probably just turned back without looking for us very long. We could see this lieutenant a quite a ways away so if our patrol had been close we could have seen anyone approaching our post. Here this officer from another platoon came out and picked us up. We didn't know how he knew where we were but; by gosh, that was really good of him to go out all by himself and pick us up.

We got back to our positions and we hadn't eaten for a long time. The kitchen crew had to scratch up some food for us. Our company commander was in a house when we first got back but later when we saw him he looked at us for the longest time and didn't say anything. We were a little bit… annoyed. We kept looking at him and I suppose he didn't really know what to say to us.

If it hadn't been for the other officer, we'd have been left out there. You couldn't ever leave your post. We'd have stayed there until the Germans might have counter attacked and came up on us. There was no other way. If you left your post you'd really be in trouble. We had been very concerned while we were waiting and waiting. There had been just a plain foul up where these guys were supposed to come and relieve us. Fortunately the tanks didn't come while we were there and thankfully the lieutenant found us before anything happened.

*Primacord is a brand of detonating cord used in blasting.

From a <u>100th division report,</u> "During Operation NORDWIND, the last German offensive on the Western Front, three German divisions attempted to encircle and annihilate the 100th Infantry Division. Near Lemberg, on the Division's right, the XC Corps attackers were stopped by the 399th and elements of the 398th Infantry Regiment after three days of ferocious fighting."

100th Division / Defeated the combined attacks of two German divisions, which were strongly supported by tanks, super-heavy tank destroyers, artillery and rockets, in early January 1945, during the last German offensive in the West, Operation NORDWIND.

After giving some ground initially, the 399th Infantry Regiment tenaciously defended Lemberg in the face of a determined assault by the entire 559th Volks-Grenadier Division and parts of the 257th; on the left, the 397th Infantry refused to be pushed out of the village of Rimling, where it blunted the attack of the vaunted 17th SS Panzer-Grenadiers,. Although the Germans had expected to surround and annihilate the 100th in two days, the Division's stubborn defense completely disrupted the Germans' efforts to regain the strategically-critical Saverne Pass. While the German offensive raged on throughout January on the Alsatian Plain, the 100th's defense in the snows of the worst winter of the 20th century was the single most significant factor in blunting the last German thrust of the war in the West.

Piano Movers Again

This was during Operation NordWind. The Germans had rocket launchers that they called Nebelwarfers and the American put the name on them, "Screaming Meemies." The Krauts fired them in bunches of five or six at a time. You could hear the shells coming at about the time they left the rocket launcher. It seemed like we heard them for a long time but it was probably only a few seconds. As the shells got closer it was the weirdest sound and I have never heard anything else like it. The Germans must have made them with the purpose of making those sounds as a means of harassment. The first time we heard it we knew it was something completely different. Beehive and I were standing a building in an old army camo that had been partially destroyed. That was our defense position.

There was a doorway where we were standing in a big old long heavily built barracks that had been damaged. We were standing on each side of the door facing the German position and things were pretty quiet. All of a sudden we heard a strange noise coming and didn't know what it was. It got louder and we figured, "boy that's got to be something different. We better get out of here." Beehive and I started running as fast as we could go down a very long hallway towards the end of the barracks. We got to where there was a turn in the hall we slid around it and layed flat on the floor behind a wall to get away from the shelling. That was about the time they hit and missed the barracks we were in but they struck a long line of buildings near us that had been stables. The noise was just deafening.

Then it was over and it was quiet while we layed there on the floor for a while. When we got up to look around to see what happened we saw that all of those buildings close to us were just demolished flat. They practically disappeared.

That was the first time we heard the "Screaming Meemies," and from then on we knew exactly what they were. Beehive said they sounded like someone was pushing a piano across the floor over gravel and then pushed it down the steps. When they came again later he'd say, "Here come those piano movers again."

The Germans must not have had many of these weapons because we didn't hear them very often. The history of the 100th division tells about "Screaming Meemies" in Heilbronn in April 1945 but I don't remember them in that battle.

Time to go out and milk

Dear Mom and All of you,   *Thursday night Jan 4, 1945 France*

Thanks so much for the package. I can sure use the gloves and the sweater. You don't know how happy I am to get those boxes. I am so glad you sent candles. Gee I can really make use of them. You see that is the only light we have and candles are so hard to get hold of over here. *(* candles)* I am eating the cake by candle light now and it sure is good. I gave the fellows in my platoon a piece too and they said it was sure good.

I didn't get that cow milked last night but I'm going to try again tonight. Some of the fellows just came in with a chicken. They just went to chop its head off. Looks like we will have fresh chicken. My mission is to get fresh milk (ha, ha). Quite an outfit we got isn't it? We get kind of tired of eating Army chow. The farmers around here aren't home tonight (tsk, tsk)

Nope it's soon time to go out and milk so I better close now. Here's hoping this finds you all well and happy and may God Bless you all.

Thanks again for the nice package.
Love, Verdie

*Candles: The K-rations boxes were coated with wax to keep them dry. When we ran out of candles we started scraping the wax off the boxes. We put the wax in one of the meat ration cans and waited until we had enough to melt it and make a candle. For a wick, we used part of a shoe lace or whatever else we could find. These candles worked okay but we were sure happy to get store bought ones from home.

Patrols

After writing letters and then eating cake and chicken we had other duties. Two of us went out together on patrol in the dark. We mostly spent two hours listening and looking and then going back to our foxholes or a house and then another two went out on patrol.

Century Division Report: German counterattacks of 1 and 8-10 January 1945 were repulsed; thereafter the sector was generally quiet and the Division prepared for a resumption of the offensive.

K Rations: The Army travels on its stomach.

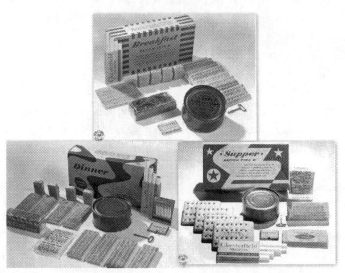

K rations, Breakfast, Dinner and Supper
Source US Army, Signal Corps
US Army Quartermaster Museum

K Rations consisted of a little packet of crackers, about the size of an overgrown Cracker Jack box, one small tin of super concentrated meat. (It said Hormel and it was drab army color), four cigarettes and one candy bar. The bar was concentrated and it was so hard we couldn't eat it very fast. We were told not to eat it and then drink water because the chocolate swelled. That was supper for a hard working infantry man.

For breakfast there were the same crackers. The Army drab green tin had eggs and pieces of ham. It sure didn't have a label that said country fresh eggs. We mostly ate the eggs cold. Lunch was the same except the tin had a real hard hunk of cheese. The round tins were three inches around and one and a half inches thick. The ingredients weren't listed on the can. I guess it wasn't any of our business and it didn't make any difference because we were going to eat whatever was given to us.

The taste wasn't too bad until we got tired of it. We constantly ate on the move. We carried the hard cheese and drank water out of the canteen. For a long time after the war I couldn't even look at cheese. Meal times were whenever we had any time. We carried our own K rations for up to two days. The supply guys never brought the K rations all the way up to us, only as far as they dared to get near the frontlines.

The rations and water were dumped off some place and then the kitchen crew radioed us telling the spot where the food had been dropped. Then we sent a detail back to get our food. We took turns getting our food. Ammunition was delivered the same way.

The K-rations didn't seem like much but somehow we kept on going. At our age and with all that we did we were always hungry but our strength and the stamina was still there. The rations must have been designed with enough nutrition to keep us going.* none of us were overweight. We were mighty lean.

*Type K, or "K-ration"; the final version totaled 2,830 calories a day.[4]

The kitchen crew gave us a hot meal of meat and potatoes and bread when we were in reserve or if we were in an area where it was easier to get to and things were generally quiet. It was sure something better than K rations. Sometimes all that was brought up was baked bread and coffee. Then we got a four inch slice of bread and a few cups of coffee. We thought, "Jeepers, I never knew how good fresh bread could taste." We really appreciated that. It was baked far back behind the lines in the Army kitchens.

The coffee came in a big four or five gallon insulated can. A hot cup of coffee made by the kitchen crew really tasted great after we had been making our own coffee with powdered coffee in a canteen cup. Sometimes we had a chance to make coffee or bouillon that came in the K- rations but usually we were on the move. You could get the coffee and bullion pretty hot with the little stove. The bullion had a lot of nutrition in it and the coffee had a lot of caffeine that kept us going. We had a little gas stove we carried in our pack. We each took turns carrying the stove and gas. The problem was that we couldn't always get gas. Most of the time we tossed the packs of coffee away. Sometimes we gave the candy and bullion to civilians or maybe we traded for bread.

The tankers carried supplies and occasionally we got C rations and that was a step up for an infantry man. This is what the artillery units and tanker units got. C Rations were the size of a soup can with pork and beans and some kind of stew. It tasted great if we could heat them up.

The tankers tried to look after us the best they could. When the infantry was close we protected them and a tank came in handy to ride on. Tanks protected us by riding over the shoe mines. This saved us as we walked in the tank tracks. Tanks had a lot of fire power that could knock buildings down. If the enemy was in a building, shells from the tanks could clear it out and make it safer for the infantry.

Two Soldiers, a Hungry Dog and a Can of Meat

My grandson Jacob asked me how our food rations were and I told him, "Well, the food wasn't too bad, but the dogs didn't like some of the rations." One day we stopped to eat and were sitting on a fallen tree or a stump. It was outside of a village in France. A dog came up, and he looked like he was just about starved. He really needed some food to eat. One of the fellas liked dogs, so he said to me, "You know, I am going to give part of my rations to that dog." He opened up his ration and he took it out. It was in a can and was like some finely ground pork. I didn't think the rations tasted too bad and we kept ourselves going by eating it every day.

The soldier who was trying to do a good turn called the dog over. He was going to give him some of his food that he had taken out of the can. Well, the dog came over and he kind of sniffed it, then he turned around and just walked off. The guy said to him, "You $#&* so-and-so, I have to eat this every day and you won't even eat it." He threw the can and the meat at the dog. The dog ran off with nothing to eat. I won't repeat the words he really used when he yelled at the dog.

When thinking back on this story I wonder if maybe the French dog was being compassionate to the soldiers who had liberated him from Nazi control. He might have decided after he sniffed the can that we needed the food more than he did.

January 3ʳᵈ to January 13ᵗʰ
Notice there is a gap of ten days without letters sent by
Verdie. His outfit was busy with the German army.

Chapter Seven

Pinned Down for Two or Three days

We were getting prepared for an offensive. Not just our company but a major push that included the entire 100th Division. At times everyone stopped until all the units like the 399th Regiment, 398th Regiment and the 397th Regiment infantries were together so we could have a coordinated move on the enemy. We sat there and waited until someone who'd planned all this figured out how to carry it. More reconnaissance had to be done to see where the Germans were and what they were doing. The Germans had strongpoints here and strongpoints there and couldn't cover every mile no more than we could. Sometimes these points were very far apart. Our usual tactics were to hit their strong points figuring we could eliminate one strongpoint, get through that and then go back far enough to eliminate a couple more. The commanders figured we could get through strongpoints to link up with the other American units. These were the tactics of both the Germans and the US Army.

In this instance we moved up during the night into position to get ready for the mission. We came in at night and had no idea where the German positions were. We went on the forward slope of a deep ravine. We got up right next to it and here was enough light during the night so we could possibly see what we were doing. We dug in the machine gun right on the edge of a ravine. We figured it was a good spot where anybody coming towards us had to come up this steep ravine, so we dug in there at night.

It was quiet during the night. Chug and I kept digging and set up the machine gun. We piled up dirt around the edges so it was just the gun was sticking out. We had no idea where the Kraut position was.

One of us layed down and rested while the other one stood listening and watching. When it was just getting daylight we'd find out if we happened to be close to a Kraut position. We were dug in deep enough to go up to our chests. We had kept digging and digging. The gun was about level with our eyes for protection and there was dirt alongside that for protection. It was just getting light and we eased up to look around to see what was going on out there. The minute we stuck our heads up just barely looking out, wham! We got a burst from a machine gun. Dirt and bark from the trees behind us just flew. The Krauts had spotted us and were probably 200 yards away on the other side of the ravine.

The Krauts had heard us digging during the night but didn't ever fire then because the minute they did, their position was given up to us. You could easily see the fire from guns at night. The first thing we did was pull a wire up and hook our phone on because we had connections with the company CP (Command Post). We immediately called back and asked for artillery support.

All day we couldn't even put our dang heads up before the guy fired. We couldn't see him because he was so well camouflaged. There were plenty of evergreen trees and brush on the other side. The only time we could get out of our hole was at night. We were on the forward slope of the ravine. We snuck up the hill and over the top where the rest of the company was dug in behind us.

So there we sat, we couldn't move and we couldn't get out of the hole. That dang son of a gun fired the minute when we even barely stuck our head out to take a look. This went on for two or three days.

No one came up there during the day while we were in the hole. Then all of a sudden we heard a noise behind us. I quickly turned around and here it was Lieutenant Nicolson coming up to our hole. We told him, "Get in the hole real quick." After not much waiting, he stood right straight up and said, "Oh f*** em."

About that time the Kraut let loose and shells starting coming with the dirt flying and bark falling off the trees. The lieutenant dove headfirst straight into the hole and was pure lucky that he didn't get hit. He crawled around and right away he asked us, "How long has this been going on?" We told him, "Oh we've been here about two or three days.

You can't get out of the hole because that sucker has a perfect bead on us. You can't leave, you're gonna stay here until dark" He told us "I'm not staying here." "He is zeroed in on us." I said. "Oh, I am not staying here," said the lieutenant. "Nope, it's too risky,' we told him.

He was down in the hole and became so doggone mad that finally he said, "I'm leaving." "Well you do what you want," we said. He crouched down, got ready and all of a sudden jumped out and zig zagged back and forth into the trees. The Kraut didn't fire and Lt. Nicholson made it back over the hill.

When he got back to his position he got us on the phone right away and told us "lay real flat in that hole because we are going to lay down the artillery on that position." So here our guys were going to lay down artillery shells about 200 yards in front of us. He said, "I'm talking to the artillery right now and we've got the position. Okay, you guys get down flat in there!" We layed as flat as possible while the artillery pretty nearly sucked us out of the hole. The shells were landing about 200 yards in front of us.

Round after round of artillery landed right across the spot where the machine gun shots were coming from. There were trees and dirt flying all around. We figured that was sure going to be the end of the machine gunner. The gun position was really plastered but we still didn't trust the Krauts. The next morning we did the same thing as before, we took a peek over our hole and-Wham!! The Kraut started firing at us again. The dirt was flying everywhere and bark flew off the trees. Even with all the artillery laid upon him, the Kraut machine gunner was still there.

We clipped the field phone on to a wire and let the company CP know what was happening. He called back and told the artillery, "The Kraut is still there." So this tactic was tried a second time to get him out of there. We laid down flat again and the artillery shells were really laid down this time, 200 yards right in front of us. The shells came right over the hole hitting right smack in front of us and it felt again like we were being almost sucked out of the hole. The shells were pretty accurate but the Krauts stayed there and we still couldn't see them. This round of shelling didn't stop the Krauts or move them out of there and we couldn't see them. We wondered... what in the world can we do? We just couldn't see where they were. It seemed like there was nothing we could do with that machine gunner.

At night when I snuck back, I got a pair of field glasses. "I'll spend the day looking for the position where all the machinegun fire is coming from," I said to Chug. We figured we could give the Kraut some fire too but we didn't want to waste ammunition without spotting him. We dug a little trench in the dirt so we could lay there in the hole and scan that area really slow. We spent all day trying to spot the Kraut and never could see him even when he was that close. So there was nothing we could do with him.

It was "Chug's" turn to be in firing position on the machine gun. We rotated like this all the time, day and night. It was my turn to lay down in the hole to get some rest for a couple of hours and I had pulled my boots off and just gone to sleep. All of a sudden "Chug" started firing. I jumped up as fast as I could and grabbed my M1. Once in a while the 81 MM meter mortars behind us fired a flare that went up pretty high. The flare went off and had a parachute that kept it floating for a while. This lit up our position almost like daylight for just a few minutes. When the flare went off there was a Kraut patrol standing right smack in front of our hole within 15 or 20 feet when "Chug" spotted them. He opened fire with the machine gun.

By the time I got up, the flare had gone out and it was pitch dark again. Chug said, "The Krauts were right in front of us and I asked him, "What happened to them?" He said, "The Krauts were right at the edge of that deep ravine and then went back over the edge." The first thing I said, was, "If they are still in business we can expect grenades right away." Sure enough in a matter of minutes a few grenades hit not too far from us. Obviously we didn't hit get in our hole during the dark night. It's not likely the Krauts just accidently arrived at our position.

We figured the Krauts' objective was our gun position and the gunner knew where we were because the Kraut who was firing at us all the time knew exactly where we were. We were lucky the flare went off when it did so we could see them and get the first shots at them. We were glad the mortars sent up flares to give us a chance to see when there was any movement around our position. The Krauts must have been sneaking up to our position between the flares going off. If the flares had not gone off the Krauts could have walked right up on us.

Later the riflemen from Company F came up and dug on one side of our position. Then E company came up on our left flank a little further down to reinforce this area. We didn't have anything to do all day so we started digging a trench to meet up together. We kept digging and digging until we got a trench over to the next hole so we could go back and forth. We dug deep enough so we were below the surface.

Close to us, E Company had a machine gun dug in and there was continuous firing from their position. We said to each other, "E company must be going in reserve. They're firing up all their ammunition so they won't have to carry it back."

Finally we left our position at night and went back to join Fox Company. When we jumped off at 0500 the next morning F Company and E Company outflanked the Kraut machine gun position and he must have run off. Chug and I figured we'd like to know where all of those shots had been coming from. Maybe it was a whole crew or something. Fox Company didn't go right in where the Krauts were but cut off on an angle because we had another objective.

Next to us was E company and they went into the area where the shots had been coming from. Afterwards we bumped into some of their guys and we asked them, "Did you go into that area where the Krauts had been firing from?" Finally we found someone who said, "Ya, we went in there." "What in the world was in there?" I asked him. "It was a concrete bunker with a little slit in the front of it just enough for the gun barrels to stick out and it was covered with dirt and brush.

There was a very small field of fire. By the time we got there, whoever had been in there had taken off because he must have decided, if we stay in here- we've had it. You should have seen the pile of empty cartridges left behind," he said. That's where the gunner had been all that time. We had figured that the Krauts had to have been in a concrete bunker otherwise our artillery would have blasted them out of there with those two big artillery barrages.

Tactics: A Rolling Barrage

When the infantry went on a rolling barrage we took a position and then holed up. Then artillery fired into the position, softening it up for the infantry and working to eliminate some of the German infantry before we got there. This was all a coordinated plan. As soon as the artillery quit firing we went in there while the Krauts were still dug in attempting to survive our artillery barrage. We kept moving and then waited while the artillery laid down another barrage. Then we headed toward the dug-in Krauts again. This didn't ever get all of the enemy so we still faced plenty of fire. At the same time the German artillery was firing at us and we didn't have time to dig in. This was the time we had the most casualties from a combination of artillery and small arms fire.

Sometimes we had air support. Thunderbolt P47s strafed the area in front of us and that helped us out a lot. The planes could only do this when the weather was favorable. It may be weeks at a time when the Thunderbolts couldn't help us out because in bad weather they couldn't fly low enough. When the terrain was suitable, the tanks helped us but many times in the Vosges Mountains they couldn't get up there. Even the artillery had a tough time getting to spots in the mountains to give us much needed support. The regimental combat team consisted of infantry, artillery and tanks. Many times it was infantry against infantry in the Vosges Mountains. We always felt much better with the support of the combat team.

We were real glad when we had air support from the Thunderbolt P47s

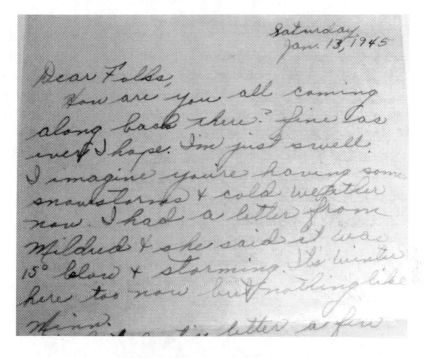

I'm just swell

Dear Folks   *Saturday January 13, 1945 France (Reyersville)*

How are you coming along back there? Fine as ever I hope. I'm just swell. Mildred said it was 15 below and storming. It's winter here too now but nothing like Minnesota. I got a letter from Curtis a few days ago and I will answer as soon as I possibly can. I hope you are getting my letters. How are things coming with Mildred and Vernice? Mildred and Lowell want a hired man don't they?

I bet you had a lot of fun with Joann, Janet and DuWayne staying there. (My nieces and nephew) Do you hear from Earl? I haven't heard from him since I've been over here. They are really giving them works over in Luzon now aren't they? I hope and pray this whole mess ends soon. I suppose Lyle is back in school now. Did you have a good vacation Lyle?

Nope, I'll have to go for now. I'll write more next time.
May God bless you all,

Love, Verdie

How the infantry moved at night

When we were moving at night through the woods we grabbed the pack on the back of the guy in front of us. We went along like a long snake and that is how we kept together at night. We were getting as close as we could to our objective to be ready to attack at 0500. I heard about another company that was moving at night through the woods when the last guy in line felt someone grab onto his pack. He thought one of his guys had joined up later. The soldier kept on going until it was getting light and when he looked back- here it was a Kraut. He had gotten separated from his unit and he had no way of knowing in the dark that it was the Americans.

Things an infantry man carried

I usually had a net on it but had been using my helmet to heat up water to shave and clean up. That's when the photographer showed up.

The best storage place for stationary, toilet paper, matches and cigarettes if you smoked was between our helmet liner and the helmet. We kept anything small in there that we wanted to keep dry. A Zippo lighter was kept in our pocket. Sometimes we used "white lightning" liquor or even perfume for fuel because we couldn't get lighter fluid.

We weren't supposed to have any American money but I kept a dime in my pocket all during the war in France and Germany. The slug that hit me on the firing range was in my pocket as my good luck charm. In my breast pocket I carried a little Bible which we all got from the chaplain. It got a little beat up but I carried it home and it's in a frame with some of my medals and pins.

In my field jacket pocket was little book about six by five inches and called "My Life in the Service" that I bought at a drug store in Montevideo before leaving for the Army. It was for keeping track of my service record and as a daily diary. In the front I wrote that the chaplain's name was Captain Frankenstein.

While in the war zone I wrote some things in this diary and didn't look at it for about twenty years. One day I dug it out of a box in the basement and took a look at it. It seemed like it was time to tear out the pages and burn them because I didn't want to look at what was written and didn't want anyone else to look. It was an attempt to erase or delete some things in my mind. Maybe it works.

Here is what a combat infantry man was expected to carry. An M1 rifle, ammo belt with as many clips as we chose, the field pack with an extra pair of socks and underwear, an extra shirt, a gas mask and an extra pair of boots. In a day or two after we got into combat, we started shedding our loaded packs because they were too heavy. Now we looked like infantry men.

We absolutely couldn't carry field packs up the steep trails in the Vosges Mountains. We had to be mobile. Mobility was more important than an extra change of clothes. We didn't get to store any equipment while we were in combat. We only kept the bare necessities. Sometimes we picked up another pack depending on the conditions.

Some guys carried a lot of grenades but mortar men were loaded down with ammunition and equipment. We kept one blanket, a shelter half which was like a tarp, a raincoat, a belt hatchet, a trenching tool, a folding shovel in a canvas carrying case, a quart canteen on a belt, a first aid pack on our belt, and at least a day's supply of K rations that fit in to the pocket of our field jacket.

We kept extra socks under our shirts by our waist in order to keep a dry pair. If we dropped blankets and other equipment we used field expediency and picked up what we needed. A blue Germany Army blanket kept me warm for a while.

We started with leather combat boots and Army green field jackets. About six week in to combat we got white hooded parkas and shoe pacs. It seemed like it was Christmas when we got these. This was a tremendous improvement. The new parkas were reversible, warmer and lighter. The new boots kept our feet warm and dry because they had rubber bottoms and leather tops. Both of these were a huge advantage for us. If your feet were wet too long there could be many problems. The new boots saved a lot of soldier's feet from frostbite and trench foot.

Shoe Pacs

"The number of American casualties (in the Vosges Mountains Ardennes) from 16 December 1944 through 2 January 1945 totaled 41,315. Less serious but more numerous, 46,107 were noncombat, cold-weather injuries like hypothermia, frostbite, and trench foot. The latter accounted for half of all injuries from exposure. Trench foot is defined in a June 1945 Army report as a diagnostic term that describes long-term vulnerability to cold at just above freezing temperature. The document concludes that most cases resulted from prolonged exposure, in immobile circumstances, to cold and damp by soldiers who lacked the opportunity to change their wet socks and boots and who did not receive warm food or drink."*

*General Board, United States Forces, European Theater, Trench Foot (Cold Injury Ground Type), Study Number 94, pp. 4–5, U.S. Army Center of Military History Library, Washington, D.C

Shoe pacs were a tremendous improvement for keeping our feet dry
Source: US Army

About the weather in the Vosges Mountains 1944, 1945

From my Grandson Matthew Gilbertson January 2015

Hi Grandpa,

I talked to Garrett Marino (weather *forecaster from MIT*) and he suggested two places to look at: National Climatic Data Center (NCDC) and World Meteorological Organization (WMO). I checked out both, and the closest location to the Vosges Mountains that seems to have data is Basel, Switzerland, which is about 100 miles from the Vosges. Basel and Bitche are about the same elevation (1000ft), so they both probably observed the same temperatures. The highest elevations in the Vosges are 3000ft, so when you were there, you could expect the temps to be 6-10 degrees colder - i.e., you can subtract 6-10 degrees off the temps recorded.

That means it was mostly been below freezing from Dec 15-Feb 1 in the higher Vosges with the coldest temps well below zero in Jan. It's hard to say how much snow they got since we only have liquid measurements from Basel, but based on a 10:1 snow/water ratio, there could have been one foot of snow in late Dec and two feet in January. It looks like temperatures warmed up in February, with highs probably in the mid-40s.

I guess it should come as no surprise that there aren't any good weather records from towns in the Vosges area during this period, except for Switzerland.

This looks like some to roads we walked on in the Vosges Mountains in 1944
From The Story of the Century (Official)

Winter in Vosges Mountains

My parents wrote in a letter about reading in the Minneapolis paper that the 7th Army was snowbound in the Vosges Mountains and nothing was moving. This rough weather lasted for a few days and the folks back home probably knew more that was going on than we did. Some of the stories about the winter of 1944 and 1945 in the French mountains said that it was one of worst in history. There were many causalities from the weather including trench foot and frozen feet. When your feet got wet and cold, you lost circulation and some lost their feet. Some of us could handle the weather conditions better than others and being from Minnesota was probably a big advantage for me because I was used to the cold and snowy weather.

We saved our feet by rubbing them to keep them warm. We rotated taking our boots off and rubbing each other's feet. We did this at night when we weren't moving. It was a top priority because I was not going to lose my feet and absolutely did not want to come out a cripple. Sometimes we took off one boot and rubbed our own feet one at a time. Taking the best care of my feet as I could in the cold and the snow was extremely important. The key to avoiding trench foot and frostbite was to act as a team and look out for each other. None of the guys I spent the most time with in the winter ever had trench foot or severe frostbite.

You could walk on frozen feet and not really feel it. You may not even know it. There was quite a bit of trench foot. How could some guys let their feet get to that point? They must not have kept close watch like I did. One of the worst cases of trench foot that I saw was when we got into house and one of the guys in our platoon was going to check his feet. He took his boots and socks off and his feet were black. He sat there and looked at his feet for a long time without saying anything. He hadn't realized what was happening because it must have been a long time since he had taken off his boots and rubbed his feet. He could walk but as soon as his feet warmed up he'd be in trouble. We didn't know what to say to him. The medics took him back to battalion aid but we never heard how he made out and if his feet were saved.

Whenever I had a chance I took my boot off to rub my feet. After the war my fingertips and toes were numb for a long time. In the spring my fingers hurt when washing my hands with cold water. We couldn't wear mittens or real thick gloves because we needed our trigger fingers.

The Army issued us olive drab wool gloves with leather palms that kept our hands fairly warm. We froze our nose and cheeks many times. Some men got gangrene from freezing their noses and cheeks. If you waited too long to take care of it right away you had a problem. I had the advantage of growing up in a very cold climate and knew what to do.

On the ship going over I got a scarf from the Red Cross. Ladies in the states used to knit Army drab scarves for the soldiers. This scarf was great to keep around my neck and I put it over my head and under my helmet. There was a hood on our field jacket but it didn't have a lining so I sewed the scarf into the hood. It covered my ears under my helmet. It also covered my mouth, chin and nose during the coldest parts of the night. The hood had buttons to cover up past my nose. With the scarf as a liner I was warm in the cold winter. Later we were issued white parkas with fur lining and were reversible with green on one side and white on the other. We used the white side when there was snow. The hood fit over our helmets so then I had two hoods and both of them really kept the wind out.

When we first got overseas we got close to a tank unit and that was where I got a good pair of coveralls with wool lined pants. One of the tankers traded with me for an extra pair of combat boots that had I kept after we got shoe pacs. He wanted the boots. The bib had straps under the arms. None of the other guys had pants like this and no one questioned that I had a different pair of pants. There were many things to do to keep warm and take proper care of yourself.

One of the problems with the white jackets was that the Germans had the same kind of jackets and you couldn't tell us apart. Two of our men got captured while on night patrol. They didn't come back from the patrol so we were worried and sent out another patrol to find them. It had snowed and our patrol found their tracks. They got to a point where American Army boot tracks and German Army boot tracks met. After the war we got a letter from Bates and he told us what happened. They got confused and decided to go in a hole to wait until light. In the morning they spotted a bunch of guys in white parkas and walked right up to them. Uh oh, they were Germans.

A 100ᵗʰ Division soldier in the snow
From "The Story of the Century" -US Army photograph

A few nights and days in a ghost town

Yes Mom,   *January 19, France (Reyersville)*
I received your very welcome letter. The one you wrote January 3ʳᵈ.
Thanks a lot. I hadn't got any mail for quite a while so I sure was glad.
I got a Christmas card from Arvid and Gilma and family so thank them
for me when you see them.

Yes, it does seem strange that it is already 1945. I was sure the war
would be well over by 1945 but it drags on. Our hopes and prayers are
that it will be over in a while and I think it will. For a time it looked like
it would last a good while longer but things look brighter now.

The Krauts decided to throw everything they had but didn't get far.
Things were a little rough for a while though. The Russians sure are
giving the works now aren't they? I'm glad you are getting my letters
now. I wrote quite a bit during December so I hope you got them all. I
haven't been able to write much the last two weeks but I am in a house
again right now so I have a good place to write. I had a shower today
and some clean clothes and a shave so I feel pretty good. I had quite a
beard. I am glad to hear Earl and Roy are okay and I hope they won't
have to take any more of those islands.

So we have a new member of the family. I'm glad everything is fine. I bet DuWayne is excited now. Have Vernice and Astor decided what to name her? I suppose a girl is want they wanted too. (*She was named Mary Jean*)

It sounds like you are having real winter back there now. We had two to three inches of snow here but it wasn't too cold. It's almost gone again now. By the way I am in the 7th Army like you figured. I thought maybe you had read about my division in the newspapers. You know what division I am in don't you? If it is mentioned it will most likely be the division and not the 399th Regiment. If you don't remember my division just look on the patch and the shirt I left at home.

I have plenty of writing paper now. It'd be nice if you could enclose some air mail stamps once in a while. We get a newspaper over here called the "Stars and Stripes" once in a while so I get some news. I was reading about that new draft bill. It sounds like they'll take a lot more 2-Gs and 4 Fs. It's okay with me. I saw that some factories are boosting war production again too. I'm glad we live in a country like America where we really get things done.

Yes, I am waiting to get the Monte American. It should start coming any day now.

Don't worry about me, I get plenty to eat and am perfectly okay. I spent a few nights and days in a ghost town a while ago. It sure was a forlorn place. It hadn't been lived in since 1940 when those dirty Krauts ruined it. Practically every building was ruined but there were some good cellars though. I wish I could tell you more about what I'm doing, but you know how the Army is.

We had chicken for dinner today and plenty of it so I really filled up. I sure could go for some lefse though. I'll make up for it when I get home. Say, do you think you could send some of those brownie cookies. Home cooked food tastes so good and it's nice to get a change from Army chow and K and C rations. If it is hard to get sugar, you better use it for something more necessary.

I'll have to close for this time now. Here's hoping this finds you all well and happy and may Almighty God bless you all.

Love, Verdie

Friday Jan. 19
1945

Yes Mom,   France

I recieved your very welcome
letter this morning. The one
you wrote Jan. 3. Thanks a
lot. I hadn't gotten any mail
for quite a while so I sure was
glad. I also got 2 letters from
Phyl. I got a christmas card
from David & Gilma & family
the other day so thank them
for me when you see them.
    Yes it does seem strange
that it is already 1945. I was
about sure the war would
be well over by 45 but I
guess it drags out. Our hopes
& prayers are that it will be
over in a little while and
I think it will. For awhile
it looked like it would last
a good while longer but
things look brighter now.

Part of my January 19th letter

I guess the Krauts tried to throw in everything they had but they didn't get far. Things were a little rough for awhile tho. The Russians sure are giving them the works now aren't they.

I'm glad you're getting my letters! I wrote quite a bit during Dec. so I hope you get them all. I haven't been able to write much the last 2 weeks. I'm in a house again right now so I have a good place to write. I had a shower today & got some clean clothes and a shave so I feel pretty good. I had quite a beard too.

I'm glad you got the $25 I sent. I'll be sending some more as soon as I get paid. Are you getting any more of my allotment checks?

Part of my January 19th letter

I've had some good ringside seats

Dear Curtis,   *Saturday, January 20ᵗʰ, 1945 France*

Thanks for the letter. So you have stopped flying for a while. I know how it is with the weather and flying. I hope you can solo in the spring and I hope you can get a hold of a ship of your own. There will be plenty of light planes for sale. The Army has so many of them. I got a "Flying and Popular Aviation" magazine from a fellow a while ago and read an article about the Army planes they're selling. They said they had them from $375 and up. They sure have plenty of light planes over here that are always flying around. Of course there are plenty of other ships too. I've seen quite a few good air shows. They aren't the kind we see back home though. I've had some good ringside seats watching bombings and strafing.

I am going to try and get a hold of a ship as soon as I get out of the Army. I sure wish a lot of times that I could have gone through with my flying career but this war mixes up everybody.

Are you going to work for Julian Ellingson this spring? I imagine the wages will be better than ever. Well Curtis, I know you don't agree with me but you're lucky to be on the farm. I wish I was there myself right now. I'd gladly haul gold dust * 15 hours a day. Whatever you do Curtis, don't get into anything military. A uniform may look good now, but there is no glory in it.

Bro, Verdie

Organic fertilizer provided by our cows, horses, hogs and chickens.

Chapter Eight

Mail is more important than food, I think.

How letters traveled from a foxhole in France to a kitchen table in Minnesota

Our family's mailbox was on Highway 29 a half mile from our house. When I was home and it was time to pick up the mail or put outgoing mail in the box, I got on our horse, Jim. After putting his bridle on and jumping on bareback, we rode down the road in a hurry with Shep racing along beside us. Jim laid his ears flat and tried to outrun Shep. Both of them really liked to race and they'd be running full out. That was my daily activity to go the half mile to the mailbox and see if we got any letters that day.

For a year or two before I left home, we were getting letters from my brother Roy who was in the Marines stationed in Alaska and my brother Earl who was in Army training at a Fort Adair in Oregon. My folks often read the letters aloud to Lyle, Curtis and I while we were sitting at the kitchen table. Roy wrote a few times saying, "Tell Verdi to stay out of this." Earl wrote wondering whether I might get a farm deferment to stay home and work on the farm. These letters from my brothers probably made even more interested in joining the Army Air Corps as soon as I could.

While reading these letters I sent home over 70 years ago, I imagined my family reading them at the kitchen table. My brother Curtis who was 14 took over my mail duties but now maybe he was riding our horse

Beauty to the mailbox to pick up the letters. We had lost Jim when he got into the flax straw which bound him up and caused him to die. Now my parents were reading all three boys letters while just Lyle and Curtis were listening. Maybe they had potato soup that night for supper and had read one of my letters which said, "I sure could go for some potato soup now." It was kind of like we were together even though we were so far apart.

It was also interesting to try to piece together just how the mail got delivered to the soldiers and to their families. Even now with jumbo jets and super highways it takes a long time for mail to arrive from overseas. My grandchildren send postcards from all over the world and sometimes it takes weeks for the cards to get here. Here are some examples of the time it took for mail to arrive home in Minnesota or to me in France 1944 and Germany in 1945.

January 3rd Somewhere in France, Dad I received your letter the other day and got Mom's that was mailed December 23rd.

Dear Verdie,   April 26, 1945 We received your letter of April 14th a couple of days ago. (I was in Germany then.)
        I am very thankful that the US Postal Service and the US Army recognized just how truly important mail was to all of us soldiers and our families.

From the United States Postmaster General (1940-1945) of the United States, Frank C. Walker: "It is almost impossible to over-stress the importance of this mail. It is so essential to morale that army and navy officers of the highest rank list mail almost on a level with munitions and food."

Here is how I imagine the path of the mail on its way to my foxhole

My parents and brothers sat down at the kitchen table after supper was over and all the work was done. Some nights it was my dad writing and other times it was my mother. Once in a while my brothers Curtis and Lyle wrote me some very welcome letters. In the morning Curt put the letters in his pocket and rode Beauty down to the mailbox. Shep raced along with him. Curt raised the little red flag on the box to let the mailman, our uncle Ole Pederson, know we had mail to send out.

If there weren't enough stamps for the letters Curt left money in the box to pay for some airmail stamps.

Later in the day Ole pulled up to the mailbox in his 1941 "Robin Egg Blue" Ford. He delivered the mail to my family and collected the letters my family was sending to me and my brothers who were also overseas in the Army and Marines. Ole finished his mail route in Mandt Township and then drove eleven and half miles from our mailbox to leave the letters at the Montevideo, Minnesota post office. From Montevideo it traveled 130 miles to the Minneapolis, Minnesota post office by train or truck. The mail was sorted again in Minneapolis. When the letters had airmail stamps they most likely went to Wold Chamberlain Field (the airport near Minneapolis now called Minneapolis-St. Paul International Airport) where it was loaded on a DC 3 and flown to New York City.

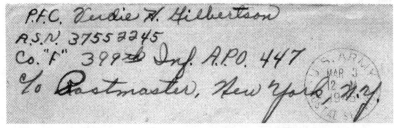

This was the address the Army used to locate our unit

After the letter's arrival in the New York City Post Office the process is explained in the diagrams. In New York the letters were placed in a package of mail for members of the 100th Infantry Division, Company F. (*My Company in this case*). The letter or package then went into a mail bag that traveled to the New York Port of Embarkation Army Post Office. It was here that the Army assumed control.

The USPS did not know locations of the overseas units. The Army knew where the 100th Division and the companies were located. If there was an airmail stamp PFC Gilbertson's letter went by cargo plane to the overseas Army Post Office (APO) through which the 100th Division,Company F soldiers got their mail. Cargo planes flew the long routes with refueling stops in Newfoundland or the Azores Islands. From there we figure the planes landed in England where the mail was sorted again and then transported to France or Germany by airplane or by a ship crossing the English Channel.

Now it needed to be transported by truck to the 447ᵗʰ APO which was a part of my address. The APOs moved along with the division as it advanced through France and Germany. They were oftentimes many miles from our positions. From here the mail orderly picked up the mail for our unit, loaded it into a jeep and then followed the supply crew or food truck up to our location on the front. We gathered around to hear our name called and were always glad to receive letters and packages from home. I wrote earlier in one of my letters "I was so awfully glad to get your letter this morning. Mail is more important than food I think. *November 20, 1944*

EPINAL	FRANCE	NY	447	10	11	44
RAMBERVILLERS	FRANCE			29	11	44
PHALSBOURG	FRANCE			6	12	44
WINGEN	FRANCE			18	12	44
DRULINGEN	FRANCE			27	12	44
SARRE-UNION	FRANCE			5	3	45
BITCHE	FRANCE			24	3	45
NEUSTADT	GERMANY			31	3	45
MANNHEIM	GERMANY			6	4	45
BAD WIMPFEN	GERMANY			9	4	45
BONFELD	GERMANY			13	4	45
HEILBRONN	GERMANY			20	4	45
BACHNANG	GERMANY			27	4	45
GOPPINGEN	GERMANY			4	5	45
STUTTGART	GERMANY			19	7	45
FST				8	12	45
CALAIS	FRANCE			1	1	46
CEASED OPERATION				16	1	46

NUMERICAL LISTING of APO'S

JANUARY 1942 - NOVEMBER 1947

Prepared by
ARMY POSTAL SERVICE
AND STRENGTH ACCOUNTING BRANCHES AGO

List of the locations for Army Post Office (APO 447) from November 10, 1944 - January 16, 1946

The path from our foxhole or civilian house back to my parent's kitchen table.

Sometimes after we cleared a town we got into a house and could letters write by candle light. Other times we sat in our foxholes writing letters home and reading letters from home. We kept our stationary, stamps and pens in our steel helmets. When the mail orderly gave us our incoming packages and letters, sometimes we took our helmets off, got the letters we had written home out of our helmets and gave them to the mail orderly. Then he put them in a pouch and brought them to the platoon leaders. They are the ones who are shown on a chart as the unit censors. I didn't know this at first but the lieutenant looked over our letters and signed his name over the Army Examiner stamp. According the flow chart after he signed the letters the orderly picked them up and brought them back to the APO. I doubt the lieutenants had very much time to read our letters.

From the APO a USPS chart we studied shows a postal regulating station and then a base censor. We only see one signature on the envelopes so we don't know if the letters were examined again by another censor. After this, my letters traveled the reverse path to the United States. They probably went to New York, then to Minneapolis and later to Montevideo. In the morning Uncle Ole Pederson drove his Ford to Montevideo to pick up the letters for Route Five. Then he brought them to his home where he sorted them in a little building close to his house. he called it the "post husen." When we were kids, we liked to go over to his place and watch him sort all the mail for his route into the little bins. When he was ready to deliver the letters he got into his 1941 Ford and drove to our mailbox.

Sometime later in the day my brother Curtis or someone else in the family went down the road to pick up our mail. My parents were happy when they got mail from their boys. We were all overseas in in combat in both Europe and the South Pacific. Even though we told them not to worry, I'm sure that when our letters arrived they gave them a bit of comfort that we were still alive and well. They probably slept better* the nights that they had received letters from their boys. It's amazing that these letters had traveled such a long distance and often arrived in a relatively short period of time.

* From an April 26th letter my mother wrote to me. *"We heard from Earl yesterday so it made us feel a little better about him. He is not in a very good place now. But it helps a little anyway as long as we hear he is all right."*

Wish I could be there driving the John Deere

Dear Dad,   *Monday January 22, 1945 France*

How are you all getting along back in good 'ol Minnesota? I 'spose you're sitting around the stove most of the day now. It won't be long until you'll be planning spring work again, will it? I wish I could be there driving the John Deere. January is nearly over too.

Well what do you think about the war? I 'spose you're reading all about the rushing Russians. It looks like this mess will be cleared up soon. For all I care the Russians can beat us to Berlin. And they're (US) doing okay on Luzon too.

Have you gotten any more snow? We had about 3 or 4 inches here the other night. How's Sam getting along? Does he hear from Julien? Greet him from me when you see him. Dad, I will have to wish you a happy birthday even if I am late.*(Dad's birthday was Jan 16ᵗʰ)* I wish I could have sent you at least a card a card but I can't get anything over here. I'll have to make it up next year. This is all I have time for now so I will have to close.

So long and may God bless you all.

Love, Verdie

I could try and slip it in

Dear folks,   *January 26, 1945 France*

This will be a short letter but I will be able to write more in a few days. I received Dad's letter written December 29ᵗʰ and Lyle's letter the other day. Thanks a lot. I also had a letter from Roy and two from Earl. I'm so glad to hear they are okay.

I was surprised to hear that my name was mentioned by Cedric Adams* over the news. Can you remember the names of the other fellows he mentioned?

Say Dad, if there is anything you'd like to know about things over here just ask me and I'll try to tell you. I've seen plenty of the rottenest things there are to be seen but I don't feel much like talking about it. You maybe wouldn't believe it if I did tell you but if there is anything you'd like to know I could try and slip it in.

I've got it much nicer now so I feel pretty good. We expect to be relieved soon and then I'll be able to rest up and catch up on my writing. I am not having it hard now so don't worry. I get plenty to eat and everything. You asked me to request things so here goes. If you could send me another box of cookies I sure would like that.

Nope, I'll have to close now. I'll write more next time.
God Bless you, Goodnight

Love, Verdie

*Cedric Adams was popular broadcaster on WCCO radio, the station my family always tuned in to. We all listened to him before I went to the Army. He was well known in Minnesota from the 1930s until his death in 1961.

A Mortar Squad

A mortar squad in action
From 399th in Action US Army photo

It took quite a long time to get in a position to attack. Many times we hiked for miles to get close to the German Army strongpoints. They had many gun positions and pillboxes in place. There weren't two days that were exactly the same. Much of the moving by our unit when we were on the offensive was done under the cover of darkness. The whole division planned out our next movements. We didn't know what the objective was beyond our own Fox Company which ranged from full strength of 184 men. The average number in action was about 100.

I was mostly with the mortar squad which consisted of eight soldiers. Each guy had a specific job to do and we were a team that worked together with one weapon. The ammunition was heavy along with the bipod, the base, the aiming stakes and the mortar. Each guy carried some of the parts. When we needed to move, it took just a few minutes to take the mortar apart and reassemble it. We were trained to do that very quickly and we all moved together as a team with the machine gunners and riflemen. The mortar squad dug in next to the machine gun squad. When there were trees overhead, we couldn't fire the mortars so our squad immediately became riflemen as we always carried a carbine or a M1.

Once the mortars were set up we sighted in and began firing as soon as we had a target. Sometimes our squad leader as a forward observer sighted in a target. He might say, "Range 450 yards, windage five degrees, set up your sights, fire three rounds to zero in with white phosphorus. Fire for effect!" This meant we were firing high explosives.

Most of the time as it got dark we quit firing because the mortars gave off such a bright flash of light that our positions could easily be spotted at night. We always wanted to keep hidden as much as possible.

CHAPTER NINE

I'll wrap my rifle barrel around a tree

From my letter of January 31

Dear Dad,   *Wednesday January 31, 1945 France*

I suppose you are waiting to see what the groundhog has to say. It seems funny to think that January is about gone. Pretty soon spring will be here again. I hope and pray that spring will bring peace. It looks good over here anyway.

How's everything back home? So you are a grandpa twice again. I'm glad to hear that everything is fine. I got Mom's letter last night written the 15th of January and I got a letter from Roy and Clarice. My mail is coming through good now

You are right about what Army I'm in. (*Notice he avoids saying the 7th Army*). I am having it nice now so don't worry about me. I'm glad to hear that those boys are home from overseas. I can imagine how happy they are. Just what kind of wounds has Marvin Jerve got? It's too bad they have to come back that way.

I suppose you really stick to the radio now with all the news about the Russians. I wonder how far we have to go before these Krauts get enough. I sure would like to hear some radio news now. We don't get the news very regular you know. What I am waiting for is the order to "Cease firing". I think I'll wrap my rifle barrel around a tree when that order comes.

Have you had any more snow lately? There is about a foot here now. It's not very cold though.

Well Dad, this is about all I have time for now so I will have to close. Here's hoping this finds you all well and happy and may God Bless you all.

Love, Verdie

American Seventh army troops continued cleaning up buildings in Hatten, where the Germans had been trying to bore through the Maginot defense system just north of the Haguenau forest.

The reinforced Germans attacked late Monday with tanks, but the Americans counter-attacked and held all their ground.

* * *

North of Strasbourg, other Seventh army troops were reported to have crossed the Zorn river and gained a mile and a half north of Herrlisheim, 12 miles above the Alsatian capital.

West of nearby Offendorf, the Seventh speared ahead nearly two miles.

Fighting continued in the woods north of Gambsheim.

No report came from the French First army front south of Strasbourg.

Americans scored some gains in the Bitche salient of the northern Vosges.

A newspaper clipping my mother saved
Courtesy of Montevideo American News

What one guy wanted to do with his M1 rifle

From 399ᵗʰ in Action p 154 used by permission

When I look at this drawing from a history of the 399ᵗʰ of the 100ᵗʰ Division, it makes me think of one time when a couple of us from our squad were sitting out in the woods on a log. As we were eating our K rations someplace in France, the other fellow was staring at his M1 rifle. He said to me, "Ya know, I think I'd like to have one of these after the war." I asked him, "Why, what would you do with it?" He told me, "Well, I'd lay it out in the front yard where I could see it from our living room when I am looking outside. I'd just watch it while it lays out in the rain, the snow and everything and let it slowly deteriorate-then disappear. That's what I'd use it for." "Wow," I told him, "That's a real good idea."

My son asked me why the guy said something like that. Well, of course we lived with our rifle. We ate with it, we slept with it, and we went to the bathroom with it. It was always within reach no matter where we were. It was always a part of you wherever you went. I guess the other guy thought there was one time he wouldn't be carrying it around. He could just watch in deteriorate and rust in his yard. That's what he wanted it for.

What's going on in the minds of the combat infantry man?

We were watching the *Patton* movie when General Patton slapped a soldier and called him a coward. Patton and many others were never in the situations that put soldiers in a state of not being able to fight anymore. While we were in a defense position one of our men shot one of his own guys who was out of the fox hole at night. We were always told if anyone was moving around at night it was a Kraut. We had strict orders to stay in our foxholes. The only ones supposed to be moving were on outpost or on patrol.

Our guy that was shot was running out to place a lit cigarette on the aiming stake which the mortars used to sight in on at night. When he was seen running our guy thought it was a Kraut so he shot and killed a fellow American soldier who was in his own unit.

It was a terrible thing for him to deal with and he was not able to continue his regular duties. We never thought anything bad about soldiers who got to the point where it was best to be taken off the line.

It's amazing what a human being's mind can do to adjust to or cope with when we are forced into it. When you get into traumatic situations something happens to you that almost becomes a way of life. That sounds kind of weird, but you kind of just accept it- this is the situation I'm in and I can't do anything about it. I can't get out of it so… you just give up any thoughts about that. You say, "I've made up my mind." Your survival instinct is just so strong and it isn't something you can do anything about- it's involuntary.

Once you say- "there's probably no way I'm going to get out of this," you accept it. This was the time when my emotions started to change. It's hard to explain. You almost think you become another person. You accept - this is me.

You almost get to the point where you… sometimes you'd say "I'm going to get so hard emotionally. When I get back to normal civilian life again, am I going to be a person that's so doggone hard that I won't have any feeling?" You feel like- what is it going to be like when this is over with?

The change back to regular life is maybe harder than the change to start with. But the sooner you accept that- chances are- you're not going to make it through this, the better you feel. It is just like giving up. It's hard to explain. The odds of making it out of this alive and whole are so small, you think about that, and pretty soon you hardly think about it anymore and then it's easier. Once you get through that stage, it's easier to cope.

The best way to cope for many of us was when you got to the point where you made fun of pretty nearly everything. It's really not normal behavior. Emotionally you can go from one extreme to the other, rage to compassion.

John Delewski: One of my buddies

We started together training for infantry duty at Fort Bragg and stayed together in the same platoon all the way to Germany until I left the 100th division when I was transferred to become an MP. For the next several months from October 1944 to May 1945, our platoon traveled together and we depended on each other for survival. I got shifted from machine guns to mortars because my training at Fort Bragg was in both mortars and machine guns. We went wherever we were needed and were told to go.

It was fortunate I got into the mortars before we left because almost the whole machine section was captured early in the fight. If I had stayed with machine guns I may have ended up a POW for the rest of the war. One man escaped the Krauts but then with only one guy left in the section I went back to machine guns.

Eventually I got back with the mortars. We went back and forth as needed. I could have been a buck sergeant if I had stayed in machine gun section and been a squad leader. Sometimes PFCs were the leaders. Being a private soldier was good enough for me and I had no real ambition to get a new rank. Rank and money didn't mean anything to me. I only carried one unauthorized American dime and kept that in my pocket for some reason.

Time didn't mean anything. It's strange how most everything became insignificant. The main thing was survival and looking after each other. We had a special bond and finding something to eat was a top priority. Delewski made a lot of jokes and that made it easier. He helped keep the morale up. Delewski was with me and "Beehive" when we were the first ones in our company to put our marks on German soil. The guys who were joking, humorous types tended to stick together. That helped a lot with our attitude and every day psychological well-being.

The infantrymen I served with were scattered all over the place after the war ended. Delewski might have been sent toward the Russian border, I wasn't sure. My next stop was an artillery outfit but we were all doing MP duty.

Our 100ᵗʰ day up at the front

Dear Mom,   *Friday Feb 9, 1945 France (Glassenberg)*

I am having a rest now and that sure is nice. I'm living in a house again in one of these little villages. Yesterday was our 100ᵗʰ day up at the front so I really appreciate a rest. I wouldn't go through those last 100 days for anything.

Say, I got the Montevideo American the day before yesterday, the December 22 issue. That sure was a nice write up about the 399ᵗʰ. I guess you know pretty much what we've been doing after you read that. I read the article to the other fellows and they enjoyed it so much too. Roy and Calmer had a nice write-up too. (*See the story in the last chapter.*)

I just had a shower and got some clean clothes so I feel pretty good now. I also saw one of those USO shows and really enjoyed that. There was a magician and some dancers, a very good comedian and some good music.

How are you all getting along back there? I 'spose you are waiting for spring now. Have you had any more snow? All the snow is gone here again. It's been about like March weather back home. How are Mildred and Vernice coming along with their hired girls? Fine I hope. I haven't got that package you sent with jam and peanut butter yet. I sure am waiting for it. We don't get much of that around here.

I 'spose you are all listening to the news more than ever now with the Russians heading toward Berlin. I get the news regularly now so I know pretty good about what's going on. I can't see how this war can last much longer. I expect it to end any day now. I guess the civilians in Germany are having a tough time. Well, the Germans are getting a taste of their own medicine now. The war in the Pacific is going so good too now.

Thanks for sending the addresses of those boys. I hope I can run into some of them.

I imagine the farmers will have a hard time getting help this spring when the Army is going to draft even more farmers. One of the fellows from our platoon that came up from the rear brought a radio so we even have a radio in here. It's so much fun to listen to it. It's the first time I've heard one in four months. There's mostly German stations on it but once in a while we get an American station and we get news broadcasts sometimes too.

Nope, I have to close for this time. Here's hoping this finds you happy and the best of health. I'm just fine. May God Bless you all.

Love, Verdie

A map of some of the 100th Divisions travels in France
From "The Story of the Century" (pamphlet)

Getting more firewood

We were in a very remote mountainous area, and there were piles of snow all around. The farmers lived in the village while farming the land out away from their homes. During the day, their cattle and sheep went out to the pastures and were brought back to an enclosure for the night. This was from the days in the medieval times when it was done for mutual defense. These French people were living the same way their ancestors had lived for hundreds of years.

The house and the barn were one building with a door between the kitchen and the barn. There were huge manure piles stacked in squares in front of the houses. By spring the piles were much bigger. There was a pump that stuck high up above the manure pile and the manure was filling up a pit.

In the spring, the manure was piled up to the top of the pump. The farmers pumped the seepage into a big wooden barrel that was mounted on a wagon. There was a big spigot on the back end. The loaded wagon was pulled in to the fields and the seepage drained into buckets. Then the farmers threw the manure seepage on to the field for fertilizer. It was called the "Honey Wagon." This was on the border between the two countries. I didn't know how to say this in French or German. This is what Google translator in 2015 says for German *honig wagen*. This is what it says for French, *miel caravane*.

The manure piles didn't smell that bad in the winter, but when we got to Germany in the spring we ran into the same farming system and the smell was pretty bad then. We joked that we could tell who the richest farmer was by the size of his manure pile.

When we took over one of these villages from the Germans, sometimes we got to stay in a building for the night. We operated from there with patrols and outposts. We were under cover for parts of the night as we went in and out of the village. It was pretty quiet because there was so much snow.

We stayed upstairs in the house where the barn was attached and in the room was a small wood burning stove. We decided we were going to fire up this stove to get a little heat and dry out our wet clothing and equipment. The farmer who owned the house only gave us a little bundle of wood even though it was heavily wooded all around the village. There was no shortage of wood, but he decided to save it for himself. Behind the house there was his wood shed attached to the building but there was a lock on the door.

It didn't take long to burn up the little dab of wood that he gave us. One of the guys was looking very closely at the building that was both the barn and the house. He said, "I think the wood shed is right on the other side of this wall." The wall was slanted and there was an old dresser standing up against it. To a couple of us, he said "If we cut a hole in the wall, we could go right on into the wood shed." This sounded like a good idea because we sure needed some more wood to keep our fire going. He shoved the dresser out of the way and got his belt hatchet. He cut a small hole in the wall and sure enough the wood shed was right there. Then he cut a hole big enough so he could crawl through into the wood shed. He grabbed some chunks and handed the wood up to us. We didn't even have to go outside.

We had a big fire going in no time. Pretty soon the farmer came upstairs to see what was going on in his house. He looked at us and couldn't quite figure out how we had a hot fire going and a big pile of wood left to burn. We had put the dresser back over the hole so he couldn't figure out how we got more wood. I'd have liked to hear him when he found the hole in the wall. He probably said in French, "Damn Amercanish soldat." It sure was nice to have a warm place to sleep that night.

I sure enjoyed getting letters from my youngest brother Lyle. He kept me informed how hunting and trapping was going at home.

125

Too many rats to hunt around here

Dear Lyle,   *Sunday morning Feb 11, 1945*   France

I received your letter about two weeks ago but haven't had much time to write lately. Thanks a lot. I suppose you are busy going to school every day. I know how you enjoy that. You are lucky anyway. The kids over here aren't going to school now. They don't seem to mind though. We had church services this morning. I hadn't had a chance to go to services for quite a while. I 'spose you had lots of fun while DuWayne and Janet and Joanne were staying there.

Have you trapped any weasels or skunks this winter? There are quite a few deer around here but I haven't had a chance to hunt any deer. There are too many rats to hunt around here.

How's the pony coming along? Are you going to use him for plowing this spring? Have you been fishing lately? Boy, I sure could go for some fried fish now.

The people here in the small villages have all got their house and barn in the same building. It's pretty handy but it doesn't smell so good sometimes.

There is a fellow from Grand Rapids here so we talk a lot about Minnesota. He is a farmer too so we talk farming quite a bit.

How's the weather now? Have you had any blizzards yet? Are you building any model airplanes now? I'll be building them again when I get home.

How's Shep and the rat terrier getting along? Still fighting with the cats I suppose. The people who own this house have a pretty nice police dog. Half police and half dog.

Nope, Lyle it's about time for chow now so I'll have to close for now. Write soon and greet everyone.

Bro, Verdie

A letter to our dog Shep

I thought about writing letters to Shep but figured the Army censors may be suspicious. Anyone reading my mail might have figured it was somebody that was writing in a special code.

Shep: Our faithful dog

Dear Shep,

I wish you were here by my foxhole, then I could get a little more sleep at night. There wouldn't be a Kraut that would dare come within a half mile of here. Things are going to the dogs here in France. I 'spose you are still fighting with the cats. I hope you are sleeping on the porch guarding the farmhouse and the family. Have you had any problems with chicken thieves lately?

I 'spose you having been helping Curt and Lyle poach some pheasants and even helping them catch some skunks now and then. I've seen some really nice dogs over here. They are German Shepherds, you know police dogs. I guess they are half dog and half police.

Well, I guess I'll have to get some shut eye now, Goodnite

Verdi

Writing letters to my brothers

One of the reasons for writing to my brothers was that it made me feel like I was still involved at home. It seemed like a better feeling for me when we were kind of visiting and talking about hunting, fishing and the farm. Lyle always liked to be out in the woods hunting and Curtis was flying airplanes like I did before the war. It was fun to talk about the things we all liked together. Keeping connected with my brothers and my parents made me feel that things were still okay at home. Lyle and Curt did the things I always enjoyed doing at the farm. My brothers liked to hear when I spotted some deer or thought about going fishing in a German stream or seeing some Thunderbolts or Piper Cubs in the air. This helped us all keep the family ties strong.

Roy and Earl were fighting the Japanese in the South Pacific and we sent letters to each other when we had time. *Editor: When we review letters sent by Verdie and letters sent by Roy and Earl we see them referring to each other and the latest news. Sometimes his parents relayed the news and other times Verdi relayed news he heard in letters from Roy and Earl.*

Roy, Curtis and Lyle while I was in the Army. Roy was home on leave and Curtis was getting ready to enlist, Lyle was too young to join up.

Taking out a German Observation Post

Our company was in reserve and there was a Kraut observation post that was continuously directing artillery toward us. It was determined that the best plan was to take that post out. A combat patrol was going to be sent out at 0500. We never liked daylight patrols since we were so visible and could easily be seen. What was decided was we'd take one platoon of riflemen and one mortar squad. Being our mortar squad was the best we were picked to go on patrol together. The objective was quite a ways in beyond our positions.

Our Captain Huberger was assigned a jeep but we rarely saw it, this time he happened to have it. We were going to carry quite a bit of mortar ammunition so he figured on taking the jeep as far as we could and then walk the rest of the way. We loaded our mortar and the mortar ammunition into the jeep.

Our mortar squad rode in the jeep a little ways and of course the rifleman were hiking. It was quite a few miles into German territory. A few miles in, as we got closer, we left the jeep because we couldn't take it in and then we carried everything. What we were trying to do was get up near to this observation post which was on top of a high hill. It was pretty steep and we were trying to get as close in as possible before the Krauts detected us.

We figured there'd be an outpost but there wasn't one. For some reason or other the Krauts didn't have an outpost so we got in before we were spotted. It was pretty heavily wooded with a trail going up the hill. The plan was for the riflemen to fan out in the woods around and scatter out. Then the mortar position was going to start shelling the buildings. We happened to find a perfect spot for the mortar. It looked like a spot where somebody had dug out in the side of the hill probably to haul some gravel or dirt. We set the mortar up and there was wide open range on top. We got the mortar set up and never heard a thing. It was all quiet. The rifleman had already fanned out and were in position.

Our squad leader, Sgt. Aime Baillargeon had what we called a handy- talkie radio. This was short range and we also had one on the mortar position. Aime crawled up a ways with his field glasses to where he could see the building. We were talking on the radio and he said to us, "fire three rounds of white phosphorus to zero in on the building."

This is a chemical and you didn't want to get too close to it.

We usually fired three rounds to bracket so we could adjust the mortar. We always fired one on the left, one on the right and then one in the middle. It gave off a white smoke that told us what we were hitting. Then we sent in the high explosives after that.

This time when we fired, the first round of white phosphorus got a direct hit on the building. It just happened to hit right square when we were zeroing in. Aime got excited and told us, "Commence firing high explosives as hard as you can." We started pumping rounds as hard as we could with one guy on each side and every one of them were hitting the building. It was just pure luck that we hit it the first time.

Pretty soon a bunch of Krauts came running out of the building; and with a mortar firing, couldn't tell where the rounds were coming from. The Krauts were getting out of that building as fast as possible because every round was hitting it and they were coming in our direction.

As the enemy got closer Aime said, "They're coming near us, lower your range about 200 yards." So we quick cranked up the mortars to lower the range, started firing and we hit the ground between the enemy and us. The Krauts turned around in the other direction and took off back toward the building. Then we could crank down again and start again on the building.

The mortar rounds looked like rockets and there was a safety pin in them. Two guys pulled the pins and handed the rounds to the men doing the firing. They dropped it in the mortar and when it hit the bottom it fired. One guy in the mortar squad got so scared he pretty near froze. His job was to pull safety pins. He got so petrified that he wasn't able to pull pins. We kept hollering to him, 'Pull pins, pull pins, pull pins!!" Luckily the other guy picked up the pace and we kept firing many, many rounds as fast as we could. We really plastered the Kraut position.

All of a sudden we had a defective round and this short round landed between us and the target. The minute that happened the Krauts knew where it was coming from and where we were. In a short time the German artillery zeroed in on the mortar and on us. The second lieutenant who was in charge of the riflemen came towards us yelling "Get the hell out of here. Pull that mortar out and get the hell out!!"

When we were firing so many mortar rounds the base plate kept pounding into the ground so now it was hard to get it out of there. The mortar and the base plate were separate so we pulled the mortar out but the base plate was stuck so hard in the ground that we couldn't get it out. The second lieutenant got so excited and he kept yelling "get the hell outta here." We finally had to leave the base plate in the ground and take off.

We headed out as fast as we could in the other direction because we knew dang well it was just a matter of minutes before the artillery landed in there. The Krauts had figured out where we were. We got to the jeep, threw the mortar in and took off. The riflemen were heading out in a hurry to get back toward our positions. We had the mortar tube and had to get back to our position. The mortar tube had got so dang hot that you couldn't touch it from all that firing. It's looked like chrome plating on the inside of the barrel. We took a look in the middle and the lining had started peeling off.

The mortar had been ruined with all the firing we did. We had kept pumping from both sides as fast as the shells went out. We had to head out fast because we were just a patrol. Everybody got back to our unit again and nobody even got hit. We were really lucky that time. A combat patrol bringing in a mortar that far was a big deal. The lieutenant that was in charge of the riflemen was written up for a Bronze Star for leading the patrol. I guess you could say I was on a Bronze Star patrol. We accomplished our mission. That was what a combat patrol was like.

We were way up in front of our unit. Talk about audacity! I bet you the Krauts probably thought, those dang Americans must be crazy to send a combat patrol in so far to go after us. The Krauts were so far back they didn't think we'd go in there. That is why there wasn't an outpost. No matter how far back the Krauts were, an outpost may have helped protect them from enemy fire. If the Krauts had outposts we may have really gotten in trouble. With that small of a unit we couldn't really defend ourselves and could have been trapped in a hurry. So speed and mobility in the infantry was the whole thing.

We were kind of heroes then since we took out a Kraut observation post.

Behind the Lines

Dear Mom,   *Monday night Feb 19, 1945*   *France*

I'm sorry I couldn't write for the past week. I've been a little busy. I received your letter about five days ago.

Boy, I am so far behind the lines I can't even hear the big guns. I am back at a rest area for a while. We eat off of a table and we have real plates and cups and I sleep on a bunk with a mattress. They treat us like kings. The Red Cross serves doughnuts and coffee every day and there is a movie every night. The band gives a concert every day. We are quartered in a big building that used to be an opera house and we eat in a dining hall. They have French girls for waitresses.

I had nearly forgotten how it felt to sit at a table and eat and have somebody serve you. I don't even have to carry a gun around here. It's the first time I have been behind the artillery for three months. It seems funny not to be hearing all the thunder all the time and am I ever enjoying that.

How are you all coming along back home? Fine as ever I hope. I'm just swell. Is it still snowing? We've been having spring weather for a while now.

I saw a movie this evening and they served ice cream and cake and of course I had seconds on that. This afternoon I had a shower and a complete change of clothes. It sure feels good to get cleaned up. I will have a chance to get my teeth checked and a physical exam tomorrow.

Have you heard from Earl and Roy lately? I hope they can stay where they are until the war ends.

Nope, I'll have to close for now. I have one more letter to write tonight. They even have electric lights here. Here's hoping this finds you all well and happy and may God Bless you all.
Goodnite,

Verdie

Monday Nite
Feb 19 1945

Dear Mom,

I'm sorry I couldn't write for about a week. I've been a little busy. I received your letter about 5 days ago.

Boy I'm so far behind the lines now that I can't even hear the big guns. I'm back at a rest area for awhile. It's really nice here. We eat off a table and we have real plates & cups and I sleep on a bunk with a mattress. They treat us like kings. The Red Cross serves doughnuts & coffee every day & there's a movie every nite and the band gives a concert every day. We are quartered in a big building that used to be an opera house & we eat in a dining hall & they have some French

A feeling I had when I was behind the lines

You think I would be so overjoyed to get back to the rear. There were soldiers in class A uniforms and there wasn't a Kraut for miles. It was quiet and I was way out of danger. I really enjoyed it there but felt out of place. This was where the "rear echelon" was. That was kind of a dirty label the infantry put on the troops that were always behind us. I didn't even know what kind of jobs the other soldiers back here had. It is hard to explain how I felt. For some strange reason I was waiting to go back to the line with my friends.

For some reason or other even when I knew what things we got into on the front lines, I wanted to go back there. It seems like I'd want to sleep in a bunk and get good chow but I felt like I should be back with my friends in the unit.

The weapon we hated the most

The weapon we hated the most was the enemy mortars. The Krauts often shot them at night and we sweated out every barrage. The shells came straight down and if you didn't have your foxhole covered with logs or something you never knew what could happen. The military now is still using mortar in wars. You hear about it in Iraq and Afghanistan. The smaller mortars are so mobile and the shells are hard to get away from.

The mortars in our squad were small and we could move quickly from one position to the next if we worried about getting hit by artillery. We could hear at night when the German shells went off. Their shells didn't leave a tracer but there was a flash that came out of the tube like a rocket. Both sides tried to get down low behind a ridge or something so the enemy couldn't see the flash when the shells were fired. The Krauts had 50 millimeter shells and they fired pretty fast. We'd hear the noise and then sweat it out before the shells hit someplace around us. There was a big flash when the shell exploded but at night the Krauts couldn't see what they may have hit.

These tactics really weren't very effective because the Krauts couldn't pick a target. It was mostly for harassment. Normally we weren't supposed to be using up ammunition randomly without having a specific target sighted in. If we were in the trees we couldn't fire back and we didn't fire at night because it was wasting ammunition but the Krauts often fired mortars mostly for harassment.

Teeth fixed for nothing

Dear Dad,   *Tues evening Feb 20, 1945*

I've been to the dentist this afternoon and my lip is still numb from the Novocain. I filled two and have to go back tomorrow and fill two more. He did a good job on them too. It's nice when you can get your teeth fixed for nothing. I am having a very nice rest now. It is wonderful to just lay down and sleep all night and not have sentry duty or anything to worry about. I needed a mental rest more than a physical rest.

They sure are getting close to Japan now aren't they? And of course the Russians are still advancing. I don't think they can be stopped now. We aren't doing so bad either are we? Well I hope and pray it all ends soon. The Krauts know it's a hopeless fight but they are the stubbornest rats on earth. I've had a little experience with these SS troops and I think they are nuts.

A few of the civilians in this town have cars. Most of them use horses though. Some of them have wagons with rubber tires on them. The civilians are pretty well dressed too. I saw a movie again this evening. I sure enjoyed that.

What did you think of the "Big 3" meeting? I got a chance to read the peace terms and they are a little tough but Germany deserves it.

Say Dad, do you think you could get hold of one of those hunting knives and send it to me? Don't get the wrong idea. I'm not planning on using it on the Krauts, they are so handy to have around. You can take some of my money and get it. Maybe they are hard to get hold of now. If you can get one I would really appreciate it. Use my money tho, it's okay with me how much you pay for it. One something like Roy's hunting knife would be best.

I 'spose you're getting the John Deere all ready for spring work now. It seems funny to think that spring is just around the corner. I got another Monte American the other day, December 29 issue. I sure enjoy reading it.

Nope Dad, I guess it's time to hit the hay. Here's hoping this finds you all well and happy and may God Bless you all.

Goodnite,
Love, Verdie

Fifty years later "Kilroy was Here" 1995

The dentist set up a chair in a house in France and he used a drill powered by a foot pedal. There was a soldier who kept the pedal going and when it slowed down the dentist pulled out the drill and waited it for it to get up to speed again. About fifty years later I was with Dr. Powers, the dentist in Monte, and he needed to replace one of my fillings. I told him, "It may be one that the Army gave me back in France in 1945 and it will probably say GI issue on the bottom." When he took it out, he looked closely and said, "Nope Verdie, it doesn't say anything about GI issue ... but it does say...Kilroy was here."

At the rate the war is going now it shouldn't last much longer

Dear Dad,   *Thursday Feb 22, 1945 France (near Bitche)*

I just finished having coffee and cake. Just like having afternoon lunch at home. They're spoiling me back here in the rest center and I am sure enjoying it. I filled two more teeth yesterday so they are okay now. I am glad to get them fixed up.

We had church services this morning. There is a very good chaplain back here. This afternoon they had a very good program too. It was a stage show with singing and playing and some good comedians.

I saw a very good movie last nite. "The National Barn Dance." It's a show made about what we listen to on WLS you know. Lulu Belle and Scotty and the Hoosier Hot Shots were in it too.

There is a radio going all day here so I hear the news quite regularly. At the rate the war is going now it shouldn't last much longer. Have you hear from Earl and Roy lately? I have been reading about the battle for Iwo Jima and I don't think either of them are there.

You should see the kids in the small towns over here whenever the kids see a soldier they beg for chocolate and chewing gum or "cigarette de poppa" (cigarettes for my father) and then they go smoke them themselves. Cigarettes sell for $8 a carton here and in Paris they sell for around $20 a carton. The civilians say they pay that much. Us soldiers get all our cigarettes free. We get one pack a day so we have plenty cigarettes. Cigarettes are pretty hard to get back there aren't they?

I haven't had any mail for a few days now but I 'spose I'll get a pile of it when I do get it. Are you getting my letters now? I can't see why some of them should take so long.

How's Sam getting along? Is he going to farm his own land this year or is he going to work out or maybe both? Greet him from me. I 'spose Julien is still in Italy. I wrote him a while ago so I hope he gets the letter. Where is Harvey now? Could you send me his address too?

It's time for supper so I'll have to close for now. They won't keep supper waiting in the Army you know. I wish I could have potato soup for supper but the Army never makes it so I guess I'll have to wait till I get home.

So long and May God Bless You all

Love Verdie
Tell Shep Hi

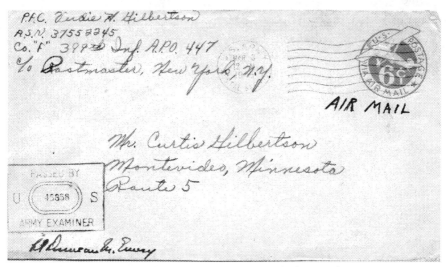

My younger brother Curtis was interested in airplanes and it was fun to talk with him about flying.

A new secret weapon

Dear Curtis, *Tuesday Feb 27ʰ France*

About time I'm answering your letter. My letter writing hasn't been very good but I hope the time comes soon when I can write more regularly. I received Dad's letter last night and I'll answer as soon as I can.

So the game warden decided to go fishing the same night you did, eh? How did Teddy and Raymond make out? I am celebrating my 2nd anniversary of Army life today. In one way it seems like I've been in 10 years and another way it seems like only a few months. A year from now I hope I'm a civilian again. I'll be satisfied if the war is over even if I'm still over here.

Have you done any more flying yet? Maybe the weather isn't fit for flying. I read in the Monte American that Bob Clagget had gone to California to get a new ship. I 'spose he's back with it now. What did he get, another Cub? I've been kinda thinking if I can save enough money, that I'll get a crate of some kind when I get home. Do you think a guy could get enough business to make some money with it? I'd like to get a Luscombe. I kinda think they'll put a bigger engine in the Luscombe. It would really be quite a ship if they put a 125 HP in it wouldn't it?

I saw a flock of geese the other day. I was tempted to let them have it but there are some rats that need it worse so I will have to wait until they have had enough. I made a slingshot* the other day. I found an old inner tube and a crotch and some leather and I made a good one. Boy, will the Krauts be surprised when the stones start flying. They'll think it's a new secret weapon.

How are you coming with Earl's car? I 'spose you've got it ready to go now. I'd like to take a spin in it myself now.

Nope Curtis, I'll have to close for now. I've got quite a few letters to write yet. Write soon Curtis and may God bless you all.

So long,
Bro, Verdie

When are you going fishing again? ha ha

Our company commander asked us to make slingshots so we could use them for sabotage when we got into towns with factories. These weapons were perfect to shoot out lights with rocks instead of wasting ammunition and worrying about ricochets. Most of us including the company commander, carried sling shots in our field jacket pockets.

Chapter
France and Germany in March

We're squeezing the Krauts

Dear Dad,   *Saturday March 3 France*

I received your letter a few days ago written Feb. 10. Thanks a lot I sure appreciate those letters. I'm just fine. I've got it pretty good now.

The war situation looks good again now both here and in the Pacific. We're squeezing the Krauts now into a pretty tight circle. They fight like rats when they are cornered. I get the news regularly now from the newspaper they call "The Stars and Stripes." We get it nearly every day with war news and home news. Of course the war isn't over until the last shot is fired.

I saw a pretty good dog fight a while ago. It's quite a racket when they start that. It usually ends with the Luftwaffe taking off for home as fast as they can go.

I sent home $50 the other day so I hope you get it. How many of my allotments have you gotten now? I have been paid 4 times since I came over here so there should have been 4 allotment checks sent out. I imagine it takes quite a while before they come through.

The way President Roosevelt talked about agreements of the "Big 3" we will be occupying a piece of Germany. Of course we are wondering who will get that job. I wouldn't mind staying over here for about 6 months or so after it' s over but I don't care to spend any length of time.

How is the weather back there now? Is it still snowing? It looks like you will have a late spring. We are having pretty nice weather now.

Well Dad, there isn't much news so I will close. May God Bless you all.

Love, Verdie

Patrols while in Defense Positions

When we were in defense positions, we sent out patrols at different times at night and take turns. We called them listening patrols and two of us went out together. Our purpose was we'd go out as far as we could and then either stand or sit while waiting and then just watch and listen for what we could hear. In one instance what we heard was a wagon that the Germans used to haul supplies. The Germans used horses sometimes in the Vosges Mountains because the trails weren't so good. We could hear the horses and wagons and one night this went on for quite a while. Finally we told the artillery about it.

A forward observer came up and his job was to pick out the targets. He laid there with his field glasses and picked out a target. This time he was interested in the chow wagon. It wasn't strategic but for some reason he wanted to find it. It wasn't going to change the war or anything. He was a young guy like us and probably thought it was some kind of prank. That one night we all decided we were going to get this chow wagon.

The observers had looked at the map, found the trail, estimated the range, and it wasn't long before we could hear the rounds being fired over us. Pretty soon we heard the horses take off running. The artillery guys kept changing their targeting to follow it. Finally one more round was fired and everything got quiet. We never heard one more sound. We figured; we got him. Then maybe a day or so later we jumped off at 0500 and had the objective to take the German position.

It was an SS position, and we went in there so fast we must have surprised them. The Germans had mine fields laid out and had put out tape for their own protection in order to walk around between the mines. Paths had been made for them to follow. We got in there so fast that the Krauts didn't have time to take the tape down. We went in there on the German paths and we captured quite a few prisoners. There wasn't a choice so they either gave up or else. After we'd taken some of the prisoners we were kind of mopping up in case there was anyone left hiding out. There was some thick woods or bushes there. Somebody said he had heard something in there. We suspected some Krauts might be trying to hide in there. We made a big circle around it and someone said in German "Get out of there or else we will start ventilating it."

It wasn't long and two SS officers came out of there wearing dress uniforms. We'd never seen anything like that before. Usually everyone including the officers wore field uniforms and here these men were in dress uniforms. SS considered themselves as the elite and were arrogant even around their American captors. The SS officer demanded to talk to a US officer before he moved from his place. We were only enlisted men. He got so arrogant that one of our guys yelled, "Raus, Raus" and kicked him in the hind end so hard with a United States Army boot that both of the Krauts took off running to catch up with the other German prisoners. It wasn't often we got this close to SS officers.

That capture was completed and we kept moving in and ran into that chow wagon further back. One horse was dead in the harness and one horse was still alive. He was wild and scared to get out away from the wagon. We finally got him untangled and thought we'd probably use him for a while. So we loaded up a lot of mortar rounds on the horse. He was pretty wild but we figured we could handle him. All of a sudden we started getting fire from the Krauts and that horse went crazy. We pulled our ammunition off as fast as we could and turned the horse loose. The last we saw him, he was going through the woods with his harness on as fast as he could run.

A little later we came upon a Volkswagen car that was stuck in the mud on the trail. When the Krauts saw us coming, two guys jumped out and ran down the road ahead of us. We yelled, "Stop," but neither of them stopped so our man shot and wounded one of the Krauts and then the other one stopped. It turned out one was a captain and the other a general. Captain Huberger was so proud that we'd captured a general. This was an unusual day for Fox Company. That was about the end of our objective.

We had tank support that came up later on and caught up with us. The Volkswagen was still sitting in the middle of the muddy road. One of the tanks drove off to the side of the road to avoid hitting the car and it got hung up on a tree. The next tank came behind and a second lieutenant got mad. He said "Drive right over it." So the next tank drove right over the top of it and crunched it. The last four tanks drove over it one by one. By the time the last tank hit went over it, that Volkswagen was flatter than a pancake. A bunch of us were standing right by the car watching the tanks drive over it and we had something to get a laugh out of. After that we dug in and held the position until we got another objective.

Prisoners of war

It wasn't often that we captured an officer. The general that was in the little Volkswagen Bug car that got too close to the line and we captured him was brought back with us. He was very arrogant and when it came time for chow his aide went up and filled a mess kit for the general. Then the aide came back and tried to get some chow for himself. The cook said, "You were through this line before." "That was for the general," the aide said. The cook told him, "Nobody waits on the general, you tell him to come and get his own food." I am sure the aide learned a few new choice cuss words in English. I doubt if the aide ever got anything to eat that time because there was no way he was going to get another plate of food from that cook.

Living in a dugout

Dear Lyle,   *Sunday, March 11, 1945*

I received your letter yesterday and thanks a lot. I was sure glad to hear from you again. You have really been doing some fishing lately I would really like to help you pull out a few of those pickerels and I'd like to help you eat them too. When I get the time and some fishing tackle I will try to do a little fishing over here. There are a lot of streams and a few small lakes and a river once in a while

I'm living in a dugout right now. It isn't so bad. I can keep warm and dry and get plenty to eat so I don't suffer any. The grass is getting green now and I see quite a few birds around. I don't see any meadowlarks though. I guess they don't have any of them over here.

The pocket gophers are busy digging around here. If I had a trap I'd catch some. I suppose you will be busy shooting and trapping gophers soon now. How is ammunition to get now? That's one thing I get plenty of. (tsk, tsk) I think I have a 9mm Belgian Browning automatic pistol to take home with me.

I 'spose you are waiting for school to be out now. It won't be long will it?

I had a letter from Earl the other day. He has it pretty nice now. I hope he can stay in that place. Nope Lyle, this is all I have time for now so I'll have to close.

So Long,
Bro Verdie
Greet Shep and Vicky from me
Thanks a lot for the Air Mail stamps

Sunning myself

Dear Mom,   *Tuesday March 13, 1945*

Received your very welcome letter today the one dated Feb 25th. Thanks a lot. I am so glad for every letter I get. I'm sitting outside my dugout sunning myself. It's about like April or May back home. The flies are even pestering me a little. I'm having it nice now so don't worry about me. I am warm and dry and get plenty to eat so I am perfectly okay. The country is beautiful where I am now. I wish I had a camera so I could send some pictures home.

I got my picture taken today. Some fellow from the Signal Corps came up to my position and wanted some pictures. He had a movie camera and another still camera. He said he'd send the pictures to our home paper so maybe you will get a chance to see it. He said it will be in a newspaper from a large town close to home so most likely they'll put it in a Minneapolis paper. I hope you get a chance to see it.

I imagine you will get some nice weather back there pretty soon. I bet there will be a lot of ponds around when all that snow starts melting. I am having it nice now so don't worry about me. I'm warm and dry and get plenty to eat so I'm perfectly okay.

I'm getting a pass to go to Paris in 3 or 4 weeks so I am looking forward to that.*

The war news looks better every day. These "supermen" over here don't look so super any more. We get prisoners all of the time and some of them are pretty sad cases. Some have been as young as 15 years old. I don't feel a bit sorry for them though. The Japs are getting a plastering too. Well, it can't be over quick enough to suit me.

That's too bad about Julien Nøkleby. I imagine it was hard on his folks. I 'spose you were at his memorial service. Say, thanks for sending the stamps, I can sure use them.

This is all I have for now so I'll close for now. Here's hoping this finds you all well and happy and may God Bless you all.

Love, Verdie

* This turned out to be another rumor. Instead of being in Paris three or four weeks later, we were busy in Heilbronn, Germany. The

17th SS Panzer Grenadier Division that we first encountered during Operation NordWind in January 1945 was still in combat with our unit in Heilbronn during the first part of April 1945.

Details about the picture taken by the Signal Corps photographer

Posing with my mortar in France March 14th, 1944
US Army Signal Corp photo

Fox Company was dug in and waiting in defensive positions and everything was pretty quiet. The Germans were pretty close to us and also dug in. Not much was going on this day. I was in my mortar position and there was a deep valley behind us with a road. As I looked down there was a jeep coming up the valley towards our area where Fox Company was. The jeep stopped and a soldier got out and came up the hill toward me. While watching him, I wondered what in the world he was coming up here for. He got up close to me and was quite nervous. You could tell he was in a hurry. He asked me, "Do you want your picture taken?" "Sure, that's okay," I told him. "Ya, you can take my picture."

The mortar was facing the other direction towards the Germans and he didn't want to get on that side. He didn't want to expose himself at all. In the picture you can see that we were behind a bank which we could fire a mortar over. He asked me, "Can you swing that thing around and face it the other direction?" That was backwards but I said, "Ya, I can do that." So I swung it around backwards and he took the picture. "Where are you from?" he asked. I told him, "Minnesota." "What's your hometown?", "Montevideo, Minnesota." I said. Then he asked the name of the paper in my town. "It's the Montevideo American." He wanted my parent's address. "Rural Route 5 Montevideo, Minnesota," I said. He was jotting all this down real quickly and I was sure to tell him my name was Verdie Gilbertson.

The machine gun was dug in next to the mortar but there didn't happen to be anybody on it at this time. "Do you want a picture of the machine gun too?" I asked him. That was exposed a little over the brow of the hill. "Why don't you take a picture of me there too?" I asked him. "No, no, no, I don't want any more pictures" he said. "I'll send it to your hometown newspaper!" Then he took off down the hill as fast as he could and got in his Jeep. He wasn't there very long.

Will he actually ever send that picture? I thought. A quite a while later after sort of forgetting about it, a letter came from my folks. My dad said, "Oh, we got such a nice picture of you with this mortar gun. It's in the Montevideo American on display. The paper told us it will be on display for a while and then you can have it."

That's how this picture happened and it was rare to ever see a photographer. That was the first one I had ever seen up close. That evening we were pulled off the line and fed a good meal. We had been in defense positions waiting for the push to cross the Rhine River.

The rumor was that we were going to be in reserve for three days. Then the lieutenant said to us. "Platoon leaders meeting." Oh no, we knew what that meant. Bam, it got quiet. We waited and pretty soon Lt. Nicholson came back and said, "All right you guys, every one of you write home. We are jumping off at 0500 tomorrow." That was the most dreaded word in the infantry, "Jumping off." That meant we had an objective of attacking a German position. There wasn't much sleep that night. Everybody was thinking hard about what might be happening in the early morning

Chapter Ten

Climax of the Game

It looks like it's the climax of the game.

Dear Folks,   *Wednesday March 14, 1945 France*

I'll write a few lines to let you know I'm okay. It's getting dark so I'll have to rush it. How is everybody back home? Fine as ever I hope.

This is a beautiful evening here just like an evening in April back home. I 'spose you are getting ready for spring work, Dad. I wish I could be there driving the John Deere. The war news sounds very good. It looks like it's the climax of the game. I hope and pray that it ends soon and I think it will. The Japs sure are getting the works too now.

You must have had a lot of snow to get the new road blocked up. Say if you don't hear from me for a while at times don't worry. Once in a while I don't get a chance to write for a while. I'm glad to hear that Earl and Roy are still in the same place. I hope they can stay there.

Nope, this isn't very long but it's all I have time for now.

Here's hoping this finds you all well and happy and may God Bless you all.

Love, Verdie

Editor's analysis of this letter: When looking over the words my Dad wrote this day and see that the next day he jumped off to attack at Bitche I get the feeling it was one time he was thinking that this could be his last letter. He speaks of the "climax of the game" meaning something big was about to happen. It certainly did when the major fortifications at Bitche were captured. He talks about the beautiful weather and his brothers. He also talks about wishing he were home driving the John Deere. If this had been his last letter- his family had pleasant memories of him even while he was at war. I believe this is what he intended.

Wednesday
mar. 14, 1945

Dear Folks,

I'll write a few lines to
let you know I'm okay.
It's getting dark so I'll have
to rush it.

How is everybody back
home? Fine as ever I
hope.

This is a beautiful
evening, just like an evening
in April back home. I
imagine you will be
having spring weather back
there soon too now. I spose
you're getting all ready for
spring work, Dad. I wish
I could be there driving
the John Deere again.

The war news sounds
very good now doesn't it.
I sorta like it's the climax
of the game. I hope & pray
that it ends soon. And
I think it will. The Japs
sure are getting the works

too now.

You must have had quite a bit of snow to get the new road blocked up.

Say if you don't hear from me for a while at times don't worry. once in a while I don't get a chance to write for quite awhile.

I'm glad to hear that Roy & Earl are still in the same place. I hope they can stay there!

I hope, this isn't a very long letter but it's about all I have time for tonite. Here's hoping this finds you all well & happy & may our Almighty God bless you all.

Love,
Verdie

The night we wrote our letters home
March 14ᵗʰ 1944

It was still light when we wrote our letters outside sitting on the ground and we had eaten a good mea and it was quiet. It was just getting dark and now we were standing, all of us a watching our artillery in a coordinated attack as they were shelling the Kraut's positions all across the horizon. We couldn't see all of it because of the mountains and hills of the Vosges. In all directions we could see the flashes from our own 155 mm artillery as it went over our heads. There was rumbling, rumbling and flashing all over the place. The shells going over us gave off sort of sucking sound. They must have been breaking a sound barrier. There was a steady rumble and we wondered how anyone could take that. This went on for hours that night and into the morning.

Our artillery was softening the krauts up before the infantry went in the next morning. We had seen barrages before but this was the most dramatic one we saw. It was sort of fascinating to see the power but maybe more sickening to me than fascinating. We were thinking, "What is going on?" We probably didn't get much sleep that night. Maybe some because you couldn't stay awake all night. You had to lay down for a while no matter what.

Of course we were apprehensive about what was going to happen at 0500 and couldn't relax enough to get any real good sleep. We expected something bigger than ever before because we had never seen this much of our artillery going over our heads. There was so much more firing than usual. We didn't really realize how big a thing it was and then a day or two later we captured the stronghold of Bitche.

Every time I see lightning flashes in the distance now I think of that night in France. The Krauts must have got the same feeling this night as we got from them we they let loose a heavy barrage of artillery with their NordWind offensive at midnight on New Year's 1945. This time the Krauts were on the receiving end like we were in January. From the experience we had it was easier to imagine what the Krauts were feeling from our guns. When reading my letter from March 14ᵗʰ, 1945 it's just like I am there again watching our artillery pound the Germans and feeling apprehensive about jumping off in the morning.

Our artillery quit firing right before we all jumped off at 0500.

Century Division Report: On 15 March 1945, the attack jumped off and on 16 March, Bitche fell to the 100th. Taking Neustadt and Ludwigshafen, the Division reached the Rhine.

"Sons of Bitche"
From the "Story of the Century"

*The Seventh Army's drive into Germany in March, 1945 was highlighted with the seizure of Bitche, a heavily-fortified town in the Low Vosges Mountains. Since the erection of the enormous sandstone citadel there in the early 1700s, the town had been continuously fortified with concentric rings of outworks, including several major Maginot forts, dozens of concrete pillboxes, and thickets of barbed wire and minefields. Although it had been invested several times, most notably in the Franco-Prussian War and in the 1940 campaign, Bitche had never fallen. From this point on the entire 100th Division became known as "**The Sons of Bitche.**"*

100th Division infantrymen move through Bitche following capture, March 1945.—*U.S. Army*

From "The Story of the Century" -US Army photograph

Membership card owned by author

History of the Society of the Sons of Bitche

"The Society of the Sons of Bitche was conceived during the occupation period of the 100th Infantry Division in southwestern Germany in 1945 "to commemorate the campaign for the City of Bitche and provide a social organization and program for the men who took part in the fight."

The Society's name was chosen to commemorate the Division's fighting for the ancient fortress town of Bitche, a key location in the then-modern Maginot Line which had withstood all attacks for over 200 years . . . until it was captured after a three-month winter siege by the 100th Infantry Division on 16 March 1945."

http://www.100thww2.org/anecd/sons.html

How Beehive got his Name.

*With "Beehive" by the Danube River in April 1945, I carried
a carbine and Beehive always had his M 1 Rifle.*

WJ Everhart and I started advanced infantry training at Fort Bragg
in 1944. He came from the hills of North Carolina and I was from the
farm lands of Minnesota. We shipped out together for the battle in
France and arrived in October 1944. For the first month or so of combat
he was still Everhart or WJ. Then one day he got his new nickname,
the one I still know him as. When we got to the Maginot Line with all
the German pillboxes the Army came out with a new explosive device
that was designed to blow holes in the top of a pillbox. The concrete in
the pillboxes was ten feet thick on the top and direct fire from artillery

154

didn't even damage these structures. Dive bombers dropped 500 pound bombs that just bounced off the pillboxes.

Someone from "rear echelon" brought up a new explosive device called a "beehive." The thing looked like an overgrown ice cream cone with legs on it. When it exploded, the point was designed to send down a sharp piece of metal to penetrate and blow up the pillbox. It was supposed to be stood up on the pill box.

Our squad was starting to discuss who was going to be the first to go up and light the fuse when it was on top of the pillbox. I don't really know why we picked Everhart but we were just joking around like we often did. Everhart was nominated to be the first to put the "beehive" explosive on the pillbox. We knew that it wouldn't do a darn thing because no one could get within five hundred yards of the pillbox. Someone in "rear echelon" had dreamed up the whole ridiculous idea.

"Beehive" never did use the *beehive* but from then on Everhart was known as "Beehive." We left the *beehive* explosive behind and decided someone else could take care of it or the planners could do the job we were asked to do. Putting this device on a pillbox was too ridiculous to even consider. There was no way this could ever work and no way would anyone just walk up on the pillbox while the Krauts were sitting there with machine guns. Even if the *beehive* was laid right on top, it wouldn't ever dent a pillbox. We watched many direct artillery rounds bounce off of those heavy concrete bunkers.

"Beehive" never did complain about his nickname. It didn't make any difference what a soldier thought about it, the names just stuck. I have always called him by his nickname when I tell stories. We spent all our days together from the advanced infantry training until the end of the war. When we got new assignments we were even MPS together. I really never knew where he went after that. I stayed in Paris and he got transferred. We only talked once after that when he won the privilege to buy an Argus C 3 camera.

Three regiments from the Century Division were the first Army in history to ever breech the Maginot Line. There were many levels of barracks located under the pillboxes and they were all connected by tunnels. The Krauts had retractable artillery that went up and down. Once we penetrated the line, the Germans could stay in their pillboxes but we were past the defenses the French had built to keep the Germans out of France. Now the Germans were attempting to keep the American forces from entering Germany. A gopher couldn't safely get across the mown grass on the Maginot Line. The Germans figured no army could ever get through there but fortunately their master plans were wrong.

The First Ones to Mark German Soil

During the last week we had been talking among the platoon about who was going to be the first man to take a leak on German soil. As we got closer and closer to the Siegfried line, our opportunity was very near so we started making our plans. Three of us, Everhart, Delewski, and Gilbertson decided to take a hike all the way up to the border line. We had to sneak out from the rest of the platoon because it would not have been good if the company commander found out about us wandering around away from the rest of our unit.

When we got to the border, we looked over the ridge and saw the Siegfried Line that was built to stop any army from ever invading Germany on the ground. The ground was stripped so bare that a gopher could not have snuck across it. There was barbed wire and the famous concrete "Dragon's Teeth" designed to keep anything including American tanks out of Germany.

We looked down the hill at the fortifications but couldn't stand up because the Krauts were waiting and watching for anything that moved. We had to lay on our sides to take our leaks, but we had told each other that we were going to be the first ones to mark German soil.

We accomplished our mission but barely made it out alive. The Krauts must have spotted us and immediately began to lob in 88 mm artillery fire. Delewski almost didn't make it but he escaped harm when he dove into a concrete bunker. I can still hear him voicing his excitement with a big laughing sound of "Wheeee." We had attempted to keep a low profile out of the sight of German artillery but it must not have been as low as it should have been.

We thought we were heroes "number one." It was probably kind of dumb but that is the kind of thing battle-worn GIs think up and I bet we weren't the only ones. General Patton was pictured relieving himself in the Rhine River. We thought maybe we might get some kind of medal for it. Dogs put their mark on trees. We put our mark on German soil.

This is just what it looked like when we looked down from
up high on a hill just at the German border
From "The Story of the Century" -US Army photograph

We've got the Krauts back in their own hole now.

Dear Dad,   *March 19ᵗʰ, Germany (Siegfried Line)*

Sorry I haven't been able to write for a while, I've been a little busy. I 'spose you see in the papers what's going on over here so I won't say anything about that. I'm perfectly okay so don't worry.

We've got the Krauts back in their own hole now. I can't figure out why they don't call it quits but the Germans are so blame stubborn that's why they keep on. They are paying plenty for it though. There won't be much of Germany left when it's all over. I don't think it will last much longer. We can hope and pray it ends soon.

So you had another snowstorm you will have a late spring this year won't you. The pussy willows are in full bloom over here. I guess that is a sure sign of spring. I'm really glad to see spring come. I 'spose you will be plenty busy with spring work in a little while. I don't think the farmers over here will get much work done this spring.

This is another short letter but I hope to do better next time

I guess I'll have to get some shut eye now. Good night and May God Bless you all,

Love,
Verdie

No more Potato Salad for our platoon

Our platoon of about thirty men had passed over the German border and was not too far into the country. Now we had the opportunity to be in reserve a mile or so behind the unit that stayed on the combat line. We didn't have this chance to rest very often. We needed to be rotated at times so we could get a little more sleep and rest. Now we could go through our equipment and get regrouped. Sometimes we even got hot meals from the chow wagon. The artillery was five miles behind the line and we were between them and the fighting. We still had to man our outposts and be on alert but we were a longer distance from getting fired on by small arms. The German artillery could still reach us.

This time while on reserve we found a family that had a big barn for all of us to stay in. Their son had been injured in the fighting and was sent home to recuperate. He was still wearing his German Army uniform. He was an enemy soldier and we probably should have captured him and sent him to a prisoner of war camp but none of us wanted to do that so we just left him alone. He was not on our list of priorities.

Our number one priority was finding some food to eat and a place to sleep. The German didn't spend any time with us and he was a little nervous about being around a bunch of enemy soldiers. We probably should have told this Kraut, "As long as we are here, you are safe but you better be careful when the rear echelon comes up." They might have got a Bronze Star for capturing a German soldier. We were not looking for any medals.

The day after we moved in the woman brought us a big bowl of her home made potato salad. She told us, "If you want to write letters home, you can come in and sit at my kitchen table." I took her up on it and sat down to write a letter or two. It was much better than sitting and trying to write on my knee.

Later in the day after a little rest, some of the machine gunners decided to clean their guns and test them by taking some practice firing.

The guns were lined up on a hill and the shooting started over a valley and into a hillside. They kept on firing for a long time. Meanwhile the farmer and his soldier son were down in the valley trying to dig some more potatoes. When both of the Germans heard the shooting and saw the dirt flying on the hillside, they dove down so as not to get hit. The farmer and son didn't know when it was safe to stand up.

After all the shooting was over the farmer came up and told the soldiers that he and his son had been down there all the time. The soldiers probably just laughed. Apology wasn't a word in the Army vocabulary. The hausfrau didn't get any more potatoes from her son and husband and even if she did, I doubt she was in any kind of mood to make us more potato salad.

My outfit took a place (*Bitche*)

Dear Mom,   *Wednesday March 21, 1945 Germany (Siegfried line)*

I'm laying on a hillside sunning myself right now. The countryside around here is very nice. There are many acres of apple trees around me, it would really be nice to see them all in bloom. I have been relieved so I am not in combat now. I hope it is a long time before I see any more action again but I suppose we won't get this war over by laying around behind the lines.

This last week was pretty rough. I 'spose you read all about it in the paper. We are doing pretty good aren't we? My outfit took a place (*Bitche*) that had never been taken before in history. I've been in Germany a little too. It doesn't make much difference but there is some satisfaction in it.

How's everything back home? Fine as ever I hope. I am perfectly okay. I had a chance to get a shower and clean clothes today so that felt good. (*We were taken back a few at a time, a few miles behind the lines to some place where temporary portable showers were set up in a big building by the Army*)

The war news sounds very good now. I can't see how it will last much longer. The Japs are getting plastered every day now. I haven't had time to write Earl and Roy for a while now but I'll write as soon as I can. You'll have to greet Mildred, Vernice and Clarice for me too and their families. I haven't had much chance to write lately and I hope it will be better for a while now. I imagine you will start having Luther League meetings again soon. Have you gotten Rev Jensen back yet?

Nope, this is about all the news I have so I'll close for now. Here's hoping this finds you all well and happy and may God Bless you all

Love, Verdie

The 398ᵗʰ and 399ᵗʰ Inf. went into assembly areas around Bousseviller, Briedenbach, and other towns to the north of Bitche, The two regiments occupied these assembly areas from 18 to 22 March. The Story of the Century P132.

"They stole our chickens"

We arrived in a German village and it was sort of a farming area where many civilians had chickens in their back yards in cages. The town was deserted because the people had evacuated before we arrived. We had cleared the town and were going to stay there overnight or maybe even a couple of nights, we didn't know for sure. The house we chose was empty with no one there so we just moved in for the night. There was a chicken coop in the back yard with probably about a dozen chickens.

Our guys Beehive, Simmons, Woody a couple others decided that fresh chicken would be pretty good eating so we made a plan to eat up those chickens the next day. It was kind of late so we figured on waiting until early in the morning. Then we were going to fire up the stove in the house and cook all the chickens. We probably should have put a guard on "our chickens."

During the night there was squad of soldiers from our company in another house close by. They came over while we weren't watching closely enough and they stole all of our chickens. These were *our chickens*- the ones that *we* had liberated. We found out the other squad was cooking during the biggest part of the night. In the morning one of our fellows went out and was going to see if the chickens had laid any eggs. He was hoping the chickens might give us some eggs before we started eating them. Not long after, he came back in and said to the rest of us, "Somebody stole all our chickens."

The German farmer, who was probably out in the woods hiding somewhere, came back to his house early the morning and was going to feed his chickens. He looked around and found only one half scared chicken left in the pen. After we were left without any chickens we went over and told the guys in the next house, "You know that was really a dirty trick, at least you could have invited us over during the night to help you eat some." For those guys to eat up all of our chickens didn't seem right. They said something to us but I don't know what their excuse was. I guess that was the only way they were going to get our chickens to eat. So we didn't get any chickens that time.

An infantry man is always hungry so when we saw a chance for fresh food we took advantage. The chickens we saw when we went by a farm had been under Nazi rule for many years so it was up to us to liberate chickens when we had the opportunity.

Once in a while some of the cooks might decide to liberate a cow for supper. Maybe the cow had attacked the cooks and they shot it in self-defense. A cow almost got one of our men one time. He had sprained his ankle so he was sent back to the kitchen crew. One day he went out with his M1 after a cow and only wounded it. He couldn't move very fast as the wounded cow came after him. He took a lot of ribbing from the crew. "You mean you couldn't even drop a cow with an M1? We thought you were a crack shot." One of the cooks finally shot the cow dead. Fresh beef steak tasted great.

Busy Chasing the Krauts

Dear Folks,   *Saturday, March 24, 1945 Germany (Rhine River Ludwigshafen & Manheim)*

Sorry I couldn't write for a while I've been a little too busy chasing the Krauts. Don't worry if you don't hear from me for a while at times. There are times when I don't get a chance to write.

I suppose you see in the paper what's going on lately. It's been a little rough lately but it isn't so bad. Germany is a lot nicer country than France. I've seen some beautiful farming country. It would be nice country if it had decent people.

How's everything back there? Are you still having snowstorms? I bet the roads will be nice and muddy when the snow starts melting. I had a letter the other day from Clarice and Vernice. I hope Earl and Roy are in the same place.

This isn't a very long letter but I guess I better get a little shuteye now. Here's hoping this finds you all well and happy and may God Bless you all.

Love, Verdie

On 24 March, 399th was given the mission of seizing the west bank of the Rhine south of Ludwigshafen. The battalion entered Altripp, south of Ludwigshafen, during the morning. The 399th, with one battalion of the 397th attached, took over the city from the 94th and continued the task of mopping up resistance within the city. The Story of the Century p. 132

I had a chance to go to services yesterday.

Dear Mom,   *March 26 Germany (Mutterstadt)*

I received your very welcome letter this evening. Thanks a million. The letter was the one you wrote March 15th. You asked me if I got that box where you had the cookies packed in a red can. No, I haven't gotten that that one. Maybe that was the one that burned instead of the one I got.

It seems funny to think that Easter is next Sunday. It seems so much more like spring when Easter has come. I had a chance to go to services yesterday. We had them in a church for the first time since I came over here. There are quite a few Protestant churches here in Germany so we use them. It was only Catholic churches in France. It was a nice church with a pipe organ in it. It didn't look like it had been used much lately though.

Germany is a much cleaner and nicer country than France. The towns are nice and I've seen some beautiful homes. I'm staying in a house right now. The people seem friendly here but we don't trust them. They have these swastika flags in their houses but they aren't flying them now. Instead there's a white flag flying on nearly every house.

I've seen quite a few of these Polish and Russian people the Nazis used in forced labor camps. They were released when the Americans took the prison camps. They look pretty bad, most of them. They are really happy now though. They even made 10 year old kids work for them. The Nazis will and are paying plenty for what they did though.

The trees are starting to sprout over here now and some plum trees are in bloom. It looks pretty nice. So the blackbirds are singing back there already. Well, I guess that is a sure sign of spring. I haven't seen very many birds over here yet. I 'spose they have been scared out of the country.

I haven't met any boys I know from home over here yet. I hope I can run into some of them. How are Mildred, Vernice and the baby girls getting along? I bet they are cute now.

We had creamed chicken for supper tonight. Boy was that ever good and we had fresh potatoes too. We have been having dehydrated potatoes and they aren't very good. I sure could go for some potato soup now. I could eat five gallons of it. I'll make up for it when I get home.

It looks like the war can't last much longer now. I thought that it would have been over before now but it drags out. All we can do is hope and pray it ends soon. I can't see why the Germans want to keep on fighting. They know they're beaten.

Well I guess I'll have to close for now. I have one more letter to write yet tonight and then it will be time to hit the hay.

Here's hoping this finds you all well and happy and may God Bless you all. Goodnite.

Love, Verdie

100th Division Infantry walking through another village
From "The Story of the Century" Army Signal Corps photo

Polish Civilian Prisoners

The war was still going on and when we came into this little village, there was a Polish displaced- person's camp. The Germans had kept these people as prisoners in a camp and forced to work, using them as slaves during the war. We had a "meeting" with the German Army and after that the Krauts decided it was time to leave this village. The Polish camp with all the prisoners was still there but now were all set free with no more German military around anymore.

When we got there the people just went wild after being locked up for so long. John Delewski from our platoon spoke Polish so he talked with them right away and then he started celebrating right along with them. Where they found it all I don't know, but there was plenty to drink. The former prisoners went into the German town and helped themselves to any beer, wine, schnapps or whatever could be found.

Now these Polish people were all free and certainly ready to celebrate as long as the food and drink held out.

One night as we were staying in the village, a German farmer who was raising sheep came down to talk with Captain Huberger and he was hoping to get some help from the American Army. He said that many of the Polish people were coming in at night and stealing his sheep. Of course the sheep were something good to eat so the Polish were butchering sheep and eating mutton like crazy. The German farmer couldn't do anything because there were too many Polish so he complained to the Captain, He said "The American Army has a duty to protect us from the Polish. While you are here, you should have an American soldier guard my sheep at night. Have him watch out so the Polish do not take my sheep."

We always laughed because one of the first American soldiers who went out to guard the sheep was Delewski. That was like having a wolf watch the sheep. If the Polish people came by looking for sheep, he most likely said in Polish, "Go ahead, help yourself."

Delewski went out with his buddy who was also Polish and came back late at night pretty well "crocked." One night the two guys stayed out a little too long and got separated during the big celebration the Polish were having. It most likely went on all night; I never went up there to see what was going on because I couldn't understand what the Polish people were saying anyway. Delewski took his time to get back with the company and he ended up having to look for his buddy. When he couldn't find him he thought; "He's got to be here somewhere." There were some barracks at the camp and Delewski kept looking in there because he sure didn't want to leave his buddy behind.

He looked all around and finally in one of the barracks, he found a body laying on a long table. It was covered up and there were a bunch of candles burning alongside of it. The Polish were probably all Catholics so that's why there were lighted candles by the body. Well, Delewski went there and he was pretty well snockerd too. He said to us, "Jeez, I went by there a couple of times because I was kinda curious about who was under there. I pulled the sheet back and here it was my buddy. All the Polish celebrators were drunk too and must have thought the guy was dead."

When Delewski looked close, he saw that his buddy was all blue. He looked like he was dead and gone. "Jeez," he said, "I grabbed him and dragged him outside then found some water to splash on him. After a little while the water worked and by gosh, he came to." Delewski helped the guy along and together they finally made it back to the company early in the morning.

Infantryman Compassion

We came hiking through a town and the civilians were still in their houses probably hiding in their cellars and they finally came out when it quieted down. We often tried to get the civilians to talk and tell us a something about the German Army. As we were looking around, we spotted a German Shepherd dog and he was in really tough shape. He was tied up and was real skinny and he sure needed food.

We tried to feed him but he was vicious and mad at everybody when we pushed some food to him. We told the owner, "We are coming through here again," and warned him. "You either take care of that dog or when we come back we will take care of you."

We hoped to put a little fear into him. Even the infantrymen had compassion for dogs. None of us liked this German civilian. He was one civilian that was arrogant and didn't impress me one bit. We all agreed, "By gosh that guy better straighten up or else." He got the message. He was "*nicht gut.*"

On 27 March the 100th Div. went into Corps reserve with orders to be ready to move on 24-hour notice. The move came on the last day of March.
Story of the Century p 133

Wednesday nite
Mar. 28/1945
Germany

Dear Dad,
Thanks for the very nice
Easter card. I recieved it yesterday.
I spose you're trying out the
John Deere now. Sure seen some
small grain already coming up
over here.

I saw a deer today. I would
have liked to take a shot
at him but I wouldn't have
known what to do with it if
I had shot him. There are quite
a few deer around here.

The war news really sounds
good now doesn't it? It looks
like will have to overrun all
of Germany before they quit.
It can't last much longer I
don't think.

How are the roads back
there now? I imagine the
new grade is a little
muddy.

The farmers here are a little more modern than in France but they are still 50 years behind us. I still see them using oxen. It's very nice farming country tho. Are you farming that forty up by the church this year too?

I'm not having it so bad now so don't worry about me. It isn't cold & I can stay dry so I feel pretty good. I sure welcome spring. I'm pretty sure I'll be home by next spring & most of the other boys too.

How are the tires holding out on the Chevy? Can you still get new tires once in a while?

I guess it's about time I hit the hay so I'll close for now. Good night & may God bless you all.

Love,
Verdie

It can't last much longer

Dear Dad,   *Wednesday, March 28, 1945 Germany*
                             (Hockenherm and Grossgartach)

Thanks for the very nice Easter card. I received it yesterday. I 'spose you are trying out the John Deere now. I've seen some small grain already coming up over here.

I saw a deer today. I would have liked to take a shot at him but I wouldn't have known what to do with it if I had shot him. There are quite a few deer around here.

The war news sounds good now doesn't it? It looks like we will have to overrun all of Germany before they will quit. It can't go on much longer I don't think.

How are the roads now? I imagine the new grade is a little muddy. The farmers here are a little more modern than in France but they are still 50 years behind us. I still see them using oxen. It's very nice farming country though. Are you farming that forty by the church this year too?

I'm not having it so bad now so don't worry about me. It isn't cold and I can stay dry so I feel pretty good. I am pretty sure I will be home by next spring and most of the other boys too. How are the tires holding out on the Chevy? Can you still get new tires once in a while?

I guess it's about time to hit the hay so I'll close for now. Good night and May God Bless you all.

Love, Verdie

Throwing Books at Hitler's Picture

March 1945

We had just cleared the town and the Krauts had pulled back. We had finally driven them out of there. We were clearing buildings looking for the enemy and anything of danger. We got close to one building and could hear a lot of commotion going on in there. We took a look in and there was a group of school children; probably grade school age. The kids were throwing books at Hitler's picture that was hanging over the teacher's desk. As we watched, these school kids kept at it and finally got Hitler's picture down off the wall. There was quite a bit of noise going on and we could tell the kids were having a good time. We just let the school kids go on with their activity. They didn't even know we were watching.

We didn't have time to do much watching as we kept on going looking in more buildings. It showed that not all of the Germans were Nazis. The German people certainly wouldn't be happy about being under the thumb of a dictator. The kids most likely didn't come up with this idea completely on their own. The parents must have been talking about Hitler now that it was safe and the kids were listening. The civilians were not afraid to express their opinions when the American soldiers arrived. Now the Nazis did not have the power. As far as the German people were concerned the rule of Hitler was over when we got there and we had driven the German Army back out of their town.

"Here comes that Old Lady (hausfrau)"

Occasionally we cleared a village in Germany. When we cleared it of the enemy we could stay in civilian's houses overnight. We were always anxious to get inside for the night. This day as we stopped, the company commander told us, "Find yourself a place to stay and report here at 0500 in the morning." Everyone in our squad scattered like a bunch of jackrabbits looking for a good place to sleep. Five of us, Simmons, Beehive, Delewski, Woody and me, picked out a house that was on the corner and it had a grocery store attached to it. We thought, 'This is a good place to sleep in and we could probably find something good to eat too."

We went up to the door and there was an older lady (*hausfrau*) living there by herself. We said to her, "We'd like to stay in your house for tonight or maybe two nights. Do you have any relatives close by that you can stay with?" Of course she didn't go for this at all because she had to move out of her house. "We won't hurt your house. We just want to stay here for a while," we told her. We kept on talking and finally she said, "Well ya, I have somebody to stay with."

We had talked her into going but first of all she gave us a set of instructions. Here this old German lady was giving orders to a bunch of American infantry men. We were really tough looking after months of combat. She took us into her kitchen and there was a door going into her store. She strictly told us in German, "You stay out of that store. I don't want anybody in there when I'm gone." We knew enough German to understand her so we said, "Oh ya, ya we won't go into your store."

She had a key and a big old lock on the door. She took the key, shut the door and turned the lock tightly. "Just remember, don't go into the store!" she told us again in German. She wasn't a bit afraid of us and we weren't going to mistreat a hausfrau. We were well armed and could have told her, "Raus, Raus macht schnell (get *out real fast*)," but once again we said to her, "Oh ya, ya we won't go in there."

As soon as she left we went in the cellar to see if we could find any eggs or potatoes. We found some potatoes and fired up her stove. We were going to put some olive oil in the kettle and fry the potatoes so we filled a cup up with oil and threw it in the frying pan. Then Beehive said, "Gee, I'd like to have some salt for flavor." We started thinking and Delewski said, "I bet there is some salt in the store but we really don't want to break her door you know." We didn't want to damage her house even if we were in enemy territory.

We all sat there and looked at it the door for a while. Finally Woody said, "You know if we took the pins out of the hinges we could take the door off." We all agreed, "Oh, that's a good idea," we said. So we got up and pulled the pins out. Simmons was keeping a lookout. We were just getting ready to lift the door off when he said to us, "Here comes the old lady back." "Uh oh," we all said, and quickly pushed the door against the doorway but we didn't have time to put the pins back in. We just sat back in our chairs and acted like we had just been sitting around in her kitchen.

Here she came in and she was going to go in her store and have a look. She took out her big key and put it in the lock. She turned the knob to open the door and here the whole door fell off onto the floor. Oh, you talk about getting told off in German. "I am going to tell the commandant!!" she said to us loudly in German. That was our company commander Captain Huberger. Well, I can only imagine what may have happened to us if he found out.

"You put those pins back in and fix that door right now," She said. "Ya, Ya, we'll fix your door," we told her. We put the door up and quickly put the pins back in again. She stayed there watching us closely until we got it done right. We got another lecture in German from her before she left. She wanted, "No more of that." It was like she was saying to us, "You are going to have to straighten up or else." We wondered what she was going to do to us if we didn't.

171

We told her, "Ya, Ya we won't do anything else." Of course as soon as she was out of sight we pulled the pins and went in her store. Mission accomplished. We looked around but we couldn't find any salt or anything else we wanted to eat. So we just went out of her store and put the door back on. We cooked our potatoes without salt but they still tasted good. Fresh food still tasted better than the nightly K-rations we were used to.

August 2015: Thinking about the "Here comes that Old Lady" story

As American soldiers who were taking over German territory we met many civilians. We could have acted as conquerors full of anger or we could treat the civilians with decency. Just think of how much better it is when we get along with people. In this instance we could have just told the old lady to leave, "Raus, Raus." We didn't have to ask her. We could point weapons at her and force her to leave. We had pride in our unit and knew a good soldier does not take advantage of unarmed civilians. Period. Granted we did take some of her potatoes and oil and tried to find some salt in her store. We didn't destroy anything and we treated the hausfrau with respect.

How's "Johnny" running?

My brothers and dad with "Johnny" the John Deere tractor I was asking about

Dear Mom, Dad and all of you,

Friday, March 30, 1945   *Germany (Hockenherm and Grossgartach)*

How are you coming along? Fine I hope. I am perfectly okay. I'm in a house now so I'm having it pretty nice for a while. I went to church today for Good Friday services. The church we went to was quite a building. Part of it was built in 1510 and part of it was built in 1707 so one part of it was 435 years old. It is still in good shape though, even if is that old. I also went to Holy Thursday service yesterday. I imagine you had services today too. I hope to get a chance to go to Easter services on Sunday.

I received two issues of the Monte American today and enjoyed them very much. Did you attend the memorial services for Julien Nøkleby and Milton Skogrand? (*Both were killed in action, Julien in Europe and Milton in the Philippines. I knew both of them from Mandt Township*) I 'spose there was a big crowd there.

Say, I suppose you got the news of an armistice with Germany that turned out to be a false report. I read about news being received in the states and all the excitement it caused. It sure would be wonderful if it had been true. It shouldn't be long before this whole mess ends.

I had a letter from Marvin Jerve today. I guess he still doesn't feel very good. He sure is glad to be home he said. I got a nice Easter card from Vernice today.

I imagine you're in the fields now Dad. How's "Johnny" running?

We had some doughnuts from the Red Cross yesterday. They bring up doughnuts quite often. I sent $35 home yesterday so I hope you get it.

This is about all the news I have now so I'll have to close. Here's hoping this finds you all well and happy and may God Bless you all.

Love, Verdie

Century Division report: *31 March, it moved south in the wake of the 10ᵗʰ Armored Division and then east across the Neckar River, establishing and enlarging a bridgehead*

On the morning (probably 0500) of 31 March, elements of the division had moved out of their areas to Rhine River. The 399ᵗʰ on the right, next to the river, encountering small arms fire. Story of the Century p 133

April 1ˢᵗ, The 1ˢᵗ and 2ⁿᵈ Battalions of the 399ᵗʰ jumped off with the 2ⁿᵈ Battalion, on the right, heading for Hockenheim. By 1042 hours the 2ⁿᵈ Battalion, with F Co. on the right, G on the left, had pushed on into Hockenheim. By 1530 the town was cleared and the objective secured.

On 2 April, the pursuit continued toward the important railroad and communications center of Heilbronn, a city of 100,000 prewar population. The 399ᵗʰ relieved elements of the 397ᵗʰ in the vicinity of Walldorf during the morning. Against negligible enemy opposition, the 399ᵗʰ Inf. pushed forward through the rain of 3 April.

At the end of day, the 2ⁿᵈ Battalion had reached Sinsheim, just northeast of Steinsfurth, while the enemy continued withdrawing southward. While the rest of the 100ᵗʰ pushed ahead, the 399ᵗʰ was assigned the mission of clearing the area around Gemmingen and Schwaigern, some 16 kilometers east of Heilbronn. The 2ⁿᵈ Battalion 399ᵗʰ, following the lead of the 1ˢᵗ Battalion, began clearing the woods north of Gemmingen. By afternoon, Co. F had completed the task.

Trouble was encountered by the 2ⁿᵈ Battalion when they tried to take Schluctern, an important rail and communications town. Exposed to heavy artillery and mortar fire along the road from Schwaigern, the battalion shifted to the north, attacking Schluctern southeast from the direction of Massenbach. By late afternoon, Schluctern was in the hands of the 2ⁿᵈ Battalion, and Co. F was on the road to Grossgartach, only a kilometer away. Capturing this important little rail town was more of a job than we had figured. For four hours the doughs of Co. F battled it out with the enemy with small arms. Finally, about midnight, the Germans withdrew, leaving Co. F in possession of the town. P 134-135.

Note; Maybe Co. F kept fighting the Krauts until midnight so we could get them to "Raus" and we could find some houses to sleep in for the night.

I hope everything will be peaceful again

Dear Mom, Dad and all of you,
Tuesday, April 3, 1945 Germany (Hockenherm and Grossgartach)

I guess it's about time I write again isn't it? My writing hasn't been very regular lately. I didn't get a chance to go to church on Easter Sunday but I hope that everything will be peaceful again so we can celebrate Easter in peace again next year. I 'spose you had services on Easter.

The way the news sounds this mess will be over soon. I can't see how it can last much longer.

I 'spose the grass and trees are getting nice and green back there now. It's getting nice and green here too and the apple trees are blooming. Spring sure looks nice this year.

I haven't been getting much mail for a while now but I 'spose I'll get a stack of it when it does come. Have you heard from Roy and Earl lately? I haven't had much chance to write to them lately. I hope they are still in the same place.

I imagine everybody is getting started with spring work by now. Is Curtis working for Julian now? So Elling Ellingson has quit farming too. Are they drafting very many farm boys now? I am staying in a house now so I have it pretty good. How's Sam getting along? I imagine he will be plenty busy this spring too,

This is about all I have now so I will close. I'll write to you again as soon as I possibly can.

Love, Verdie

Easter Sunday, 1 April, was just another day to us. As much as possible was done by our chaplains, but our sudden movement nullified detailed plans for religious services. In some cases, however, ceremonies were conducted in the woods where apple blossoms and early spring flowers were laid out as altars. The Story of the Century p. 133

"Here, that will spice it up a bit."

We were doing a strategic withdrawal near a German village when "Beehive" and I got left behind and separated from our unit. The German Army was also moving around in the area so we needed to find someplace in a hurry to hide out. As we were looking, we began to get hungry and didn't have any of our K-Rations to eat. We found a little German house and went up to the door. When the door opened, we told the old man and woman living there that we needed food. They said, "Ya, ya." The German hausfrau got out some eggs and started to fry them in a big pan. Then she got out a real big coarse loaf of bread, slid it under her arm and sawed off a few slices for both of us. The woman

175

told us the only time they had white bread was on Sundays. It was sort of like cake or a treat.

We sat down at the table with the husband and wife and began to eat. The woman put down some cups and filled them with some ersatz coffee. It was made out of some kind of beans other than coffee beans and didn't taste real good. The German man went to the cupboard and got out a bottle of schnapps. He walked over to the table and poured some schnapps into our coffee cups. "Here, that will spice it up a bit," he said. This man wasn't even afraid of us. If he was, he could have just given us the ersatz coffee by itself. He didn't have to pour in the schnapps.

We left after eating and decided to get up to the highest three-story building we could find to hide out in. All of a sudden, here came a weapons carrier from our unit. We saw him coming and when we got to the vehicle, the driver said to us, "Get in. I'll give you a ride." How he knew we were there I don't know but we were sure glad to see him.

The driver was real nervous being so close to the enemy at the front but he brought us back to our company. I often think of that German couple. It seems like these folks might have shown some fear of American soldiers. Instead, they gave us a good meal and made the "coffee" taste a little better.

It can't be over too soon for me

Dear Dad,   *Fri night, April 6 Germany (outside of Heilbronn)*

How is everything getting along? Fine as ever I hope. I am perfectly okay. I would like to be home of course. I imagine you are busy in the fields every day now. I 'spose there is plenty of moisture this spring. Are you having much rain? It's raining here a little tonite but I am in a house so I don't mind it.

They have these town criers here that go through the streets ringing a bell and telling the people the latest news. They use that instead of newspapers I guess.

Our boys are really getting close to the Japs aren't they? Next thing it will be Japan itself. Of course the war news sounds good as usual over here too. It can't be over too soon for me or anybody else too. I hope you are getting my letters now. I haven't had any letters from home for a while. I got one today but it was a month old.

This is about all I have time for now so I'll have to close. Here's hoping this finds you all well and happy and may God Bless you all. Goodnight

Love, Verdie

Tell Shep Hi

Dear Dad,   *Sat evening April 7, 1945   Germany (Heilbronn)*
This letter was written the night before the 399th crossed the Neckar River to reach Heilbronn.

Received your very welcome letter this evening the one you wrote March 27th. I'm glad to hear you are all fine at home. I'm okay as usual. I see you got another snowstorm. In the paper we get over here it said that Minnesota got another 17 inches of snow. I hope it didn't hurt the trees. I suppose there weren't very many fields seeded yet.

Yes, the war news sounds very good. I can't see why the Krauts keep on fighting but it drags out. Well it looks like the Germans want their whole country destroyed and are certainly getting it. I don't feel sorry for any Germans, soldiers or civilians.

I am glad you are getting my allotment checks regularly. Yes, they will come in handy when the war is over. I haven't heard from Roy or Earl for a few weeks. I hope they won't have to invade any more of those islands. They sure are getting close to Japan now aren't they?

I imagine you won't be able to get in the fields for a while with all the snow. The grass and trees over here are sure getting nice now. There is some small grain up but I think it is winter wheat. The grass and the trees over here are sure getting nice now.

Say, thanks for the stamps I was nearly out of stamps. I can sure use them. That's about all I have for now. It's about time to hit the hay. Here's hoping this finds you all happy and in the best of health and may God bless you all. Good night.

Love Verdie

Tell Shep Hi

I kept thinking of our dog Shep even when far away from home.

CHAPTER ELEVEN

Taking Heilbronn

Details about our division entering Heilbronn, Germany in April 1945

April 7-8. While Co. C 399th was fighting alongside the 1st Battalion 397th across the river, the rest of the 399th was in Bockingen and Frankenbach, directly opposite Heilbronn, still protecting the right and rear of the division. Patrols were dispatched to clear the remnants of enemy resistance on the west side of the river, and a patrol from Co. A reconnoitered the Neckar southward to a point opposite the town of Sontheim.

Fought one of the last major battles of World War II in Europe with the assault river crossing of the Neckar River at Heilbronn, 3 - 12 April 1945. **The Story of the Century**

How we crossed the Neckar River

The bridges across the river were all destroyed so the engineers tried to build pontoon bridges for tanks to cross for support. The infantry crossed the river in assault boats that could carry a squad of eight men. We paddled the boats across so we could establish a bridgehead on the other side and eliminate the Kraut observation posts so the artillery wasn't able to fire on the engineers that were working on building pontoon bridges for the tanks. It sure helped the infantry to have tank support.

The chemical company of the US Army laid down a smoke screen that covered the river so the infantry had some protection when we crossed. The Krauts couldn't spot us when we were in the smoke. The current was quite swift and the other bank had rip wrapping that was slippery and this caused problems for us trying to get up on the other bank. This was flat stones used to keep the river from washing out the bank. So with a swift current and slippery stones it was difficult to get out of the boat and ready to fight

Loading into an assault boat for the hazardous Neckar crossing.

This looks like the boats we went across the river in
From "The Story of the Century" Army Signal Corps photo

Army Signal Corps photo

Crossing the Neckar River
From "The Story of the Century" (Official)

April 8. The 2ⁿᵈ Battalion 399ᵗʰ took over positions vacated by the 1ˢᵗ Battalion on the west side of the river. Co. E moved from Schwaigern to the former positions of Co. B along the west bank of the Neckar. Co. F remained in Grossgartach, sending one platoon to Schluchtern as added protection for our right flank and rear. On 8 April, the U.S. 399ᵗʰ Infantry crossed the

Neckar to the south of Heilbronn, moving into southern industrial suburbs and the village of Sontheim. Most of Heilbronn was under U.S. control by 9 April, but not until 12 April was the rubble of Heilbronn cleared of Germans and a bridge built across the Neckar. **The Story of the Century 151-153**

*   ***Century Division report:*** *4-11 April. Heilbronn fell in house-to house fighting. The 100th Division fought one of the last major battles of World War II in Europe with the assault river crossing of the Neckar River at Heilbronn. In the teeth of fanatical resistance, fueled by an errant RAF bombing raid which had mistakenly hit the city center and turned the enraged populace into enthusiastic helpers of the city's defenders, the 100th launched an amphibious assault across the narrow but swiftly-flowing Neckar. While under constant observation and direct fire of dozens of guns emplaced on the hills surrounding Heilbronn to the east, the men of the 100th clawed their way into the city center and destroyed the German garrison by 12 April. 10*

100th Division in streets of Heilbronn April 1945
From "The Story of the Century" Army Signal Corps photo

Fox Company mopping up along Adolf Hitler Strasse . . . "Give me five years and you will not recognize Germany"

*This is most likely our Fox Company platoon because
the guy in front is carrying a carbine.*
From "The Story of the Century" US Army photo

House to house, room to room, over dead Krauts, through rubbish, under barbed wire, over fences, in the windows and out of doors, sweating, cussing, firing, throwing grenades, charging into blazing houses, shooting through floors and closet doors.

— U.S. soldier of the 399th Infantry Regiment describing combat in Heilbronn

From "Heilbronn, One Last Place to Die" by Edward E Longacre

I sure could go for some potato soup now.

Dear Mom,   *Monday evening April 9, 1945 Germany (Sontheim)*

Just a few lines to let you know I am okay. How are things back home now? I am in a house now so things are pretty nice. I just hope and pray this terrible war ends soon. I can't see how it can possibly last much longer but it seems to drag out.

I'm getting good chow now. It's nothing like your home cooking but I can't expect that much over here. I sure could go for some potato soup now. How are Mildred and Vernice's little girls getting along? I had a letter from Arnold the other day. He was in San Francisco waiting for shipping orders.

I saw Orice Larson's outfit the other day but I didn't get a chance to look him up. I sure would like to see somebody from back home. How are Henrietta and Olaf getting along? You'll have to greet them from me.

That's about all the news so I'll have to close for now. It's about time to hit the hay anyway. Here's hoping this finds you all happy and in the best of health and May God bless you all. Good night

Love Verdie

This is what Heilbronn looked like
From "The Story of the Century" US Army photo

Sontheim: Hard on the Ears

It was in April of 1945. We had crossed the Neckar River and completed our objective in Heilbronn. We kept on going towards Sontheim which was almost like a suburb of Heilbronn. The rumor was the Germans had moved out of Sontheim. According to the reconnaissance from the light planes the report we got was there wasn't any resistance in Sontheim right near Heilbronn, Germany. The reconnaissance told us that the Krauts had all left and some thought it was time to relax and celebrate.

Sometimes we saw the L4 planes that were used for air observation. They looked like Piper Cubs. We had heard rumors many times before and don't really know why we believed this one. We had never even talked to the pilots in the planes. One of our guys was laughing and clowning around. He found a big top hat and was walking around town having a good time. We were walking through behind the railroad grade towards Sontheim and we certainly didn't expect any action from the Germans.

Then all of sudden-jeepers- a tank that was parked on higher ground in the town and he let loose! Jeepers did we get it! Maybe the Krauts were not out on the streets when the L 4s went over. Maybe what we heard about the town being clear of the enemy was only a rumor. There were always rumors in the Army.

It was the 17th SS Grenadier Panzer Division that was there. We were planning to go over the grade and there was a little opening between that and the first buildings. Well, as soon as we stuck our heads over the railroad grade we started getting direct 88 artillery fire. It must have been tanks up there because it was direct fire not like lobbing from heavy artillery. We started running as hard as we could cutting through the orchard to get into the buildings. The shells were landing in among the apple trees. There was deep cut in a hard surface road nearby and our company made it there where we had some protection.

We were laying in the ditch on one side and the 88s were hitting the bank on the other side. The noise was deafening and the shrapnel was hitting the road. You could see the sparks from the shrapnel as it was hitting the road. Right up above us was a tall metal mesh fence so we were pinned down. Our squad happened to be one of the first that made it to the cut. The rest of Fox Company was strung out behind us.

We had been there quite a while taking fire and I said to the guy next to me, "I don't know what you're going to do but I know what I'm going to do. I'm going to get up the grade and over that fence and head to the building nearby. It'll be a matter of minutes before mortar is fired in here and then we won't have any protection." So we quick got over the ridge, climbed the fence and fell over to the other side. We got up and started running as hard as we could and made it to the building. From here we could see some of our guys who were behind us running up through the apple orchard and fire from the 88s was hitting all around them.

Then from behind the building we started taking small arms fire from a Kraut machine gun position. In the building there was a window for a cellar and the first thing Simmons did was go through it by himself. Simmons jumped into the cellar and he was coming out again to take a look. Just then a mortar hit the soft ground blowing it up sort of like an ice cream cone. The concussion from the shell blew Simmons back into the cellar. Now he knew to stay in there until the shooting ended.

The rest of the squad was behind the building trying to decide where to go from there. We hollered at Simmons to come out because we were planning to take off for some more buildings. The shrapnel missed us but the noise was terrible.

A short time later the rest of the company started coming across at different places so eventually we were all there in the town. There had only been a half dozen of us there for a while. We were taking a lot of fire so we had to wait before we could get out in the street. As we waited somehow we got word that our artillery was going to zero in on the German tanks and gun positions that were firing on us. The Army called it "Time on Target" when every artillery piece in range zeroed in on that one target. Lt. Nicholson told us to get into a cellar or whatever we could while our men laid in the artillery. It was practically like our own artillery was firing on our positions.

We stayed under cover in a cellar and the walls were just shaking. It was unreal with our own artillery coming in and this lasted for quite a while. Then it stopped and the infantry was supposed to get out and start moving. When we got out there were hardly any Krauts left. That pretty well took care of the problem. Some moved out or the ones that were left were taking cover. So we didn't really have a very hard time in Sontheim. Well, it was hard getting in there but once we were there the artillery pretty well took care of it. We didn't get up to see where the Kraut 88s had been coming from.

It was one of the loudest guns of the entire war. The combination of incoming fire was close and hard on the ears. It is hard to pinpoint just when there was some hearing loss because it happened so many times over the course of over 175 days on the line from late October 1944 to early May 1945.

It was hard on the ears with helmets flying off our heads. We couldn't wear straps on our chin because the concussion of a blast could break your neck. With all the confusion and running for cover a helmet could fly off your head. It seems like we lost our helmets there.

The shooting ended in a while and then Simmons and I along with the squad went on to another objective.

The 399th Regiment had told the vaunted 17th SS Panzer Grenadier Division in Heilbronn, Germany to, "Raus, macht schnell."

Devastation: Heilbronn, April 1945.—U.S. Army

From "The Story of the Century" US Army photo

Complaints

If we wanted to complain about the bad information someone could have punched our TS card. We joked about that once in a while if we were running into events that didn't seem fair. We said to anyone that was even thinking about complaining. "Why don't you take your TS card to the chaplain and have him punch it?" If you did that every time that events didn't go your way, the card would have been so full there wouldn't be any place left for new punches.

<u>*Century Division report*</u>: *12 April, the Division resumed its rapid pursuit of the enemy reaching Stuttgart by 21 April.*

Gather up the Guns from the German Homes

After we cleared a town and the Krauts had pulled back, the company commander talked to the burgermiester (the Mayor) of the town and told him we wanted every rifle and shotgun in town brought here to the center of town within a certain time. We didn't go looking for all of the weapons because there wasn't time to search all the homes. The burgermiester was the boss and the people listened to him. Within a short period there was a big pile of guns in the town center.

The people were scared of what may happen if they hid their rifles and shotguns. They had spent many years under the threat of the Germany army and now the Americans were in their town. These were not military weapons but ones they used for hunting. There was no shortage of beautiful, fancy engraved hunting guns and rifles. I'm sure they hated to give their guns up.

One of the shotguns was a real nice Belgian Browning 20 gauge that looked like new. Wow, I'd like to have that, I thought, so I quickly grabbed it. After looking at it awhile I didn't know what to do with because it was too hard to carry a gun like this around with me when we were still on the move. Infantrymen didn't need anything to slow us down. With some hesitation I threw it back on the pile.

Another one of our guys came by and saw it back on the pile. "Wow, look at that shotgun, I'm taking it. When the kitchen truck comes up they can mail it back home for me," he said. The chances of that Belgian Browning getting through the APO weren't too great. We never heard him tell any of us that "his" shotgun had made it all the way to his home in the states. One of the guys in the APO might have ended up with it.

We didn't stay around long enough to see what was done with this pile of guns. The support crew probably loaded all of these guns up in a truck and destroyed them. Many of the best guns probably ended up as souvenirs of war.

That sure is bad news about President Roosevelt

Dear Folks,   *Sat nite April 14, 1945 Germany (Tulhiem)*

This will have to be short I have to go on duty in a few minutes but I'll write a few lines so you'll know I'm okay. That sure is bad news about President Roosevelt. *(He died April 12, 1945)* It's hard to believe it is true. I don't think there will ever be another president like him. We still have a lot of good men in Washington so everything will be all right anyway. I haven't had any mail for a while but I suppose it will catch up with me pretty soon.

I will try to write a longer letter soon. Here's hoping this finds you all happy and in the best of health and May God bless you all.

Love, Verdie

A Letter from my Dad

Some letters from my parents were able to be saved because they arrived after the war was over and was able to keep them in my duffel bag and bring them back home.

Dear Verdie,   Montevideo,   Minn April 22, 1945

Hello and how are you getting along? We are always thinking and wondering. I hope that you are okay and feeling all right. We hear and see by the news that you boys are going places over there one city after another. Tonight we hear that the Russians are inside Berlin. I think it's funny that them fool Krauts do not quit but it will and cannot be long now before the fighting in Europe is over. May God help and speed that day. I hope and pray that the Japs will not last much longer.

We have not heard from Roy and Earl for quite some time. According to the news we know Earl is on Okinawa Island. The 96th Division is there and we hear there is some pretty hard fighting there too. We have not found out yet where Roy is. We think that he has moved from Saipan. Well, wherever they are we hope and pray that God will keep his protecting hand over them.

We have had a lot of snow and cold weather but when it finally warms up it will be nice and green in a hurry. We are all through with the seeding of course and will have to get busy with the manure pile and then the corn.

If the war in Europe should come to an end soon it would probably not be so very long before you could come back to the states and get a furlough home but we hope the whole mess is over soon.

Well, Verdie this is all I have to write about at this time. May God Bless and Keep his Protecting Hand over you and bring you safely home soon.

Dad

P.S. We are all well. I hope the shooting is over by the time you get this letter. (It *was over and I was able to save this letter in my duffel bag*). Hello from us all including Shep but he is getting so deaf the only thing he can hear is a 12 gauge shotgun shell.

A letter from my mother

Dear Verdie,   *April 26, 1945*

We received your letter of April 14th a couple of days ago. We are so glad to know that you are all right. We are thinking and wondering about you if you are in the front lines as we hear about the Seventh Army so much in the news. Our prayers are that you can be released soon and get to a rest camp again.

We heard from Earl yesterday so it made us feel a little better about him. He is not in a very good place right now but it helps a little anyway as long as we hear he is all right. He was in a foxhole in Okinawa when he wrote and said the bombs and shells were flying around so it sounded plenty tough. Our prayers are that God is with you in the foxholes as well as any other place and that he holds his protecting hand over you and saves you for us.

We haven't heard from Roy for four weeks so we are getting quite worried about him. In Earl's letter he thought Roy might be in Okinawa too. We haven't heard in the news about his division being there but he might have been put in another. We don't know but hope we hear from him soon. And that he is alright too.

May God be with you and bring you home sound and well soon, Greetings from us all including Shep and Vicky.

So long then Verdie,
Love, Mother

Plenty of stories to tell

Dear Folks,   *Tues morning, April 17 Germany (Winneden, Nulligen)*

How's everything and everybody back there? I haven't had a letter from any of you for quite some time now. My mail should catch up with me pretty quick now.

I imagine everybody is busy in the fields now. I see some small grain that is about 4 inches over here.

I saw a bunch of deer again the other day. I sure would have liked to take a shot at them. How's Curtis coming with his flying? I 'spose you have pretty nice flying weather now. I really would like to do some flying myself. So they are going to build an airport north of Monte now? I hope they build a good one this time where you don't have to hedgehop trees and high lines when you come in for a landing.

I am not having it so bad now so don't worry about me. The war news sounds better every day. There are so many things I would like to write about that censorship doesn't permit but I'll have plenty to tell when I get home which I hope is soon.(*When we all got home there wasn't much talk about what we did overseas. Everyone was sick of war and didn't want to talk much about it with any graphic details. You often hear that World War II vets never talked much about the war especially with their families*)

I am in a house again right now. It's pretty nice when we can stay in a house. I suppose it won't be long til Lyle is out of school now. I bet he doesn't like that very much. Are you going to have a school picnic this year? Have you heard from Earl and Roy? That is about all the news I have now.

I'll try to write again as soon as I can.

Love, Verdie

Complaints and Heroes

While I was sitting in fox holes in France and Germany, more than one time I made a vow to myself, "If I ever get home I will never complain about anything again."

None of us thought of ourselves as heroes as we often joked, "Who wants to be hero number one or hero number two." It is kind of strange in a way that people never find out much about the infantry. That was where the war was.

The Church Bells are ringing

Dear Mom,   *Sunday morning, April 22 Germany (near Stuttgart)*
The church bells are ringing in this little village this morning. It sounds so nice and peaceful to hear them. It makes me homesick. They sound so much like the bell we have in our church. I bet you will be plenty busy when you get all those chicks. I suppose Dad is busy in the fields.

I suppose Curtis has soloed by now. I hope he came out okay on his physical exam. I bet you will be plenty busy when you get all those chicks. I 'spose Dad is busy in the fields every day now.

Have you heard from Earl and Roy lately? I imagine you know where Earl is now. I saw something about his outfit in the paper the other day.

I am in a house now so things are pretty nice. It sure beats a foxhole. It isn't so cold now. I don't mind being outside so much but it's much nicer being in a house anyway.

The war news sounds good as usual. It can't last much longer. It will be a wonderful day when this whole mess ends.

This is about all I have time for. Here's hoping this finds you all happy and in the best of health and May God bless you all.

Love Verdie

This was most likely the day our unit captured 30 German Army prisoners.

Refugees in War Time

We saw long lines of refugees that were leaving the areas where the heaviest fighting was. There was still heavy artillery bombardment and airplanes strafing all over the place. Where the civilians were going we didn't know and they most likely didn't really know either. Just getting away from all of the fighting was their priority. We met people coming through our lines while they were all trying to get as far away as possible.

There were old people walking and pulling carts with all of their belongings that could be salvaged. The carts were piled high and sometimes there were little kids riding on top of the pile. Once in a while we saw a horse or an oxen helping out but most it was hand pulled in small carts. Many people were carrying a bunch of belongings on their backs.

The infantry was heading up into the area where the fighting was going on and the civilians were heading out the other way. We had seen this in France with civilians who were heading back home as the American Army advanced and pushed the Krauts back. The French figured now it was safe to go back home because the war was over in the place they had evacuated. If the civilians could make it through our lines they would be in much better shape.

Now the Germans were leaving their homes to escape the fighting. Once in a while we could see big encampments set up out in the woods with tents and makeshift shelters the refugees made out of whatever could be found. It was still winter and very cold. How could this large group of people possibly survive while attempting to find enough food and water to live on?

We helped the civilians when we could. If we had any rations that we could give away, the kids got them. We didn't particularly care if who they were if we could help a little… German or French, it didn't matter to us. We just saw kids who were hungry and weren't wearing any uniforms.

Money to the Wind and to the Civilians

One time our unit was advancing into Stuttgart, Germany and as we approached, we jumped off the tanks and walked behind. As we got close to the city, we could see our big American tanks outside of a building with the barrels pointing toward it. A bunch of Kraut soldiers, probably thirty, were in a Biergarten and were all drinking beer. This unit had left their rifles and packs outside and now with our tanks pointing directly at them there was nothing to do but become prisoners of war. We were going through the German soldier's packs when one of our guys found a stack of money with plenty of big bills. We found out that it was payday for these Krauts and the paymaster had not distributed the cash yet. We gathered up… I don't know how much money in German Marks. But it was a great big stack of paper money.

When things quieted down, civilians started coming out of their cellars and other hiding places. Many people gathered around in order to see the American soldiers and were all pretty curious to see what was going on. The German prisoners were standing there with their arms all held up high. The guys in the tanks were yelling in German, "Hände Hoch, Hände Hoch!! (Hold em higher, Hold em higher!!")

Well, it was a little windy that day and the guy who had found all the money took that the whole stack of bills in his hands. He looked around a little and then all of a sudden he threw the bills up in the air towards the civilians. There was money going everywhere in the wind. The civilians just went wild picking up bills, running around, and filling their hands as our Kraut prisoners just had to stand by and watch. I can just imagine what the German soldiers were saying to themselves. "Amercanish swine." Boy was there scrambling as every one of those bills disappeared in no time into the hands of the eager civilians.

Compassion for a German hausfrau

Another one of our guys kept a stack of the bills to give away later. As we moved into Stuttgart, Captain Huberger told us to find places to stay in. We found a house with a young woman who had a couple of kids and her husband was likely in the German Army. We didn't stay there very long because we had to get moving the next morning. The German woman treated us very well while we were there. As we were leaving, the guy with us who had the stack of bills, took it out of his pack and gave it to the haus frau. We felt sorry for her because she sure didn't have much in her home. When he handed her all the bills she was amazed. How much it was worth to her I didn't know but it must have been a lot because she was very pleased with it. We couldn't use the money and we knew she could. I bet the woman thought that the American soldiers weren't so bad.

Pulled off of our tanks

As we reached the outside edge of Stuttgart we quit walking and got on our tanks. We were ready to get through this town in a hurry. The civilians were all hiding in their basements and other places in town. As we were going through the streets of Stuttgart, the civilians came out of hiding out to see us. Soon our tanks were surrounded by civilians and the first thing I knew someone grabbed me and pulled me off the tank. This was happening to the rest of the guys too, I wasn't the only one. At first we were surprised and it wasn't something we expected.

You wouldn't think the Germans would be happy to see American soldiers but we soon realized that we were being welcomed. Maybe the civilians knew that the war was over in their homes when the Americans cleared the German army out of their town. After a while we got lined up again and spread out into buildings to clear out any German infantry that might still be holed up in there. We looked for shelter and found a place to sleep.

CHAPTER TWELVE

170 Days on the Front

Dear Dad,   *Wednesday, April 25 Germany (Fuerbach, Duran, Tomers, Asch)*

I am having a little rest now. The house I'm in now is pretty nice. There are electric lights and even a radio. I've been listening to the news broadcasts and it's so nice to hear the news over the radio. There isn't much left of Germany that isn't occupied now and I can't figure out why the Krauts keep on fighting. (This *was a time when we started to use the German word kaput more often. We'd say, "Alles kaput mit Deutschland. Prima" This meant, "Everything is ruined in Germany. Excellent")* (Hitler used to say, "Deutschland tag i morgen der ganska welt." This meant, "Germany today, tomorrow the whole world." Now it was obvious Germany was not going to rule the world.)*

Say, I am getting a pass to England. The Capt. asked if anybody had relatives in England so I showed him my Cousin Harvey's address. It will be a three week trip. It will be nice to get away from the front lines for a while. I've put in about 170 days on the front now so I could go for a little rest, relaxing and give my nerves a chance to settle down.

Say Dad, if you can't get a knife like I asked for, don't go to too much trouble. I have a pretty nice knife now. I got it off a Kraut the other day.

The Russians beat us to Berlin. Oh well, it doesn't matter who got there first just so they take good care of it. The Russians are the boys to do it. The American Army is about ready to link up with the Russians.

We've been joking so long about running into Russian patrols at night and it's a reality now.

It's time for chow so I better close for now.
Love,

Verdie
Greet everybody, Shep too.

After the German Army moved out

The minute we got into a village the white flags were flying all over the place. The townspeople most likely were taking the Nazi flags down as the German army left and hurried to get the white flags in the holders when the American Army arrived. These must have been homemade from bed sheets because I doubt the local stores had a bunch of white flags for sale.

No one waited as much for the end of the war as the German civilians did. We came into the villages that the Nazis had left and now the people were not living in as much fear. In a way we were liberating the people. Many were happy to see Americans, especially if they hated the Nazis. The civilians knew we were looking for Nazis. Many said over and over to us, "Nix Nazi, Nix Nazi," wanting us to be sure to know… We are not Nazis.

They've got Mussolini now and Hitler is sick.

Dear Curtis,   *Sunday night April 29, 1945 Germany*
I've really got it nice right now. I'm in a nice house with electric lights and radio. I tell you that radio doesn't get a chance to cool off. The news just came over that we have taken Munich so it doesn't look like it will be long now. They've got rid of Mussolini now, and Hitler is sick. I can easily see why. The Russians feel sorry for him, so I feel sure they can take good care of him, (tsk, tsk). (I *was joking of course*)

I imagine you have soloed by now and I hope you can keep on putting in time pretty regular now. That sounds like a beautiful ship, blue fuselage and yellow wings is a nice color scheme. So he is getting a Luscombe too. I hope you get a chance to fly it. You'll notice quite a difference in it from a Cub. I'm hoping to get a chance after the war to do some flying in some of these Army Cubs and Stinsons they have over here. That Stinson 105 is really nice. It's got a 180 H.P. Franklin 6 cylinder in it.

You should see these Cubs dive down between the hills when a Kraut plane gets after them. I wish you could see some of these Thunderbolts and Spitfires in action. It's really something. I've wished a lot of times I was in the cockpit of one of them.

There is a Kraut plane that comes over every night. We call him, "Bedcheck Charlie." He is a peaceful guy though. I don't know what he flies for because he never does any harm. For a while we could practically set our watches by him.

So, you are hauling gold dust* for Julien nowadays? Well Curtis, it may not be fun, but I've wished I was hauling gold dust a lot of times the last six months. How's the Chevy percolating? I bet it doesn't stand still much, eh. How's Monte now? Is it still as lively as ever on Saturday nights? It sure will be fun to get back again to everything.

Well, it's time to hit the hay. Write soon.
So long,

Bro. Verdie

Gold dust- Organic fertilizer provided by our cows, horses, hogs and chickens.

Another letter from my Dad

"I feel sure this war will be over even before you get this letter." Dad
This letter from my dad most likely arrived during the time I was on leave to visit my cousin Harvey in England. It was saved and we still have it. My dad was sure the war would be over by the time I got this letter. He was right.

Dear Verdie,   May 1, 1945 Montevideo, Minnesota

Your letter from April 17th was received on April 28th and we were sure glad to hear from you again and that you are okay and feeling alright. I think it is fine that you can write once in a while and get time the way your army is moving along. Germany is getting pretty small the way it sounds and looks on the map. Am wondering if you are close to Munich or up in the Alps or close to that big prison camp you boys liberated.

Of course the main thing to us is that you are alright and I feel sure this war will be over even before you get this letter. It was just about a month that we did not hear from Earl or Roy and were of course getting a little worried but we got two letters from Roy yesterday and have had three letters from Roy since he moved to Okinawa. We don't know where Roy is now but wherever you boys are we hope and pray that God will keep his protecting hand over you.

Say, we got a swell picture of you the other day. We went to the American office and got it. It's a picture of you by a mortar gun it is 8x10 and very clear. They want it back to put in the window for a while but then we can keep it.

Fishing season starts pretty soon so I may go over to Lac qui Parle and catch a few of them big ones as usual.

May God Bless and keep His protecting hand over you and bring you safely home soon.

Dad

We are rid of both Hitler and Mussolini now.

Dear Folks,   *Friday May 4, 1945 Germany*

How is everything back there? Fine I hope. I'm swell. I heard you had another false peace report in the states again. It's too bad it's put out when it isn't true but it won't be long until it is true. We are rid of both Hitler and Mussolini now. That's two less rats and the rats that are left better start looking for some new holes. I heard the news last night and I think it's only a matter of days till the fighting stops.

I got me a nice revolver the other day. It's a 32-30 caliber. I'll take it along home with me. I got another knife with a swastika on the handle. A German civilian gave it to me. It belonged to his son who was in the German Army and was killed in action. He wanted me to have it so I took it.

Say I got the package that Clarice sent me with cookies and stationary. The cookies were really good. I was so glad to get it and I sure needed stationary too. I suppose it won't be long before corn planting time comes. The farmers here are busy now. They use oxen and horses in the fields.

Here's hoping this finds you all well and happy and may God Bless you all. So long.

Love,
Verdie

Hitler Youth Knife

It was close to the end of the war but we didn't know it at the time. We were in a small village in Germany and were assigned to set up a roadblock to check civilians coming and going. A civilian and a soldier were assigned to work together on the roadblock. The civilian acted as interpreter and I kind of got to know the man as we stood and talked while waiting for people to come through. He was a middle-aged man and too old for the military. One day when he came in the morning he told me that Roosevelt had died. We had all heard that news already but the man wanted to talk about it. He said to me. "Now Roosevelt is gone and Hitler is gone too."

The kitchen had sent up hot food in a jeep. This was something extra special to get a hot meal. Here this German came walking down the street and he saw me sitting on the curb eating out of my mess kit. He stopped and said. "After you finish eating, come up to my house, I've got something to give you."

I knew where he lived so I walked up to his house. He lived alone. "Come in and sit down," he said. So I went in and sat down in his living room. Then he walked into another room and when he came back out he gave me a knife. It was a knife that was given to young men who had finished their Hitler Youth training.

Engraved on the blade in German was "Blut und Ahre" which means "Blood and Honor." The Hitler Youth was an organization that got young German kids and indoctrinated them. The knife was a symbol of completing the program. "This belonged to my son who was about your age. He lost his life in the German army. I want you to have it," he said,

Why did he give it to an enemy soldier? It was hard to comprehend why he gave it to me. He could have given it to his relatives or somebody he knew. Then he also gave me a tiny Bible written in German. It was a miniature that was real thick and small. "I'd like you to have this too," he said, I took it and said, "Thanks."

The dad was speaking only German but I had learned enough German so I knew what he was saying and knew enough words to answer him. "Speak slowly, *Sprekesie longsome,*" I said. We understood each other because German was a lot like Norwegian.

Why did a man who was my enemy give me something that had belonged to his son? The passage, "Love your neighbor as yourselves," comes to mind. This was an example of that. This was like forgiveness. An American soldier may have been responsible for his son's death. Why did he show a friendship with me? That was strange. Every once in a while I thought about that.

The knife itself wasn't the important part. Here I was an American farm kid from Minnesota and he was a German dad who had lost his son in the war. If he had given me his address I could have written to him. He might have been the only one left in his family; otherwise he'd have given the knife and Bible to a family member. In one hand the German father gave me a Bible and in the other hand he held knife with the words in German, "*Blut und Ehre.*", "Blood and Honor." Why me?

I'd like to have kept the Bible but someone else in my outfit wanted it and took it from me. I never knew where it went and never did find it. I managed to hang on to the knife because it was kept on my belt or hidden. It was rare and I never saw one like it before or after that.

(Editor) Why? Verdie treated him with respect and spoke his language as a son and a soldier along with mixing German and Norwegian words.

May 1945
"All is quiet on the western Front"

These were words I wrote in a letter to the folks after hearing the war had ended in Europe. This was the title of a book we read in high school. (*All Quiet on the Western Front by Erich Maria Remarque, a German veteran of World War I.*)

We had a quiet night with our first good night's sleep in months. There was no gunfire, no patrols, no mortars, and no artillery. No wondering if any German soldiers were out there. The war was over but there was no celebration yet. We were somewhere in Germany near a beautiful village in the Rhine River Valley. The apple orchards were in full bloom. The pleasant smell of the apple blossoms was a sharp contrast to the smells of combat. In the village there were grape vines growing to utilize all the space and furnish their livelihoods.

It was a sharp contrast to the Vosges Mountains and war conditions. It was a complete change. We really appreciated ***listening to the quiet***.

Whether we realized it or not for the past months we were always listening, listening for every noise. Now the quiet sounded wonderful.

While in combat noises usually meant something and were seldom pleasant. If a twig snapped it didn't happen by itself. If we heard a footstep, someone was there. We were trained to hear every noise and react as needed.

The Army kitchen brought us regular food like meat, potatoes and bread so that was sure a treat. We got to sit down and rest for a few days with only a little mopping up to do. We were still looking for any pockets of resistance but we were finally off the line and out of combat. The weather was beautiful and we could afford to relax.

Even now my radio is never on just for noise. Sometimes I play classical music when I'm woodcarving. To this day I still enjoy the quiet. Maybe it's a throwback to that time after the war. Since 1944, I have not been able to hear birds sing due to hearing loss caused by noise of artillery shells, mortar shells and small arms fire. The noise was unreal. You can't even imagine the sounds of battle unless you were there.

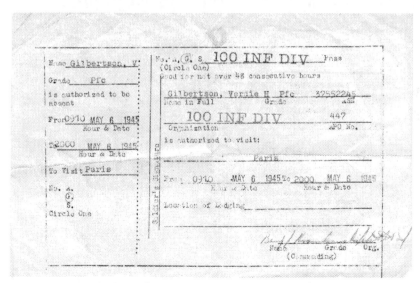

A one day pass to visit Paris May 6, 1945

Mon. night
May 7

Dear Mom & all of you,

Well, the war ended today. Tomorrow is officially VE day. Thank God Almighty that at last we have peace over here. We can't really be happy as long as we have boys fighting on the other side of the world but it is also a big step toward the end of the war over there too and we hope & pray that it ends soon.

I'm in France right now, on my way to England. I'm right on the coast of the English channel. I'm going to England tomorrow. I'll be staying in a small town over there.

It looked like the fourth of July here tonite. The French civilians were shooting up flares & rockets of all colors. The soldiers aren't celebrating very much tho. Of course everybody is happy.

It's after 12 o'clock midnite now so this is VE day. I'm sitting in the day room listening to the news. I guess everybody is really celebrating and the stations too. They say there will be a 3 day holiday.

The radio announcer just said. The order to "Cease Firing" has come. I just can't help but think of our buddies whom we left behind on the battlefields and never will hear the order.

Well I guess May 8th will go down in history. And this time it isn't an armistice either but a total unconditional surrender & there won't be another war in 20 years.

It's about time to hit the hay so I'll close for now. Here's hoping this finds you all well & happy & may God bless you all.

Love, Verdie

CHAPTER THIRTEEN

The war ended today

Dear Mom and all of you,   *Monday night*   *May 7, 1945*
By La Havre, France

Well the war ended today. Tomorrow is officially V - E Day! All is quiet on the western front. Thank our Almighty God that at last we have peace over here. We can't really be happy as long as we have boys fighting on the other side of the world but it is also a big step towards ending the war over there too and we hope and pray that it ends soon.

I am in France now on my way to England. I am right on the coast of the English Channel and staying here in a small town tonight. It looked like the 4th of July here tonight. The French civilians are shooting up flares and rockets of all colors. The soldiers are not celebrating very much though. Of course everybody is very happy. It's after 12 midnight now so this is V-E Day. I am sitting in the day room listening to the news. I guess everybody is celebrating in the states tonight the way the news commentator says. He said there will be a two day holiday.

The order to "Cease Firing" has come. I just can't help but thinking of our buddies who were left behind on the battlefields and never will hear the order.

Well, May 8th will go down in history and this time it isn't an Armistice either but a total unconditional surrender and there won't be another war in twenty years.

It's about time to hit the hay so I'll close for now. Here's hoping this finds you all well and happy and may God bless you all.

Love, Verdie

Which Unit Won the War?

Well, sometimes I think the 100th Infantry Division did win the war but may have to admit we got some help from a bunch of the other divisions. We couldn't take all the credit. The generals sure bragged about us. We always heard the 100th Division was a crack division. We actually did win the war but I suppose other divisions thought their unit won the war too.

Accomplishments of the 100th Division

Nickname: Century Division. Slogan: Success in Battle.

"The Division went into combat in early November as part of the US Seventh Army's VI Corps, with the mission of penetrating the German Winter Line in the High Vosges Mountains on the edge of the oft-disputed province of Alsace.

The Vosges terrain was formidable and the severe winter weather added hundreds of casualties to those inflicted by the tenacious German defenders. Nevertheless, the 100th led the attack through the Vosges Mountains as, for the first time in history, an army succeeded in penetrating that vaunted terrain barrier to the Rhine Plain and Germany. Within the first month of combat, the German Army Group

G Chief of Staff, General von Mellenthin, referred to the 100th as "a crack assault division with daring and flexible leadership."

While falling back toward Germany, the enemy bitterly defended the modern Maginot fortifications around the ancient fortress city of Bitche. Just after reducing these intimidating defenses, in the last hour of 1944, the Division was attacked by elements of three German divisions, including a full-strength SS-panzer grenadier division, heavily supported by armor, in Operation NORDWIND, the last German offensive on the Western front. As the units on the left and right gave ground, the men of the 100th stood fast and the Division quickly became the only unit in the Seventh Army to hold its sector in the face of the massive enemy onslaught. In the brutal fighting which ensued, the Division stubbornly resisted all attempts at envelopment and despite heavy casualties the 100th completely disrupted the German offensive. Ultimately, the 100th Infantry Division captured the Citadel of Bitche in March 1945, and passed through the Siegfried Line into Germany.

The Division's last major battle was the attack on Heilbronn in April 1945, which required an assault crossing of the Neckar River in small boats, in full view of the crews of dozens of German artillery pieces which laid fierce direct fires over the crossing site. In over a week of savage urban combat, the Division defeated elements of several German Army and Waffen-SS divisions, seized the key industrial city, and pursued the beaten foe through Swabia toward Stuttgart.

In all, in 185 days of uninterrupted ground combat, the 100th Infantry Division liberated and captured over 400 cities, towns, and villages; defeated major elements of eight German divisions; and took 13,351 prisoners. In doing so, it sustained 916 soldiers killed in action, 3,656 wounded in action, and lost 180 men missing in action.

Born in war, manned by many of America's best, trained to high standards and consistently victorious in battle, the legacy of the 100th Infantry Division is one of singular excellence: its soldiers earned the *first* EIB, were the *first* to ever fight their way through the Vosges Mountains, seized the Citadel at Bitche for the *first* time in its 250-year history, and were the *only* unit to hold its ground during the last German offensive in the west in World War II."

marshallfoundation.org/100th-infantry/who-we-are/

"Considering that infantry units were rarely maintained above 80% strength, about 50% of all the infantrymen in the Division became casualties in the course of achieving the Division's magnificent record. In liberating or capturing over 400 cities, towns and villages, they defeated major elements of eight German divisions. In this process, the men of the 100th inflicted untold casualties on the enemy, the only calculable number of which is the 13,351 enemy prisoners taken." *www.100thww2.org/100wund*

The Division

"Tore through deeply-entrenched German resistance in the craggy High Vosges Mountains in two weeks of savage fighting."

"Practically destroyed the brand-new, full-strength German 708th Volks-Grenadier Division in the process of penetrating the Vosges Mountains by assault for the first time in history Since the 1st century BC, Romans, Huns, Burgundians, Swedes, Austrians, Bavarians, Germans and even French forces had tried and failed, but in the late autumn of 1944, in the face of nearly constant rain, snow, ice and mud, the US Seventh Army did what no other army had ever done before."

"Overcame stiff resistance by the 361st Volks-Grenadier Division at Mouterhouse and Lemberg and advanced on the Maginot Line. Attacking into the Maginot, elements of the Division seized Fort Schiesseck, one of the Maginot forts attacked by the Germans in 1940, from the same direction, i.e. the south. In December of 1944, the 100th Infantry Division took the 14-story deep fortress with 12-foot thick steel-reinforced concrete walls, in a four-day assault, 17 - 20 December 1944." *The Story of the Century (booklet)*

Another letter from my dad. My family knew the war was over in Germany but did not as of May 9th, 1945 know whether or not their son had made it through to the end.

Montevideo, Minn
May 9, 1945
Dear Verdie,
And how are you feeling and getting along after the big change over there? I hope and pray that you got through the last part of the fighting

in good shape. We have not heard from you for some time but of course we know that you have been pretty busy chasing them Krauts. You really did move along the last days of the war and we are awfully glad and thankful that it is over, over there. We bet you boys are feeling the same way. We are wondering and waiting for the day that you boys can come back here again.

We had letters from both Roy and Earl two days ago. Earl had been wounded on Okinawa. He was hit by some pieces of shrapnel in his hip and neck and was taken to a hospital in the Marianas Islands. Wasn't it an act of our good Lord that island happened to be the one that Roy and Calmer were on? They had visited with Earl so Roy wrote in his letter to us that Earl was not seriously hurt and that he was up and around. We are certainly thankful to our good Lord. According to the news it has been a pretty tough place over on Okinawa. Even if Earl was hurt it is some consolation that he can be out of the fight for a while. The Japs will give up pretty soon being they have not one chance in a million to win the war which I am sure they realize after Germany was knocked out.

Well, yesterday was VE day here at home of course and all business were closed all day. There were thanks services in all churches last evening and we had a pretty nice crowd in our church too. I better sign off for this time and we hope that you are feeling OK and will be coming home soon. May God Bless and Keep His Protecting Hand Over you and bring you safely home.

Good Bye, Dad

England
Mid May 1945

It was in May and the company commander, Captain Huberger, said, "There is one guy in the unit who can go on furlough to England." This meant one guy out of a company of 180 men. We were bivouacking out in the woods in Germany just a couple of weeks after the war had ended. Captain Huberger asked if any of us had relatives living in England. "Yes, I have a cousin, Harvey Gilbertson, who is in the Army Air Corps," I told him. Another guy wanted to go too so the captain said, "Okay, we will flip a coin to see which of you gets to go. He flipped the coin and I lost out. The captain thought about for a minute and then he said, "Oh, why don't you both go to England."

When we got off the cargo truck in La Havre, France on the English Channel to catch a ship to England, all the soldiers were dressed up in class A uniforms. These non-infantry men laughed at the way we looked. We hadn't had any haircuts in several months while we were fighting on the line. "Ya, laugh you dang so and so rear echelon," I thought. They had probably never seen an infantry man before. The first thing we did was go into a room in a big building. We got a little cloth bag and were told, "Put whatever your belongings are in the bag. Take off every last stitch of clothes and throw them in a pile. There is the shower room. Get a shower."

That was fine to get rid of the old clothes which probably could stand by themselves in the corner. Then we got brand new uniforms. We got everything, Class A uniforms with whatever ribbons we had coming to us including the Combat Infantry Badge. We couldn't go into mess hall until we had a fresh haircut. The people in there looked like soldiers, not like us. After we got our haircut we could go in the mess hall. To get into get some chow we had to look like real soldiers just like back in basic training. We couldn't be seen before that.

A day or so later I got passage and went to Southampton, England. After getting there I took the train to London because there were Red Cross rooms that you could rent for twenty five cents a bunk and get something to eat. The war had only been over for a couple of weeks. London was full of soldiers and the streets were crowded with people still celebrating the end of the war.

The streets were a madhouse of people, soldiers but mostly Air Corps men. I spent two or three days in London doing some sight-seeing and didn't really know anybody there. While looking at Piccadilly Square, an English civilian started talking with me. "Would you like to have a tour of London, I'll take you," he said. We got on the subway and we went to the palace, the cathedrals and Westminster Abbey. It was still covered with sandbags to protect from bombings. We saw a lot of rubble from the bombing by the Germans and we spent most of the day together. When we were saying goodbye I told the man, "I'd like to give you something." "No," he said to me, "I won't take anything."

Then I went to the railroad station and tried to find my cousin Harvey. There were literally hundreds of Air Corps men who were on pass and going back to their bases. How was I going to find out where to go? It seemed like finding a needle in a haystack. There were two men standing there so I asked, "Say, could help me out?" I knew the number of Harvey's unit so maybe they happened to know where that unit was based and how to get there.

"Yeah, we know where that is and that happens to be our unit," one guy said. This was out of the thousands of Air Corps guys that were there. So they asked, "Are you looking for relatives or someone?" "Yes I am," I told them. "Well, what's his name?" they asked. "It's Harvey Gilbertson," I said.

Both of the guys started laughing and with smiles on their face asked me, "Are you related to him? We are in the same barracks. Yeah, we know him." How could I have possibly happened to meet someone that knew Harvey Gilbertson out of those thousands of Air Corps men? It was about as remote as getting struck by lightning. This was really hard to believe.

"No problem," they said, "You come with us on the train and we will take you there." We got on the train together and when we got to the base they showed me just where to go to find Harvey. The orderly room was the headquarters for that unit so I walked in and said, "I am looking for Harvey Gilbertson" and told them who I was. "Oh yeah," the sergeant said, "He is out on the base working on an airplane. We'll call him and he'll come up here."

The clerk didn't tell Harvey that his cousin Verdie Gilbertson was there to see him. It wasn't long before Harvey came in to the orderly room. He had probably run all the way up there. He was completely surprised when he saw it was me. To the sergeant, I said, "Well, I suppose there is a little village to stay in as I am going to be around for a few days you know." "Oh no, don't worry about that," Harvey's buddies said, "You can stay in the barracks with us. Just go to the supply room and get a bunk. You can go to the barracks and move the bunks a little."

It was great to sleep in the barracks for about ten nights, eat in the mess hall every day and hang around with the Air Corps guys down at the field. They practically gave me free run at the air base and I took my time looking closely at all the airplanes on the field. "You could fly these airplanes just as good as some of these pilots. If you want to fly one I'll start it up for you, just get in," Harvey told me. "Nope, I don't want a career in an Army jail," I said. As a corporal in the Air Corps, Harvey probably wasn't authorized to let me fly a Thunderbolt.

May 1945: With my cousin Harvey Gilbertson and a P47 Thunderbolt fighter at the 8th Air Force Base in England.

Harvey's squadron had P47 Thunderbolts and there were some B 17 Bombers and a few flying boats for Air Sea rescue who patrolled the English Channel looking for pilots that had bailed out over the water. I could only sit and pretend to be flying one. Harvey was deathly afraid of airplanes. "Oh no, I'm not getting in one of those," he said, but he thought I could fly one. Harvey's buddies treated me really swell there.

I was standing in the chow line waiting to get into the mess hall with all the Air Corps guys when two pilots walked by the line. While wearing a different uniform than the Air Corps I kind of stood out. Are you from the continent?" one of B 17 bomber pilots asked me. That meant Europe not England. He could see I was infantry. "We thought of you guys when we flew over on our missions," he said. "Ya, we thought about you guys too when we saw you going over," I told him. "How'd you like to go for a ride over Germany?" one pilot asked. "I'd love to go!" I told him. "We are going early tomorrow morning so you come down and report to the field," he told me,

Very early the next morning I was there but it was so foggy we couldn't fly. The pilots were there but had to say, "The weather just doesn't permit us to fly. Come back tomorrow and we will do it then, weather permitting." The next morning the weather was the same and we were grounded again. My furlough was up before the weather cleared so I never did get to go and that was sure disappointing. That was the end of that. It would have been quite a trip for me to see Germany from the air after walking all over the ground for the past few months.

It was amazing to me that these pilots didn't think about any regulations when asking me to go for a ride. The rules probably didn't allow taking a guy along who wasn't in their air crew. Why even go to the effort to go out of the way to do something for a guy who they'd never see again? It was like we knew each other. They were young guys too just a little older than me and had got in the Air Corps earlier on. If I had gone in a few months earlier and they had joined up a few months later we may have traded positions and I would have been the one flying.

Dear Mom,   Thursday night   May 18ᵗʰ London
    Written on American Red Cross Stationary Free postage (it took a month to reach home)

Well, here I am in London. I got here this afternoon after I left Harvey's airbase this morning. I sure enjoyed my visit with him.

I'm terribly sorry I couldn't get a chance to send you anything for Mother's Day but I'll have to make up for it next year. Maybe everything will be a little more settled by then. Anyway I wish you a happy and blessed Mother's day. I am late as usual you know.

I'm starting back on the way to Germany again on Saturday. I don't care much to go back there but I guess there isn't much to be done about it. I don't know yet what I will be doing. I'll maybe find out when I get back to my outfit.

How is everything back there now? Fine I hope. It's plenty warm here now. It doesn't get dark until about 10:30. I'm staying at a Red

Cross club right now. It's very nice. It's a big hotel and we eat here too. The chow is very good.

I took quite a few camera pictures when I was with Harvey so I hope I can get them developed soon and I will send you some.

Well I guess I'll have to hit the hay now. Here's hoping this finds you all well and happy and may God Bless you all.

Goodnight,

Love, Verdie

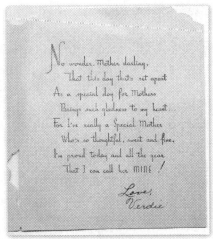

Somehow I must have found a Mother's Day card later. This card was found close by the letter from May 18th. I'm very happy my mother kept it.

"Hitler count your men"

Dear Dad,   *Sunday eve May 28*   *Germany (Ulm)*

Well, here I am back in Germany. I got back here the night before last. I'm glad to be back with the outfit again. It sure was a long trip back by boat, train, truck and the last twenty miles in a jeep. I really enjoyed my trip to England it sure was nice to see Harvey again. We had quite a time talking Norske you know. We hadn't spoken it for so long we had nearly forgotten how. Harvey was expecting to go home in the near future.

I'm sorry to hear that Earl was wounded. I had a letter from him yesterday and he said he was getting along fine. I'm glad he didn't get hit any worse. I hope he can go back to the states now. It is really swell he is so close to Roy. I had a letter from Roy and he said he had been to see Earl and they were really two happy boys.

I sure had a stack of letters when I got back. I had two from you written April 23 and May 2nd and one from Mom written April 27 and from Roy, Clarice, Vernice and Aldora Goulson.

I am in a nice place now. In a nice house with electric lights and a radio. This is a small village about two miles from Ulm. It's right on the banks of the Danube River. All I do is guard duty. I am even starting to gain some weight. I must have gained nearly ten pounds. I get plenty to eat and plenty of sleep so I can't see why I shouldn't gain weight. Of course I can use a few extra pounds.

So you got a picture of me. Well I've been keeping pretty close company with that mortar for the last 7 or 8 months. It has thrown a lot of shells at the Krauts. I was a machine gunner for a while and a rifleman for a while but I liked the mortar the best. We used to say, "Hitler count your men" after we laid down a mortar barrage. *Tsk tsk.* Of course the Krauts used to throw them back at us pretty regular.

I just about got the same dose as Earl got one of the last days I was on the front.

I've had a lot of shells land pretty blame close but this one topped them all. We were taking a town and I was behind a house. I was just getting up to run to the next house when a big mortar shell hit only a few feet away. The blast knocked me back against the wall and luckily all the shrapnel missed me. The concussion kind of knocks a guy silly for a little while but it didn't hurt me a bit. (*I never wrote about anything like this until after the war was over. Why make my parents worry even more?*)

I don't know yet if I will come home this summer or not. I am really hoping so of course. In case I have to go to the Pacific I'm pretty sure I'll get a furlough in the states first and maybe some training too. Of course I don't have the slightest idea whether I'll go to the Pacific or occupy here or come back to the states for good.

I've got over 40 points and it's quite a ways from 85. I don't expect to get a discharge but I sure would like to come back to the states for good. That furlough in England didn't have anything with my coming back to the states. In other words it doesn't count as a furlough.

I will have to close for now it's time to go on guard duty. Here's hoping this finds you all well and happy and may God bless you all. Good nite.

Love,

Verdie

Greet Shep

With my mortar in a photo that was published in the Montevideo American in spring 1945. Now that the war was over I could now tell a few stories in my letters without worrying about censors.
Photo by Army Signal Corps photographer

Verdie Gilbertson is Mortarman in the Seventh Army

With the Seventh Army, Germany.—Pfc. Verdie H. Gilbertson of Route 5, Montevideo, a mortarman with an infantry unit of the 100th division is shown checking his mortar on the Seventh army front in Germany on a picture received this week at The American office. The mortar is used as a close supporting infantry weapon and is described by most doughfeet as their own 'artillery.'

Courtesy of Montevideo American Newspaper

Back from England to the 100ᵗʰ division in Germany

Military life in England was completely different than France or Germany. England was almost like going back to the United States. When leaving Southampton, England I got together with three guys who were also heading back to Germany. We landed at La Havre again. From there on we couldn't just go to the station and ask for a ticket. The railroads weren't running because the tracks and bridges were all blown up. It some places a train may go intermittently so we were on our own to get back to our outfit. We roamed around looking for something to eat. That was our problem. We found Army outfits and got in their chow lines but sometimes we didn't get fed because we weren't from their outfit. I was surprised and mad at the Army units who told us to get food from our own units. But somehow or other we got enough to eat and made it back.

We slept in abandoned houses and wherever we could find shelter while we were trying to work our way back. We weren't thinking that this was a big deal because we were used to living like that. We didn't really think it was any hardship.

Sometimes we rode on Army trucks and sometimes trains. It was so mixed up that it's hard to remember all the details but somehow we got back to our units. No one ever checked our furlough papers or asked where we were going. According to my furlough papers I had to be out of England by the day it said and not be overdue.

When we got on French soil we were told not to worry about time. In England our papers were checked all the time. It seemed like MPs were looking for trouble and acted arrogant. If they had been in Germany doing the same thing they might have got beaten up a few times. My days as an MP taught me that it was best not to make too many enemies.

The four of us stayed together all the way back to Germany and then they went looking for their units. When I left my unit it was based in the woods not far from Stuttgart and from there it took me a week to get to La Havre. From there I had been in England for ten days. Getting back to my unit was probably 600 miles to near Thalfingen, Germany so it probably took a couple of weeks to get there and my furlough time was long over.

When meeting different units I asked questions and finally found out the 100th was up around Ulm, Germany. When I got back and reported to Capt. Huberger, the company commander, all I said was, "I'm back." "Oh good, your platoon is up at Thalfingen. You can ride up in a supply truck today," he said. There were no questions about where I had been and he didn't say I was supposed to be back sooner. After getting back to my unit some of the guys were fishing in the Danube River. The bait was some leftover hand grenades. After "fishing", a few fish floated up to the top but we probably didn't eat any.

HEADQUARTERS, SIXTH ARMY GROUP
OFFICE OF THE COMMANDING
GENERAL — APO 23

Europe 1945

My pride in you is deeper than the simple pride of a commander of victorious troops, for we fight to preserve for our own people and for people throughout the world the chance to learn or to continue learning how to govern themselves and how to live with one another.

Before the German people can learn how to govern themselves and get along with the rest of the world they must be firmly impressed with the fact that they have been defeated, that their acceptance of Nazi leadership made their defeat necessary, and earned for them the distrust of free, peaceful people.

The fight is not over with the laying down of arms. You and your conduct in relation with the German people will largely determine whether they will realize we mean business, or whether you and your children must again be called to fight and die on foreign soil.

To help you in doing your part I give you these " Special Orders ". I charge you personally with the responsibility of strict compliance with their provisions. It will be hard for you, for you have not been trained this way ; but it is only through this means that complete victory over Nazi ideals will be won.

JACOB L. DEVERS
LIEUTENANT GENERAL, U.S.A.
COMMANDING

A letter from Lieutenant General Jacob L. Devers included with a pamphlet detailing specific orders about how American soldiers were to treat German civilians.

I'm so thankful it's thunder

Dear Mom,   *Wednesday night*   *May 31, Germany (Ulm)*

It's raining here tonight and thundering and lightning. I'm so thankful it's thunder and not artillery pounding away. The artillery did used to sound a lot like thunder when it was a ways off and it used to light up the whole sky. I hope I never hear or see that again. I don't mind the rain now when I can be in a house.

I just came off guard duty and fried myself two eggs. We have three radios and I have been listening to the radio and reading the Monte American. I got the April 27ᵗʰ issue today. Oh yes, I read that article about my mortar and me and the article about Julien. I enjoyed it very much. I sure enjoy the Monte American. I get a kick out of some of the hair raising stories some of the guys write and tell about. (tsk, tsk)

I bet your chicks are nice and big now. You sure had good luck with them. I hope I will be home in time to eat some of them. (tsk, tsk)

I haven't heard anything as to what I'll be doing yet. I am pretty sure I'll get a furlough home first though in case I go to the Pacific.

I heard from both Earl and Roy the other day. Earl was fine he said. It's too bad he had to get yellow jaundice too. I'm so glad he and Roy could get together. I know what that means to both of them.

It's about time to hit the hay so I'll close for now. Here's hoping this finds you all well and happy and may God bless you all. Goodnite.

Love, Verdi

German Prisoners after the war

A photo I took of load of German prisoners after the war ended

When looking at some of the pictures I took after the war I came across one that had a truck full of Krauts. It was a trailer like a semi-truck that was used for supplies and the sides were open a few feet up about to their waists. The Americans were taking these prisoners to another place. The trailer was loaded full with prisoners, the tail gate was closed, the driver got in, put it in gear and took off. Then he quickly slammed the brakes. Wham! The prisoners all moved forward. Then the tail gate was opened again and more prisoners were loaded.

The German soldiers were standing there with their caps and packed in liked a bunch of sardines. I took a picture because it looked so comical. It maybe wasn't funny for the prisoners but I don't think the driver did this more than once. He and the guards probably figured now there were enough prisoners to fill the truck. It may have been called abuse but it didn't really hurt them. These Krauts were probably thinking, "#$% Amercanish swine." It was a good time for me to have a laugh.

I hoping to come back to the states

Dear Curtis,   *Tuesday June 5 Germany*

How are you coming along back there? Have you done much flying lately? I suppose you are still working for Julian. I haven't heard from any of you for a week now but I imagine the mail has been delayed again.

I'm having a pretty easy life now. All I do is guard duty and that isn't very hard. I'm really catching up on my sleep now and my eats too.

I don't know yet what I'll be doing or where I'll go. I am hoping to come back to the states of course.

I tried fishing in the Danube River but it's so swift that it's no use trying to make a hook stay under the water. Some guys used hand grenades, throwing them in the water. It works pretty good.

Have you heard from Earl lately? I hope he is getting along fine. It sure would be nice if he could go back to the states.

I imagine you are busy haying now and I suppose there are plenty of jobs now. Have you still got the fox? They must be getting quite numerous around there now. I suppose you go to Monte quite often. How is the Chevy percolating? I hear that gas coupons will be increased to six gallons now. I bet you don't mind that.

What kind of car did Julien buy? I bet he really tears around now. I don't blame him either. Have you done much fishing yet? The season on sunfish and crappies is open now isn't it? I suppose it's open for everything on June 15th.

Have you soloed yet? Has Bob gotten the Luscombe yet? That should be a pretty nice airport when they get it ready.

Well it's time to go on guard duty again so I'll have to close for now. Write soon and greet everybody.

So long,

Bro. Verdie

PS: I got a lot of pictures of airplanes when I was up at Harvey's field. I'll try and send some as soon as I get them developed.

7th Army will be occupation army in Germany

Dear Mom,   *Monday June 11, Germany*

How is everything coming along back there? I heard you had some more snow. I hope it didn't get too cold so it hurt the crops. It has been raining here practically every day the last four or five days. It's nice again now tho.

I suppose you hear from Earl and Roy regularly. I haven't heard from them for a little over a week. I hope Earl is getting along okay.

I suppose you have heard by now that the 7th Army and the 3rd Army will be occupation armies in Germany. Of course that doesn't necessarily mean that my division will occupy. They transfer the division around to other armies quite often. So I still don't know whether I'll be occupying or not. I suppose we will find out what divisions will be occupying soon. So far I have 38 points so I don't expect a discharge. I might get 5 or 10 more points but I don't know for sure yet.

Well I suppose Julien will be leaving again in a couple of days. I bet it will be hard for him to leave. He has enough points for discharge doesn't he?

I have to go on guard duty now so I will have to close for now. Here's hoping this finds you all well and happy and may God bless you all.

Love, Verdie

P. S. I am enclosing a little souvenir from Paris. I mailed another souvenir yesterday so I hope you get it.

Letter from My Mother
News about my brother Earl

Dear Verdie, Tuesday June 19th, 1945

Curtis received your letter today that you wrote 5th of June. Glad to hear you are well and having it better in every way.

I suppose guard duty gets plenty tiresome too but then it's nice when you can get enough sleep and get enough to eat it means so much to know that. We got a letter from you yesterday that was exactly one month old. It was written in London May 18th so it took exactly a month to get here. I suppose it was because it was free mail and was delayed someplace.

We had a letter from Earl and he is still at the hospital at Saipan. Roy and Cal were still there too. Earl has shrapnel removed from his neck but said it is still sore. His ears still bother him yet, you know he was shell shocked. He was supposed to go to the doctor and maybe find out if he will get out of the infantry.

This morning we had some nice bright sunshine and I hope it stays like this now for a while. Hope this finds you in the best of health. We are all the same as ever at home here. May God be with you and all of us until we all meet again.

So long then Verdie and God Bless You,
Love, Mother

Free mail traveled much slower than Air Mail

CHAPTER FOURTEEN

Found out I will be
going to the Pacific

Dear Dad,   *June 19, 1945 (Kirchheim, Germany)*

I received your letter yesterday, the one you wrote June 5th. Thanks
a lot. I have moved since I wrote last. I'm still in the vicinity of Munich
or what is called Bavaria. I'm living in a paper factory now. We have
fixed it up like a barracks and we have bunks and a nice mess hall and
radios too. I'm training again but we play ball or go swimming every
afternoon. I went swimming this afternoon and my back is plenty
sunburned. We have a very nice swimming pool in this town.

Yes, I sure had a nice time in England. Harvey and I had a lot of fun
talking over old times. I saw so many interesting places too. I've seen most
of Europe now or the main parts anyway. London, Paris and Marseilles.
I might get a chance to go to Munich and Berchtesgaden, Hitler's home.

Oh yes, I'll get to see the other side of the world too. (*How do think
my parents felt about this news?*) We just found out that we will be going
to the Pacific. (*They had just announced that our division was scheduled
to ship out to the Pacific on September 12th, 1945*) I will come home on
a furlough first though. (*We found out later we were going directly to the
Pacific with no furloughs.*) I don't know yet when I will leave here for the
states. I imagine it will be sometime this summer. I don't like the idea
of going into combat again but I guess that is the Infantry's job and we
just have to grin and bear it. I don't think it will be any worse fighting
Japs than Germans. They can't be much dirtier and I doubt if I can see
anything worse over there than I have here.

Anyway I thank God that I can come home before I go over there. Yes, I sure hope that Earl can come back to the states and Roy too. I am glad Earl is getting along okay.

I bet the crops are nice back there now. Do you think the corn will be knee high by the 4th? The small grain is all headed out over here now and the corn is about a foot high. The strawberries are getting ripe too. (tsk, tsk) They are releasing so many Kraut soldiers to help on the farms. It seems funny to see these Krauts walking around and not being able to take a crack at them. One of the German civilians came up to the American military government the other day and asked if they would release some SS men because they were younger and were better workers. I guess that guy went out faster than he came in. If they ask me, every SS man should be shot between the eyes. *(I must have been thinking about the 17th SS Panzer Grenadier Division that we had met up with at NordWind and again in Heilbronn.)*

I bet you had a swell time on the fishing trip. We will have to take one of those trips again if I come home this summer.

Say Dad, could you tell me how much money I have in the bank now? It doesn't make much difference but I'd just like to know. I'm planning to buy a new car or an airplane when I get enough. I've walked so much since I came in the infantry that I'm going to make up for it when I come home. I suppose it would be better to invest my money in something else but I guess there will be jobs to get after the war. Anyway I'm not worrying about that until the Japs have had enough.

The country around here is really beautiful. I wish I could get camera film so I could take some pictures. The country is hilly and mountainous and a lot of woods. The Germans are very clean people and they keep everything spic and span. There are a lot of deer here but we aren't allowed to hunt. We aren't allowed to associate with the Germans except on business. (*See our orders below*). They have a lot of beer over here so we are permitted to go into a place and have a few glasses of beer or apple cider.

It is pretty warm here now, but there are plenty of shade trees, (tsk, tsk). I am enclosing a picture of Harvey and me (See *story about my trip to England*) I took when I was over at his field. It is time to hit the hay so I'll close for now. Good night and May God bless you all.

So Long,
Verdie Greet Shep

6. Never to associate with Germans.

a. We must bring home to the Germans that their support of Nazi leaders, their tolerance of racial hatreds and persecutions, and their unquestioning acceptance of the wanton aggressions on other nations, have earned for them the contempt and distrust of the civilized world. We must never forget that the German people support the Nazi principles.

b. Contacts with Germans will be made only on official business. Immediate compliance with all official orders and instructions and surrender terms will be demanded of them and will be firmly enforced.

c. American soldiers must not associate with Germans. Specifically, it is not permissible to shake hands with them, to visit their homes, to exchange gifts with them, to engage in games or sports with them, to attend their dances or social events, or to accompany them on the street or elsewhere. Particularly, avoid all discussion or argument with them. Give the Germans no chance to trick you into relaxing your guard.

Orders from the Lt General Devers

A letter from my dad in response to the letter above

Dear Verdie, July 2, 1945

We received your welcome letter of June 19th today and see you are still in Germany. We would like to see you home again but as long as the war in Japan lasts we would rather see you stay where you are. You know what I mean. We see by the news that the 7th Army and 3rd Army will be the occupation or police troops in Germany but we understand now that a few divisions were picked out for Japan. You say you might be coming home sometime this summer. Well we can't tell, the Japs may make up their mind to quit at any time and then you won't have to go out there anyway. (*My dad was always an optimistic man with plenty of faith in God. This was always good to know.*)

We hope and pray it will turn out that way. It seems strange that they want to keep on and get all their cities and factories blown to pieces and not have one chance in a thousand to win this war anyway.

Earl's ears are not back to normal yet. We hope he will not be sent back to combat. The crops here look very nice especially the small grain oats and the wheat is almost headed out. The flax is in full bloom. The corn is a little behind but some warm weather will do it wonders. Your allotments have been coming in regular every month. This money you have sent will certainly come in handy for you when you come home.

Goodbye and May God Bless and Keep his Protecting hand over you and bring you safely home.

Dad

June 1945: Standing outside our new barracks by Kirchheim, Germany. Before we got there it had been used by the German army. Notice the bullets holes on the outside wall.

Busy training now

Dear Mom,   *Sunday June 24, Kirchheim, Germany*

I'm sorry to hear you had the flu so hard. I'm glad you are alright now. Are there very many cases of flu around now?

I went to church this morning. We have a very nice big church here. It's nice when we can go to a real church every Sunday. When the war was going on we'd have services out in the woods, in bombed out buildings and any place that was handy.

I don't know yet when I'll be leaving here but the way it sounds it won't be long. I'm hoping I'll get a 45 day furlough but I guess I can't expect more than 30. I guess the longer I stay home the harder it will be to leave again. I'm glad Earl is getting along okay and I hope he can come back to the states. I'm planning to write Roy and Earl this afternoon.

We are busy training now so I put in a 12 hour day but we usually play ball or go swimming part of the afternoon. The squad leader isn't here now so I have a squad to take care of today.

Say, you better not send me any more packages because I might have left before they get here. So Curtis has soloed. I bet he is proud of that.

We heard from one of the fellows from our company that had been captured by the Germans last January. He got lost in a snowstorm one night and the next morning he found himself in the German lines. He lost 40 pounds while he was a prisoner. I remember the night he disappeared. It was snowing and blowing so hard that you couldn't see your finger in front of your nose. I'm sure glad those days are over. We all nearly got captured about that time but thanks to a heavy machine gun outfit, the Krauts didn't get into the gap behind us.

We had a parade yesterday and it looked pretty good. The German civilians came out to look too.

Well, this is about all the news I have so I'll close for now. Here's hoping this finds you well and happy and may God bless you all.

Love,
Verdie

Back to the service and orders to Japan

We moved to Pforzheim and we acted like soldiers and had to get up in the morning with reveille and the mess hall. We were organized just like back in basic training. Then we started having a variety of school classes we could take. After taking an electricity class I did a little electric hookup at the German Army barracks where we stayed. Later I took a photography class. Then we got orders that the 100th division was scheduled to leave on September 12, 1945 for the invasion of Japan. That was the end of the schooling because we began retraining for the Japanese invasion. There was an abrupt switch back to business.

We could hardly accept it because we thought we were going home soon. It was emotionally upsetting. Everybody just detested starting in again. It was a shocker. First we were going home and then we were going to Japan. We trained all the way up until the second Atomic bomb was dropped.

Well I guess I will be staying here until the year is over

Dear Mom,   *Sun Morning*   *July 15, Germany*
I wrote this letter on Co. F 399ᵗʰ Infantry stationary.

This is a beautiful Sunday morning. It reminds me of Sunday mornings at home. I imagine you are having services today.

Well I guess I'll be staying over here until this year is over anyway. I read in the paper the other day that the 100ᵗʰ Division will stay over here through 1945. It's alright with me. I'd just as soon stay over here until next spring. I figure I will have enough points* to get out of the Army next summer at this time. It's too bad Earl didn't have enough points for a discharge. I had a letter from him a few days ago. He said he had been over to see Roy and Cal. He said he might be able to get into a noncombatant outfit. I hope he can. The infantry has to do all the dirty work. If Roy had been in the Army he could have gotten out now with all the foreign service he has. Time does go fast though. I am going on ten months overseas and 29 months in the Army. I've got two battle stars now and I expect to get one more for the Vosges Mountains.

I spose the small grain is nearly ripe now. It won't be long before fall is here.

Japan is sure getting a pounding now. It can't be too long before they have had enough. I'm training every day now. It's about like being in a camp back in the states. I got 2 issues of the Monte American last week. I see there are quite a few service men getting discharges now. It's good to hear that things are starting on the way back to normal again. I hope by next summer that all the fighting has ended.

I suppose Curtis is out flying today. If the weather there today is as nice as it is here it would be a nice day for flying.

We have church services at 11 o'clock so I better get ready to go. We haven't got a church here but we'll use a day room in the barracks I guess.

Here's hoping this finds you all well and happy. So long.

Love,
Verdie

Outside our barracks in Germany, with Beehive,
Verdie, Clyde Simmons, Lew Hirst,?

*The **Advanced Service Rating Score** was a scoring system that awarded points to a soldier and was used to determine who was sent home first. At the end of the war in Germany and Italy, a total of 85 points were required for a soldier to be allowed to return to the States. Otherwise, if you had less than 85 points, you could expect to continue to serve in the Army and most likely be sent to fight the Japanese.

How to Score Points

Points for discharge from the Army will be totalled as follows:

1. Each month in service .... 1 Point
2. Each month in service overseas .... 1 Point
3. Each combat award (includes each medal and each battle participation star) .... 5 Points
4. Each dependent child under 18 (maximum of three) .... 12 Points

The four items above are the ONLY ones for which points will be awarded. No points will be awarded for age, marriage or dependents other than children under 18. A complete list of medals and campaigns for which points are to be awarded is published on page 5 of today's paper.

From Stars and Stripes May 1945

Occupation in Germany
Thalfingen near Ulm, Germany

> c. American soldiers must not associate with Germans. Specifically, it is not permissible to shake hands with them, to visit their homes, to exchange gifts with them, to engage in games or sports with them, to attend their dances or social events, or to accompany them on the street or elsewhere. Particularly, avoid all discussion or argument with them. Give the Germans no chance to trick you into relaxing your guard.

Orders from Lt General Devers

We stayed in civilian's houses in the villages. Lt Nicholson got a hold of the burgermiester and told him we would take every sixth house. The burgermiester told the people to find someplace else with friends or family. Lt. Nicholson asked the burgermiester where his house was. "I'll take yours," he told him. It was the biggest house around. We never saw Lieutenant Nicholson much after that. There were about four of us in each house and we really only took up about a half dozen houses in the village. We had beds to sleep in after months of sleeping in holes and on the ground.

The lady that owned "our house" had two kids named Rudy and Umpka. She had some relatives close by and she came back once in a while to check on the house and do some cleaning. The two little kids often came back to their house and pestered us. They couldn't speak any English. When the kids talked they kept asking us if we understood. "Verstehen Sie," you understand? "No," we said. This got the kids going. Sometimes Rudy and Umpka got a little mad at us because they figured we were teasing.

We didn't have much to do and we were tired so we laid down by the river soaking up the sunshine. We were supposed to be guarding the train that had some ammunition but we didn't think that was real important so we were mostly just loafing. We ate pretty well when hot food was brought up. You could call it rehabilitation from being animals to being human beings. We had become experts on the types of European soil in France and Germany and used to brag about that. We had been surviving for months by digging holes in the ground. In the winter time the ground was mostly frozen. Sometimes we utilized the holes left by artillery.

Relaxing our Guard

them, to engage in games or sports with them, to attend their dances or social events, or to accompany them on the street or elsewhere. Particularly, avoid all discussion or argument with them. Give the Germans no chance to trick you into relaxing your guard.

Orders from Lt General Devers

We followed orders most of the time but this time the Germans civilians in Thalfingen used an Oompah band, cookies, cakes and some wine to trick us into relaxing our guard.

We were ordered not to fraternize with the German civilians after the war. One day in our area of the town, the Germans were all celebrating and they invited us to join them at the apple orchard on the edge of town. There was a platform set up with lights all around it and there was wine and food for all of us. The people went to our platoon leader (he was called, "the commandant") to give him the invitation. Here these German villagers had invited our whole platoon to come to their party to celebrate. We weren't even supposed to be talking with them much less going to a party.

Lt. Nicholson came and told us the villagers had asked us to attend their party. "You guys can go if you want to but don't tell Capt. Huberger. It won't go any further than right here," he said. Our whole platoon went to the party where there was a polka band playing and plenty of celebrating along with old time German music. The civilians danced with the American soldiers. We thought it was fun and the people in town sure had a good time.

The war had been very long for all of us and for German civilians it had been going on for many more years. The lieutenant might have gotten in trouble but Capt. Huberger never said anything about us fraternizing with the Germans. The civilians treated us like neighbors and didn't hold the war against us. They knew we just wanted to go home. It helped that this little village had not been bombed.

When the same people found out we were leaving town, many gathered up whatever sugar could be found and baked us cakes and cookies. Sugar was hard to find. The German civilians wanted the whole platoon to gather at one of their houses, so we piled in about four Jeeps and went up there. When we left, the villagers gave us a good sendoff waving to all of us, the enemy soldiers. That was the end of my occupation service in Germany.

Reviewing the troops and military courtesy

This is another after- the-war story that still makes me laugh.

Military courtesy was not practiced very much in the infantry during the war. After the war was over it took a quite a while to get us retrained on courtesy for higher rank and all of that. One day Captain Huberger, the company commander, said we were going to a parade review. Some high ranking officer- it must have been a general- was coming and he wanted to review the troops in dress uniforms. We weren't used to this after having spent the past six months in combat. We had to hike a quite a ways to get to a great big open field and the whole regiment of about three thousand troops was there. We lined up by companies just like we did in basic training when we had formal retreat. So there we were standing and waiting for this high ranking officer to come and do whatever he was supposed to do.

We didn't have to stand at attention but were on parade rest as time went on and on. We were all getting disgusted as we stood around waiting for the general. He finally arrived and there was a big reviewing stand on the field that he was supposed to get up on and give his speech and whatever else he was going to do. The stand was up high so he could see all the troops out there and it was a hundred yards from us. He finally got his speech started and not too long after that- here came three Thunderbolt fighter planes overhead whose pilots must have seen the formations in the field. The planes started to circle around and I thought to myself, "I know just what those pilots are thinking and if I was a fighter pilot I'd be thinking the same thing if I was in their place."

The three Thunderbolts circled around and looked at us when they were fairly low and then all of a sudden- peeled off and came real close behind each other, right smack over the ground between us and the reviewing stand where the general was speaking. You can imagine what might happen if three fighter planes went right between the reviewing stand real close to the ground. There wasn't very much room between us and the Thunderbolts. I still don't know how the pilots ever dared to fly that low.

When thinking about this I still laugh. It was so comical. These three fighter pilots were just patrolling around getting bored so they probably figured the war was over now and it was time to have a little fun. The general got flustered when the Thunderbolt pilots upset the whole business but he finally did give most of his speech. That was insubordination of the highest order. These pilots who were just having fun were disrupting an officer's review of his troops. All of the men in formation either laughed or cheered. We could just see the faces of the pilots as they pulled out of there and I bet all of them were really laughing. They most likely figured- we showed them. The pilots had their fun and were smart enough not to come back again because if someone had gotten the ID numbers from the planes, they would have been in big trouble.

August 1945

After the fighting was over in Germany and we got our duffle bags returned I was able to keep and save a few letters from home. This one was written by my dad in two parts on August 9th and August 10th, 1945 as the war in Japan was coming to the end.

A pile of Lefse and some Lutefisk

Dear Verdie   August 9, 1945 Montevideo, Minnesota

I hope you are in the best of health and so are we at home. I see from the letter Curtis got from you that you are on guard duty. Suppose you boys are getting a little tired of staying out there and we don't blame you. We here at home are waiting and hoping for you boys to come home again. Our hopes are running high these last days. Say isn't the war news sounding very good these days and isn't it great about that new bomb and the Russians declaring war on the Japs? They are sure a goner now. I feel sure that that the Japs will surrender soon perhaps before you get this letter. We believe you boys will be home for Christmas. Ma would make a pile of lefse with as many pages as a Montgomery Ward catalog and I would get the biggest lutefisk on the market for that supper.

We are just about through with the harvest and the small grain is certainly small this year. I suppose we will start threshing the last part of next week, the corn is just starting to tassel out and looks good but it is about two weeks behind. If we get some warm weather soon it might turn out all right.

Roy is back on Saipan and Earl is still there too.

There is a big shortage of harvest help again but the businessmen have been very good to come out evenings and help with the shocking and say, some of the Krauts you boys over there have taken as prisoners have been around here putting up shocks. They come from a prison camp up in Ortonville and are accompanied by guards of course. Ed Laumb had a bunch of them over in his field the other day. The prisoners are not so bad on shocking but of course don't come close to what our boys can do. They will work in the corn canning factory too.

We can see more and more service men on the streets nowadays. Some got a discharge but most are slated for the Pacific. I don't think any of them will ever have to go there.

You mentioned in your letter to Curtis about buying an airplane and of course Curtis is enthusiastic about it but don't you think it is just as well to wait until you come home as that will not be very long anyway and you could handle your own money yourself.

Dad

P.S. There are pheasant broilers around again this summer

CHAPTER FIFTEEN

Good God. I'll go up to the church and Ring the Bell

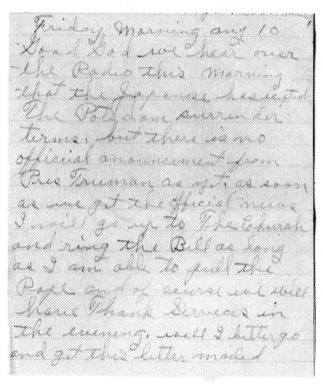

My dad wrote this on Friday morning August 10, 1945

Good God, we heard over the radio this morning that the Japanese have accepted the Potsdam surrender terms but there is no official announcement from President Truman as yet. As soon as we get the official news I will go up to the church and ring the bell as long as I am able to pull the rope. Of course we will have Thanks services in the evening. Well I better go get this mailed.

Dad

Japan Surrenders

On the night of August 6th, 1945 we had gone to Stuttgart, Germany to the USO show with Bob Hope and Ingrid Bergman and there were thousands of GIs there. We were going back to our base and waiting for everybody to get loaded. We were just getting in the truck when a guy came running towards us and he was really carrying on. We wondered what was going on. "We dropped a big bomb on Japan" he said, "Now we should give Russia one," another guy said. The Russians were our allies and also Communists. He could have just as well been positive because everyone else was elated.

We didn't know for quite a while what kind of bomb it was. We were training to go to Japan and had set up mortars. Three days later on August 9th, 1945, a guy came running up to us and said, "We dropped another bomb on Japan and they have surrendered." When the second atomic bomb was dropped on Nagasaki, Japan our training for the Pacific War and Japan was stopped immediately.

Everyone was celebrating because the war was over without even knowing what the big bomb had done. All we knew was that it was over. With forty four points, I was eligible to go back to the states. The orders had me scheduled for shipping home in September so I wrote home telling my family I planned to be home by Christmas and I was transferred to a unit that was ready to leave. Little did I know my stay would be for another six months in France. The Army never told me what had happened to the first plan. There was no point in complaining because I had it pretty easy during the time I was waiting to go back home. In fact I was not too disappointed. That was another strange feeling. Maybe I wanted to relax and settle down a little before meeting everyone back home. It was a good time to put on a little weight and return to normal.

With a class A pass I could come and go as I pleased. What other time in my life could I have a chance to spend a month in Paris, France? My buddies and I spent time roaming around Paris, we ate good food and the work was easy on the switchboard. When I get home, I thought, I suppose it'll be time get a job and go to work. Here I was getting $90.00 a month with room and board, free clothing and they took care of my teeth. Peace time army was a racket for us. None of my buddies or I spent any time complaining about us having to stay longer in France. You may notice in my letters that I didn't tell my parents anything about these feelings.

Happy Birthday from my Mother August 18th, 1945

*A 1945 Birthday card from my family who always
kept thinking about and praying for us.*

Dear Verdie
As each year adds
New reasons, Son, for being proud of you
So each year prompts more wishes
For good luck in all you do.

Now we will be looking forward to having you all back again soon.
It's going to be wonderful when you are all home again. We can all start
to live again and plan for the future. I sent you a box for your birthday
but it won't be there on time but better late than never. (*My birthday is
September 7ʰ*) Hope this finds you in the best of health. So long then
Verdie

Love, Mother

Wonderful to know that the war is over

Three weeks after Japan surrendered

Dear Mom, Dad and all of you,   August 30th, 1945

    Thank you so very much for the nice birthday present. I sure can make good use of the stationary and the socks and handkerchiefs too. It sure is wonderful to know that the war is over isn't it? I can hardly believe that it is actually over. We aren't training anymore now. We are having school right here in this camp so I am going to school now. I'm studying bookkeeping, Algebra and auto mechanics. It sure is nice to be learning something that will be useful in civilian life instead of learning how to fight.

    It is sure a relief to know that we don't have to go into combat again. Even when the war was over in Europe I'd always have the combat in the Pacific to look forward to.

    I consider myself pretty lucky to get out of this war without a scratch. There's only about 30 men left in this company of the 170 that came over here. We lost about 60 replacements too. Counting the replacements we lost about 200 men in this company alone so you see what chance there is in the infantry.

    It's soon time to hit the hay so I will close for now.

Love, Verdie

*The words below were written in 2015. The letter
written in August 1945 verifies what I still remembered
almost 70 years later. That is a lasting memory*

How many of made it through the battles?

    After the war was over we were sitting around talking with a few of our buddies and someone asked, "I wonder how many of us are still around." We made an attempt to count up how many of us we could remember since our training days at Fort Bragg, North Carolina. We could only account for 29 out of the 184(full company strength) men we started out with on that first day in France. The others were wounded, killed in action, missing in action, captured, or lost with weather related causes like frostbite, trench foot and sometimes combat fatigue.

Roll Call

*Process: Battalion commander said to the company commanders
"Report" Four company commanders reported.*

Morning roll call Fort Bragg, North Carolina September, 1944 "Fox
Company report." "184 present or accounted for, Sir!"

*If the same process were used in Germany this could
have been the report.*

Morning roll call Germany May 5th, 1945: "Fox Company report."
"29 present or accounted for, Sir!"

Dear Lyle,   Wednesday Sept 12   Germany
(*My brother Lyle was about seven years younger than me and starting 9th
grade*)

I spose you are busy threshing nowadays or maybe you are all
through by now. Maybe you have started school. Are you going to
Milan this year? I hope you like it. It may not be much fun at first but
you have to go a while before you begin to like it. Don't quit though
even if you don't like school at first because you will never be sorry you
went there. I didn't like it at first either but it was a lot of fun after I
got used to it.

I imagine you are at Vernice and Astor's tonight being it is Vernice's
birthday. I would sure like to be there. I could go for some cake now.
I'll make up for lost time when I get home.

It won't be long before pheasant season now will it? When does it
start this year? I was hoping I would get home for pheasant season this
year but I guess I will open my own pheasant season when I get home.
You will have to shoot my limit for me this year. I've had guard duty the
last two days, a guard at the guardhouse. There are only three prisoners
in there so it isn't a very hard job. I don't like being up nearly all nite
tho. I'm pretty lazy you know. I had today off so I slept all forenoon.

We have movies nearly every evening so I go to them. I get to see
plenty of shows. The film breaks just as often as the film we used to see

at Earl Tobiason's station but of course it's fun to see anyway. We don't draw for money here though.

We get a quite a bit of cigarettes and candy bar each day and we get Coca Cola quite often too. A Cub landed down on the field a while ago but I didn't see him before he took off or I would have gone down there. How is Curtis coming along with his flying now?

Well Lyle, I see the boys are going to chow now so I better go too or I won't get any. These Army cooks don't keep any food for slowpokes so I better scram now.

So long and write soon,
Love Bro. Verdie

Greet Shep and Vicky and the pony too. And the cats.

Lyle with his pony and some cousins on for a ride

Sunday Afternoon
September 23, 1945 Germany

Dear Dad,

It's raining here again today. It won't be long until it will be snowing again.

I didn't go to church services today. It was at 9:30 instead of the usual 11 o'clock and I didn't know until I got there at 11 o'clock. I imagine you folks went to church today. How is Rev Jensen getting along now? I suppose you will start having services in the afternoon now.

I guess I'll have to say the same thing about me coming home. I still don't know anything for sure. I hear over the radio now that the troops in the states will be discharged now regardless of points. General Marshall also said that the point system will be discontinued this winter and all men with two years of service will be eligible for discharge. I hope that goes through. I will have three years in February you know so I could be getting a discharge this winter then. I don't like this point system and I've heard very few men that do. I think discharges should be given according to length of service. A man doesn't live long enough in the infantry to get very many points. Are they still drafting men there?

I am glad to hear that the small grain turned our good and that the corn wasn't damaged too bad. Have you had any frost yet? So you have to have a permit to sell grain now? Well we can thank God we live in the USA especially Minnesota where we never have to worry about going hungry. It's a wonderful country compared to Europe where starvation is so common. There are some German kids here that meet up by the garbage cans after every meal here and eat the garbage we throw away. There's always a line of children begging for anything we have left over in our mess kits. I don't feel sorry for the Germans but it is too bad that small children should be that hungry.

I haven't heard from Roy or Earl for a few weeks. I hope they can be home by Christmas. The way McArthur talks there won't be a need for a very big occupation force in Japan.

This is about all the news I can think of so I'll close for now. I hope this finds you all well and happy.

Love,
Verdie

Dear Folks,   October 2, 1945 Reims, France

Here I am in France again. I got here Sunday afternoon. I left my old outfit last Friday. It sure was a long ride in a boxcar so it wasn't real comfortable. I came to this outfit yesterday and we all went to one camp first and then they split us up into different outfits again. This is a field artillery outfit. I don't know just yet what I'll be doing yet. I'm living in a big tent and we have a big stove and a radio in here so it's pretty nice. The chow is very good. Much better than in my old outfit.

Reims is a pretty big town. It hasn't been bombed hardly at all. There are camps all around here that take care of the outfits that are preparing to go home. I don't know when this outfit will be going. I hope it is before Christmas. It's warmer here in France than in Germany but the nights are pretty chilly though.

How are you folks doing back there? I read in the paper that there was a snowstorm heading for Minnesota so maybe you have some snow now. I guess I won't get any mail for quite a while now. I hope it doesn't take too long for it to get here. Say will you pass my new address around. I haven't got any address cards to send.

I can't think of more news so I'll close for now. I'm a little busy getting settled down now.

Love,
Verdie

Dear Dad,   October 14th, 1945 Reims, France

Has Roy come home yet? I hope so. I got Mom's letter of September 28th yesterday. I am so glad to hear that Roy is on his way home. I know how happy he is and you folks too. It doesn't seem like almost four years since he left. I hope Earl is on his way home too.

I am an MP now. It's a pretty easy job. I don't exactly care to be an MP but I haven't much choice you know. This town is pretty rough. All these redeployment camps are around here and there are plenty of soldiers around and they do plenty of celebrating you know. There have been quite a few soldiers shot and knifed in fights so I guess they need MPs around here. A Negro soldier killed a white soldier. They know who he is so I suppose he will get caught.

I am on duty four and a half hours one day and two and a half the next day & then have a day off. The chow here is very good.

I can't say just when I'll be coming home. I suppose you read in the papers about the strikes they are having in the docks in New York and that the British taking their ships backs will delay redeployment quite a bit. I don't expect to leave before Jan. or Feb. now. The way it looks they don't care much whether the troops get home or not. There are still a lot of men with over 80 points left over here.

I've seen some interesting things in this town. As you know the peace treaty with the Germans was signed here. I went up to that place today. It was very interesting. They also exhibit all kinds of war machinery here.

Have you had any snow yet? I spose pheasant season opens next week doesn't it? I bet Roy will enjoy that. You'll have to shoot the limit for me and eat the limit for me too.

Well if Roy is home you'll have to greet him from me and congratulate him on being a civilian again. This is about all the news I have for now so I better close. Here's hoping this finds you all happy and well tonight. Goodnight.

Love,
Verdie

Chapter Sixteen

How I Became an MP

I was sent to the 208th artillery that was scheduled to go home. When I got there in my new unit was doing MP duty so I got a uniform and a new job. There were not enough ships to take me home.

With our Military Police Jeep

Verdi Gilbertson

Visiting with German prisoners after the war

When I became an MP after the war was over, one of my duties was to be a guard in the mess hall from late at night until early the next morning. It was a big place with many units coming and going. The German prisoners did all the cooking and cleaning in the mess hall. There were a lot of Germans working there and I was the only MP on duty to stand watch. We weren't even supposed to get close to them but the prisoners really wanted to come over and talk to an American soldier. When their work was done they walked over to me. I was the only American on guard but wasn't particularly worried.

The German soldiers wanted to learn about Americans and kept asking me about my experiences about growing up in United States and being a soldier in this war. I really shouldn't have been visiting with the prisoners but thought this was my best chance to find out what their part of this war was. There was nothing wrong with that I figured and I wasn't being sympathetic with Germany. After all we had been fighting their army for a very long time. These soldiers were people just like me and I was interested in their stories. There was always a German officer close by who was in charge but he never talked to an American soldier. He went off by himself and he never said anything against his men talking with me.

Some of the German soldiers had been on the Russian front and said, "Nix Ruskies, they are like bears coming and coming in charges, you just couldn't stop them," The German soldiers had no time for the Ruskies. "Ruskie" was slang for Russians just like we called the Germans, Krauts. What the Krauts called us, I don't know

There was always a 45 caliber pistol on my belt but there was no way these prisoners were ever going to start anything with me. Even though these Germans had lost the war- they were plenty glad it was all over just like us Americans were.

Military Police Duty
An Unlikely MP on Mission Impossible

Standing outside by the gate to an Army post. We had to check all vehicles to be sure they had a trip ticket authorizing them to drive an Army vehicle.

"Beehive" and I had been together all through training at Fort Bragg, North Carolina and during combat. Now we found ourselves teamed together again as MPs in Verdun and Rheims, France. "Beehive" was a true hillbilly from the mountains of North Carolina and I was a true Norwegian farm boy from Mandt Township, Minnesota. As Military Police we were supposed to be looking for trouble but mostly we tried to avoid it. Rheims and Verdun was easy duty but I really didn't want to put on the MP uniform. A lot of infantry men ended up doing MP duty.

We showed up for our MP duty and there was a first lieutenant who was the perfect guy to be an MP. You couldn't have picked a better guy to lead MPs. He had no sense of humor and it was business only for him. By gosh if you got out of line it was trouble. We were battle worn infantry men and we never saluted or stood up when this officer came in the room and he just had to put up with it. What could he do, complain to someone? We were infantry men. We only saluted infantry officers.

My duty with "Beehive" was to go out in our Jeep looking to see if there was any disorderly conduct. We were expected to take any American soldiers out of the establishments that were off limits. We had a daily route to patrol around Verdun. Most days we found the same place to take a break, have a cup of coffee and eat some good rolls. It was a two story place and we took our break downstairs. When we stopped in, the French couple was always very friendly to us. Both of them smiled and greeted us with, "Bon soir MP, voulez-vous café?" We answered, "Tres bon." "Oui, Oui." "Parle vous café?" they asked us. "Oui, Oui," we said. We sat down and had a good long coffee break. We patrolled the area and we stopped at this same place a quite a few times.

One evening before dark, the Lieutenant came up and told us, "Let's get four Jeeps together. I found out about a house of ill repute and it is off limits. We are going to go and raid it. I'll lead the way. This is an important mission and we will catch them by surprise." We figured this top secret mission must have some element of risk

"Beehive" and I followed him in our Jeep and as we got closer we recognized the streets and the buildings. Soon enough we could see it was the place where we had been having our coffee breaks for the past few days. We started laughing as we saw a bunch of American soldiers running out the door between buildings and down the alleys.

"Rush the place and get all the soldiers that are running away," the lieutenant yelled. He was very serious about this. There was no way we could have caught any of them as they were running down the streets. Neither of us was going to head out after them so the culprits all got away. Maybe they were "rear echelon" and this was the only action they ever saw. We figured there must have been a lookout in the house that spotted the MP Jeeps before we stopped.

When we were drinking coffee at the place "Beehive" and I never had even the slightest suspicion that anything unusual was going on upstairs. We must have thought the man and woman lived up there. Then we started to think, "No wonder the man and woman serving coffee and rolls were so friendly to us in our MP uniforms."

"Well, we are going to load up the girls and take them to the civilian jail," the lieutenant told us. So we loaded three or four into our Jeep and the other MPs loaded the rest. The smell of perfume coming from the girls was so strong I pretty nearly passed out. All of the girls were giggling and laughing. And Beehive and I were laughing too.

We pulled up to the French jail in Verdun and the Gendarme came out to meet us. We were still laughing and so were all the girls. The lieutenant was talking to the Gendarme who was speaking French and waving his arms all over the place. Pretty soon the girls were all led into the jail and the lieutenant was satisfied. I suppose he thought he had accomplished his very important mission.

We laughed and figured the girls were let out almost before we got out of sight. "Beehive" and I figured that we probably needed to look for another place for our coffee breaks.

It wasn't a very pleasant year and I wouldn't want to go through it again.

Dear Dad,   Tues. October 23rd, Reims, France

I received your letter of October 4th yesterday. It's been raining on and off for a couple of days. I guess it's about time for the rainy season to start now. It started about this time last year too. Last Saturday was a year I've spent in Europe. I left the states October 6th last year and landed at Marseilles October 20th. It wasn't a very pleasant year and I wouldn't want to go through it again.

I hope Roy is home by now. He should be home by the time you get this letter. I can imagine how happy he is. I hope Earl is on his way too. As far as I know I expect to leave here in Jan. or Feb. I hope it's sooner but there are a lot of boys that want to go home you know.

How everybody is over at the Swenson's now? Is Teddy still trapping? You will have to greet them for me.

I suppose pheasant season is in full swing now. Did Alf and the Dutchman and that other fellow come out this year? I sure would like to go out and shoot a few pheasants now. And of course I would like to eat them too.

There is a boy here that has a little deer or fawn for a pet. He caught it in Germany. It's just as tame as a dog. There are a lot of deer in Germany. We saw a lot of them when we were flushing Krauts out of the woods.

So you got that sword. I didn't really expect it to get there. I could have sent home a carload of rifles and other Kraut equipment but it isn't much to see.

I'm sorry it froze a little too early for the corn but I spose you can make use of it anyway.

So Curtis wants to enlist in the Marines. I know exactly how he feels but if I were him I would wait a couple of years. I spose he would have to enlist for four years. Well if I were him I'd be darn careful what I signed my name on. Anyway as you said, I wish he would wait until us boys come home.

I haven't been paid for September yet so I will be sending 2 months' pay at the end of October. I'm glad my allotments are coming regularly.

I should think they would be easing up on the tire rationing now. It is sure good to know that things are approaching normal now. Say Dad, there's a movie they made about the infantry. Ernie Pyle is the one who helped make it. I'd advise you to see it when it comes around there. "The Story of GI Joe" is the name of it. It's about the infantry in action over here and it's supposed to be the best war picture ever made. I haven't seen it yet myself but from what I hear it's pretty good.

Well I better close now. I hope this finds you all well and happy and may God bless you all. Goodnight

Love,
Verdie

Greet Shep, I spose he's busy helping hunt pheasants now.

The letter of October 23, 1945 was the last letter from me that we found in the attic. In my dad's letters he mentions later letters he received from me. The letters I wrote were probably less frequent and maybe my parents didn't always save them like they did while I was in combat. We are very grateful that my mom and dad saved as many letters as they did.

Important MP duties

Another MP post in France

One night I was dispatched from MP headquarters to pick up a medical doctor from a military hospital in Verdun, France. When I picked him up he directed me to a civilian house in the residential area of Verdun. When we got there he went in the house while I sat and waited outside in the cold jeep. There was snow and it was cold enough to put up side curtains on the jeep. I didn't believe that military doctors were supposed to be treating French civilians but didn't say anything that night and just took him back to the military hospital. A day or two later I was told to pick up the doctor again. I figured he was going to another place but he told me to go to the same house as the time before.

We returned to the same place and I waited outside in the Jeep again while he was in the house. When he came out the second time I asked him, "What were you doing at a civilian's house." It was none of my business but I was curious to find out what he was doing. "There is a woman here that has pneumonia and the only thing that will help her is this new miracle drug called Penicillin. She is recovering and maybe we won't have to go back again," he told me. We never did go back again and I took it for granted that the woman had recovered. That was the first time I had ever heard about Penicillin. So there were some humanitarian things I did as an MP.

The Unlikely travels of a Dollar Bill

The dollar bill that we signed in Verdun, France

One day while we were sitting up at MP Headquarters in Verdun, France a US Army truck driver came up to ask us for some help. The truck he was driving had been stolen while he and a load of GIs were celebrating inside a French wine shop. The GIs had all their belongings in duffle bags and were on their way to La Havre to catch a ship back home to the states. He came up to the MPs and said, "When I came out the truck was gone. I guess it was stolen", "Did you lock it up?" we asked him. "No I didn't," he said.

The French stole trucks if the Americans didn't lock them up and then they drove the trucks up into the mountains. The driver was supposed to put on a chain and lock the wheels. The GIs also should have kept someone outside to watch but all of the guys went inside to go drinking or in to the wine shop. "You will never see it again. The Army won't even look for it. Forget it about it. We can't leave our post to look for it," we told him.

The MPs could only report the stolen vehicle. We told him to call his outfit and tell them that the guys were stranded. We arranged to transport the driver back to Germany and the rest of the GIs found a ride to La Havre but all their belongings were lost forever.

Now the driver needed to stay in Verdun for a few days before he could get back to Germany. I told him he could come to our barracks to stay a few days. While he was there we started visiting and he told me he was from Boyd, Minnesota. That is about fifteen miles from Montevideo, Minnesota. He stayed for a while and got to know us. When it was time for him to leave he was very appreciative. He pulled out a US dollar bill which he wasn't supposed to have and said, "I want all you to sign it and I will keep it as a souvenir." A few of us went ahead and signed it. I never even thought about it again.

About fifty years later, an envelope arrived in the mail and when I opened it there was that same dollar bill. With it was a note that said, "I found this in my cash register and your named is signed on it so you might like to have it." It was from a woman who ran a café in Clarkfield, Minnesota. I used to stop and eat there when I was working on the road with the telephone company.

The only name I recognized on the bill other than mine was W.J. Everhart. It was all kind of strange that this same dollar bill that I had signed in Verdun, France in December of 1945 showed up in a Clarkfield, Minnesota café cash register over fifty years later. I didn't really investigate much because I figured the woman who found it didn't know how it got there. I didn't remember the name of the soldier truck driver from Boyd so there wasn't much to go on. Who knows how it got there but this was as good as any dollar for buying a cup of coffee at the café in Clarkfield.

A letter from my brother Roy

Hi Kid,   Monte, Minn Mandt Township
                                                  Monday November 19, 1945

Yes, I finally got home and it sure is grand. I suppose you know all about it already. Everyone is fine and looking great. How are you over there? Coming home soon I hope. I should have written sooner Verdie but you know how it is. This is the first letter I have undertaken since I came back and I am <u>Joe Blow Civilian.</u> Mom wrote to Earl yesterday and right now Dad is sitting across the table writing to Curtis. It's 8:30 in the evening now.

I suppose Mom told you about Eleanor and me getting spliced next Saturday the 24th. Yup, I'm going to do it Verdie. I hadn't planned to get married quite this soon after I got back but the ways things are now it's the only way out. You see I have no car to run around in and the tires are poor on Earl's car too so it's a little difficult to get around going forty miles up to Ell's folks you know. It would be an awful lot of driving if we were going to see each other every night of the week.

On the way back we stopped in San Diego for 10 days and I was sure surprised when Ell told me Curtis was there. He was only across the street from me so of course I saw him as soon as possible the next day. He is so big and tall now that I hardly knew him at first glance. "ha, ha." Neither him or the folks ever mentioned a thing about him wanting to enlist so I was struck dumb-founded that night. I know he doesn't like it but it's too late now eh? It will do him good though after all there is supposed to be peace time again. I guess he was getting pretty impossible about it at home now he has what he wanted. I wish he had waited until I got home but maybe it's best this way. Had I interfered with his wishes perhaps he never would have forgiven me. What do you think?

My old car is up on blocks in the shed with no tires on it. I bought a license and applied for tires but haven't had any luck. I haven't enough pull with the ration board I guess. "ha, ha." It's in pretty poor shape all around so I don't know whether I'll fix it up or not. I'll just forget about it until after our honeymoon. "ha, ha."

It really seems strange to be sitting here at home writing letters. So quiet here in the country it seems. It's kinda strange when a fellow is used to a lot of racket. I can hear the neighbors for miles around here every time they let a fart. "ha, ha."

So long Verdie. Hope you are fine and will be home soon. When you receive this letter I will be an old married man.

Love
Bro. Roy

Hello from Mom, Dad and Lyle

Another letter from my dad
You don't have to lay around in a
cold foxhole this winter

Dear Verdie,   Montevideo, Nov 25ᵗʰ 1945

How's everything? We are waiting to hear that you are packing up to leave for home. I bet you are too especially now when the big job is done. It's about 6 months since VE day so you should be entitled to start for home pretty soon but there are so many of you there that it takes a lot of transportation. We hope it will not be so very long before you show up here in the Town of Mandt again. We think Earl will be here by Christmas the way he writes. Curtis thinks he will get a furlough for Christmas so you should have been here to but we will make up for it later.

Clifford and me got through the corn about a week ago. We got about 800 bushels here at home so it wasn't so bad after getting that big hailstorm last fall. The rationing has been taken off everything now except sugar and tires. Roy applied for two new tires for his 36 Chevy but so far has not got any. We have not used his car since Curtis left when we took the best tires and put them on Earl's car. We will try to get both of them over hauled and some new tires as soon as we can get someone to do the job.

I have tried all fall to get somebody to do the work but they just give you a dirty look because they are so busy. We will be very glad when all you boys come back to help out. It seems funny but there is a bigger labor shortage now than during the war especially in this part of the country. You will not have to worry about work or a job when you get back.

As you know everything was put into the war effort so there is a lot of stuff we are short of. There is a big housing shortage and also very little farm machinery manufactured the last four years. There will be a lot of electric line and road building around here next year. We farmers are told to produce about the same as last year. (Provided our good Lord will help us along of course.)

It's kind of lonesome here tonight after Roy left it's just Ma, me and Lyle you know. Hoping you will be shoving off for this country pretty soon. I will say goodnight and may God bless and be with you.

Dad

P.S Will try and get the cars fixed up by the time you get home. We still have plenty of lutefisk and lefse and also pheasants.

It is so good to know that you don't have to fight and lay around in them cold foxholes this winter.

Og magne tak.

Dear Verdie,   Montevideo, Minn Town of Mandt
December 8, 1945

Hello there how are you? Received your welcome letter yesterday from November 26. Og magne tak. We are expecting Earl to show up most any day now. We hope he sends a telegram like Roy did. We like to be there when you boys step off of the bus or train.

The weather will not affect you as much when you come home as the boys from the Pacific. Roy was close to the stove when he had a chance. That 100-110 climate made the blood thin I guess but they will soon get used to this Minnesota again and feel pretty comfortable I believe.

Well the big shots in Germany are certainly getting their payment for the war crimes they committed and they are starting to deal it out to the Japs too. Well we don't feel a bit sorry for them either. Good riddance. They were the cause of a lot of pain, sorrow and misery in these last four years and you know a lot more about that than we do.

You asked about the corn crop, well it was not so bad. We got about 1000 bushels but nearly all of the corn is soft because of the cool and wet summer. It makes good hog and cattle feed. We have 59 hogs at present. We have only two cows milking but expect six next month so there will be plenty of cream when you come home.

We are hoping to see you home soon. Goodnite and May God Bless and Keep His protecting hand over you and bring you home safely and soon.

Dad

1945 Christmas card from Mom, Dad and Lyle

*1945 Christmas card from my sister Clarice, her husband
Clifford and their kids Delores and David*

*We went to Verdun, France. By this time it was about Christmas
and I got to go to a Christmas show there in 1945.*

January 1946 Paris, France

Posing by the Eiffel Tower in Paris 1946

Gourmet food after the war.....

In Paris after the war, the Army contracted the French to cook meals in the MP Barns and cafeterias. Now there were authentic French chefs and the food choices got real fancy. There were even menus on the wall but the words were all in French so we couldn't really read it. It didn't make any difference because we still were expected to eat what was served. Anyway I didn't recognize any of the names on the menu. There were always a few hundred GIs in line. When we got close in the chow line there was some breaded meat on a platter and it had a real fancy name.

I can still hear one guy who put some of this breaded meat on his fork and tried it. He yelled out for all of us to hear…SPAM!!!. I wish I had written down the French name it was called. There were always lots of remarks about the food and what we got to eat. The United States Army supplied the food for this cafeteria so I am sure it was the same as we got in our K-rations. It was made by Hormel and it was finely-ground meat. It never said Spam on the can but that is what we all called it. How could all of that meat be squeezed into a solid round piece in the can? It stuck together and we ate it with our hands. While in combat we never used a fork or spoon to eat it. We did have either a spoon or fork in our boot in case we needed it for a C rations that came in a bigger can.

Now in this fancy French cooking cafeteria we sat down at a table with some pieces of this bread meat the guy identified as spam and we ate with forks and spoons and drank out of real cups instead of metal canteen cups.

Switchboard Operator in Paris

After Christmas I "volunteered" for switchboard duty in Paris and this lasted until February. One time in Paris the GIs had a big protest because so many of us were still in Europe so long after the war. The protests didn't work and there still weren't enough ships for us to go home on. Another thing slowed everything up and that was a big dock strike in New York when the workers wouldn't unload any ships. The dockworkers figured it was prime time to get a settlement because the ships were needed to bring soldiers home.

Looking for a Good Camera in Paris

With a French camera that I bought at a store in Paris after the war was over.

In Paris there was PX where we could buy stuff like candy, cigarettes, and stationary and sometimes they may have a camera for sale. I wanted some pictures from Paris and thought I needed good a camera but you couldn't buy one just any place in the city. I had a French camera but I wanted a better camera. I hunted around in Paris trying to find one. It took a while because the French hadn't been making much of anything other than war materials during the war years

Occasionally the PX got a camera and here I found a 35 mm Argus C3. It was one of the first 35 millimeter cameras and top of the line. I knew it was the latest because my Cousin Arnie Gilbertson had bought one before the war and I knew that this was quite a deal at the PX. Cameras were quite expensive and the only way to purchase one was through a lottery. You couldn't just buy it; names were drawn to see who would get it. Both "Beehive" and I signed up for the camera lottery.

Then "Beehive" was transferred to another unit before the drawing. Most every day I went down and kept checking at the PX. Sure enough "Beehive" won the lottery to buy the camera. "He will never want the camera because he was never interested in taking pictures," I thought. If he didn't want it he could transfer his name to me so I could buy it. I got on the switchboard to try to trace him down calling all over to different outfits looking for him.

Finally, I found where he was located and got an answer. "I want to talk to WJ Everhart," I said. Nobody would have known who he was if I had called him "Beehive." "Beehive," I said, "You just won the drawing to buy the Argus camera in Paris. If you don't want it, somehow or another you could transfer it over to me and I will buy it." He decided he wanted it because if he brought it back to the states he could probably sell it for full price. It was an expensive camera in the states but a lot cheaper in the PX. He figured he might get a pass and come to Paris to get it.

As far as I know he never came back. I ended up using the French camera that pulled out in bellows. The film was probably 126 and it had a long focal length. It took pretty good pictures. It's an antique now. I used it a few times when I got back to the states.

After the war I brought the film home and got it processed at Brown Photo in Minneapolis. I still have the photos in an album and look at them when the kids and grandkids ask about my days in the Army.

CHAPTER SEVENTEEN

Ready to go back home
La Havre, France

L to R Douglas Woodard, Verdie Gilbertson, WJ Everhart

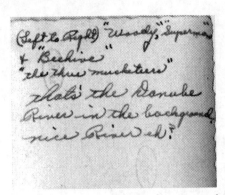

While waiting for the ship to take me home to the United States, it felt kind of like leaving a family. Here I was alone among hundreds of GIs. There were no familiar faces. Before this I figured I'd be so glad to be going home that I wouldn't care if I ever saw any of those guys again.

I thought of W.J. "Beehive" Everhart, Clyde Simmons, John Delewski, Douglas Woodard and others who had helped me make it through the rigorous training and the tough combat days in France and Germany. Beehive and I were together from Fort Bragg, North Carolina and all the way to serving as MPs in Paris, France after the war.

I had dug many a fox hole alongside these guys. Some dug real deep holes and others dug in just enough so their nose was below ground. Usually while one of us was in the foxhole asleep the other was in the same hole standing up wide awake and on guard listening and watching. We tried to time it for an hour each. One hour up and one hour down. We got pretty good at catching a quick sleep and then getting up to listen some more.

February 1946: Leaving the port of La Havre, France for Good Old USA

The duffel bag next to me is the same one I was issued at Camp Campbell, Kentucky when I first joined the Army in 1943. We carried our duffel bags on the ship to France and then left them there. We got them back in Germany after the war was over. Our name and number was stamped on the bag. Keeping track of the bags was probably the job of the quartermasters. Everything I had left in the bag when leaving the troop ship in October 1944 was still in there in May of 1945.

A list of approved items I brought back to the states

Souvenirs

When boarding the ship I had a "38 Caliber Belgique pistol" *(it was actually a 9mm Belgian Browning)* on my belt. On the gangplank there was an Army transportation officer that was checking our equipment as we loaded. "You can't take that on board," he said, "You have to turn it in to me. I'll take it." So I said, "This is personal property and I have a permit to carry it." "I still have to take it," he said. "Well if you take it you have to keep good care of it because I don't want the salt water to rust this good pistol. You'll have to clean it every day."

He took it and after we had been at sea for a few days my name came over the loudspeaker telling me to report to a certain place on this big ship. When I got there, here it was the same officer and he said to me, "Here, take your pistol, I am tired of cleaning it. Do you have any ammunition for it?" "No I don't," I told him. "The reason I took it," he said, "is because sometimes guys get in fights and we don't want anyone to get shot over a card game or something." I got my pistol and had to take care of it myself. It may have been better if he had kept it all the way to New York. I couldn't leave it anywhere because someone would be sure to take it so I had to carry it all the time while on the ship.

Atlantic Crossing

Leaning on the railing of our Victory ship heading home to the USA in February 1946

On a "Victory" ship traveling home via the North Atlantic Ocean in late February 1946

We left La Havre France in the last part of February 1946. We followed the Great Circle Route which was in the North Atlantic Ocean. It was a normal Atlantic crossing. This time we were only one ship unlike the 150 ship convoy we had going over to France in October, 1944. The first three or four days the sea was smooth, just small waves. When you get closer up to the North Atlantic in March it's the roughest time of the year. We were about 400 miles off the coast of Newfoundland and then the seas started getting rough. We started getting bigger and bigger waves until it got to the point that we were not allowed on deck anymore.

The water washed right over the top of the ship with the waves. Everything was locked down and we just rode it out. At night, as I was laying in the bunk the ship pitched and rolled and pitched and rolled. Sometimes it seemed like I might roll right out of the bunk as it lay right over on its side.

There was a lot of noise. Sometimes the bow came out of the water and when it hit the next wave there was a loud bang. The bow went down in the water again and then the propellers in the rear came out of the water. You could hear the engines speed up. Then they'd dig back in the water again. This kept up sometimes all night just pitching and rolling. That went on for probably two or three days and nights.

Finally we got out of that area which was the roughest part and it was a lot smoother with still some high waves but not near as bad. Of course this was in iceberg country. There was a bulletin board on the ship and I went there to take a look at the charts and maps. Each morning a pin was put in the map to show our location and how far we had come.

One morning I went down to the board and there was a note attached to the pin. It said, "Today we are passing over the same spot that the Titanic sunk in 1912." The note said the ocean was five or six thousand feet deep. We didn't know the exact location of the Titanic, but we probably passed right over it. The Titanic hit an iceberg but we didn't see any icebergs this time. Even though we didn't see any icebergs, we were a little bit concerned.

Many of the men were seasick much of the time. Of course the young guys still liked to have some fun when someone was in the bunk so sick he couldn't get out. Someone might say to the guy, "You know what I'd like to have now?" "No, what?" "A big fat pork chop." You know what happened of course.

There was a great big barrel down the middle. If a seasick guy couldn't make it to the bathroom he ran for the barrel. Sometime there were well guys standing around the barrel and there was no sympathy if you were seasick. Anyway, I was fortunate, I wasn't ever sick.

We had good meals and I don't remember missing any. There was a big container of boiled eggs up at the mess hall. The cooks said, "You can have all the boiled eggs you want." I'd take a bunch and stick them in my pocket. I'd be laying there on my bunk at night and once in a while, I ate a boiled egg. We were told, "Keep eating, the more you keep eating the less chance you have of being seasick." It seems like it should be the opposite. I was fortunate because I got by pretty well.

When we loaded at La Havre, I had made up my mind ahead of time that, "I'm going to get down in the troop department so I can get a top bunk." That was right below the ceiling or deck and was painted white. The top bunk had a quite a bit of room so you could sit up and everything else. I quickly threw my duffel bag on the top bunk and claimed it. It was pretty comfortable up there as I could sit up and read.

Coming over I had been stuck between two bunks and you were pretty tight with one guy below and one guy above. There were at least three levels and you had to climb from one bunk to another to get to the top.

Up in the mess hall when the sea was real rough the cooks tried to put food in our mess kits and sometimes missed. Some mashed potatoes and gravy might land on the floor. You could have stood on one side of the mess hall and slid to the other without even moving your feet. We stood up and ate. We never sat down. Luckily the crew picked up the food off the floor and always kept it clean.

Our entertainment was to sit on deck and ride up and down on the bow. Sometimes when the sea got rough someone from up in the bridge called down, "All right, get off the bow, you are going to get washed overboard." Sometimes we maybe stayed a little too long. It maybe wasn't the smartest thing to do but we thought it was fun.

I'd have given a week's pay

Finally on about February 12th, 1946 a ship was ready to leave La Havre, France with room enough to take us home after almost two years of infantry duty in France and Germany. The ship was busy filling up with battle- weary soldiers eager to make their way home to the good old USA. As I stood up on the deck watching soldiers come aboard, I could see one man was determined to bring his little dog friend along for the ride. It was against regulations to bring a pet on board so the MPs were very alert to keep the poor little dog from running up the gangplank. The dog was sent away a couple of times and then the master got on board. That seemed to be the end of the story but lo and behold that little dog showed up the next day as the ship was out to sea. Somehow he snuck onboard.

During the ten day voyage the little dog appeared every so often and the soldiers were glad to see him. Finally the ship landed in the New York Harbor. We were war- weary troops who were ordered to line up in a formation. A high powered second lieutenant dressed up in pressed officer's pinks and shiny boots started giving us battle hardened soldiers a lecture. We were all eagerly waiting to get processed and head for home.

Our patience was wearing thin as the officer went on and on. He was looking for us to show him some respect. Just then that little dog appeared and walked up to the front. The lieutenant kept on talking and didn't even see the dog but the men in the formation sure did. Just as the lecture got to a point where we could hardly stand it, the little dog lifted his leg and leaked right on the officer's leg. Well, the soldiers started laughing so hard that the lieutenant had to stop and just let us all move on. I laughed so hard that still to this day I'd have given a week's pay just to see that dog lift his leg on the officer's pressed pants.

Ready to Get Back Home

I sent this telegram to the folks back home on the farm on March 9th, 1946

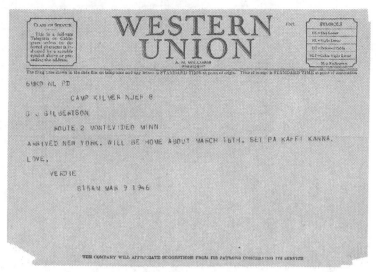

Telegram Western Union
From Camp Kilmer New Jersey

GJ Gilbertson
Route 2 Montevideo
Arrived New York. Will be home about March 16th. Set Pa Kaffi Kanna (translation, put the coffee pot on)
Love,
Verdie
8:15 AM March 9, 1946

Date__ **March 26**_____194**6**

OFFICE OF REGISTER OF DEEDS
STATE OF MINNESOTA
COUNTY OF CHIPPEWA

HONORABLE DISCHARGE

BY__ **United States Army**_____

TO__ **Verdie H. Gilbertson**___

Filed for record__**March 26, 1946**___

and recorded in Book__**"3"**_____

of Discharges, page__**523**_____

VERDI CLAGGETT
Register of Deeds

By_____Deputy

 # 105565

My honorable discharge registered by Verdi Clagget,
Chippewa County Register of Deeds

Transition from Military to Civilian Life

From a report written by my grandson Jacob. "Once back, Verdie tried to adjust to a civilian life but he said it was kind of strange and hard getting used to after being away for so long. To try and take his mind off of some of his memories of the war, he finally fulfilled his dream of becoming a pilot and even purchased a plane of his own."

My Stearman was my Psychiatrist

With my Stearman which helped me transition from soldier to civilian

The day was April 29, 1946 and I just bought a Stearman open cockpit airplane. I took it up for forty minute ride from the Montevideo airport. This was my first experience flying in an open cockpit biplane. It was very different from the Piper Cub and Luscombe and I enjoyed it very much. There was a big radial engine and there was a lot more wind and noise than the Piper Cub I had flown earlier in the day. I went from a Lycoming sixty five horsepower to a Continental 220 horsepower engine.

After the war, cars were hard to get and I had to get put on a waiting list. I checked back a few times and I wasn't moving up on the list. Then a guy told me that I would move on up the list if I slipped a few hundred dollars to the car dealer. I said there is no way I will do that. I loved to fly and there was a Stearman for sale. I had enough money from my years in the Army because I had sent it home and saved it. I decided to spend my hard earned Army money to buy the airplane for $1400. I hadn't found a full time job yet and wouldn't until I went to work for the telephone company in September.

During my transition from military life to civilian life, that Stearman was my psychiatrist. I was flying an open cockpit airplane and I could go up and enjoy the scenery. I was just sitting up there flying in the smooth air all by myself and it was three dimensional on all sides. I wasn't ground bound. I was more comfortable flying than driving.

CHAPTER EIGHTEEN

Civilians during and after the war

After people read my first book, some wanted to know more about my time in the war. It is very important to let people know what the civilians went through during the long war. What happened to them and what were their experiences? Civilians were a very big part of the war and we don't see their stories in war movies.

The story is not often told

For the civilians there was always a shortage of food and water and there was a very major shortage of living quarters. In some of the villages and even more in the cities, families lost their homes that were destroyed by bombs and artillery fire. They couldn't have gone to the insurance company and said, "My house was completely destroyed; will you pay for it?" There was no insurance company that was even close to big enough to cover expenses for all of the complete destruction. The civilians lost their homes and often a big part of their families in all the rubble.

Some small towns we came into we called "ghost towns." These were sort of spooky in a way. As we came in late at night the moon was shining and everything was white with snow piled on the rubble all around us. The roofs on the buildings were all gone. We could hardly find our way around because there was a Minnesota- type blizzard going on with blowing snow. We went up the stairs of a house and found a perfect place to set up our fifty caliber machine gun emplacements. I didn't think then about this being a home where a family had been living in peace before the bombs and the armies arrived. That night back in 1944 we were busy fighting a war and setting up our defense positions.

We were moving into one little village and there was no sign identifying it. The only way we knew where we were was by looking at the map. It was still really cold and before we had crossed the Rhine River into Germany. We were in Hottveiler, France. It was very close to the Maginot Line. This used to be a town filled with people in their homes. It was a community before the bombs, and now it was abandoned with not a soul in sight. We used some of the buildings for shelter but the town had not been lived in by anyone for a long time.

Civilians suffered even more than the military did. The old people, women, and babies were left behind when their husbands and sons were gone. They were struggling and trying to get along on their own. We actually talked to people and met face to face so I knew firsthand what they were going through. The infantry went into the towns to patrol on reconnaissance missions. The survivors told us the terrible things that had happened during the massive bombings.

Pforzheim, Germany had just been bombed; out of a population of 20,000 people, 12,000 people had lost their lives. The refugees who were left were living on the high part of town on the edges. When I had a chance to talk to some of the civilians up there, one middle- aged man told me that his daughter was downtown working in a factory when the bombs hit, and now she was down there in the rubble. He told us all about what happened when the bombers went over. He talked about his daughter and how she had been to the United States to get some education. There was probably no way to recover her remains because so many were buried in the rubble from all the destruction. The fires were still burning all over and the odor was just unbearable. When we talked with the survivors all of them were still kind of in a daze.

You don't hear too much about what really happened to the civilians during the war and the story is not often told. We saw so many civilians evacuating their homes and towns carrying their few belongings on carts sometimes with little kids riding on top. Some of the people had horses but most were just walking. As they moved along I watched and wondered, "Where are these people going to find food and water?" We met the civilians leaving town as we were going into a town. The people were fleeing to escape the violence of war and there wasn't much of anything we could do for them.

If we ran into homeless kids and we had some extra rations, we gave away whatever we could spare. We didn't particularly care if people were French or Germans or anyone else. To us they were just civilians; kids, old women, men and babies. That's just a lasting image that has always stuck in my mind.

Then there were all the homeless kids running around after the war in little bunches, and we were stationed in Pforzheim, Germany in an old German Army camp. There was a mess hall for us and we were using what the Germans had used before us. These homeless kids hung around the mess hall waiting for soldiers and when we came out- if you had a crust of bread or anything from the mess kit they'd grab it right out of your hand. Whatever went in the garbage cans the kids tried to fish out.

They carried a little tin can with a wire on it, reached their hand over the edge of the garbage can, and if there was a little bit of coffee in there, they'd pull it up—anything that was solid enough, went into their cans. Some of them were ten or twelve years old; some were smaller and some were bigger. These were just plain homeless kids separated from their parents during the war.

We gave the children whatever we could, and as far as I was concerned we could have let those kids come in the mess hall and eat. Later on, the Army started rounding up these homeless kids. I didn't get involved but talked to some who were. They went around in trucks and when a bunch of kids were spotted, the soldiers had to catch them on the run because the kids were scared. The American soldiers ran out, gathered the kids, and put them in the trucks. The German kids thought for sure that if the military grabbed them something bad may happen. The kids were taken to a center for homeless, displaced kids, where relief services fed and took care of them.

Parents came to the centers trying to find their lost children. The parents stood near the chow line or the food line when the kids went through to get their food. Mothers and fathers stood there and watched and see if their kids were waiting in the lines. I don't know how long this went on and how many were reunited. I do know that there were still many homeless kids running around for a long time afterwards.

Motivations of Civilians after the war

As we were walking back through Germany and France after the long war, it's difficult to explain my feeling while seeing the French civilians. When thinking about them I wonder about the motivations in the hearts and minds of the people in these towns. We saw a typical family that had been living in a house that was made of brick or the older ones were made of stone. There were very few wooden frame houses like I grew up in. One minute their houses were intact; when one artillery shell or a bomb hit a few minutes later, there wouldn't be anything left. Their homes were gone and most likely part of their family lost their lives.

We saw people very soon after it happened: a bomb hit and then they stood around just staring - not even talking because they were still in a state of shock. We hiked right through towns and saw civilians standing in the rubble looking at what used to be their homes. These people were the fortunate ones that had survived. Well, we had to think: this is war. Yes it was, and of course it was war at its very worst.

Months later, we came back through Germany and France after the war was over. As we were working our way back through, we went through some of the same villages. We saw people sitting on stools, boxes, or whatever there was to sit on. They'd be sitting next to the piles of rubble with a chipping hammer, chipping the mortar off the bricks, and cleaning them in order to salvage the ones that weren't broken. You could see stacks of bricks in neat piles and there were little piles of bricks all over. Some people grabbed other bricks and sat there, tap, tap, tap, cleaning and salvaging bricks and putting them up on the many piles.

Standing there wondering and looking, I asked myself, "How could you get enough motivation to sit there looking at all of the destruction and then even get started?" How in the world could any of them even know where to begin? It looked like it was impossible to get something out of all those piles of rubble and make something out of it so you could work to rebuild a house to live in. It took minutes to completely destroy their home and other buildings and now it may take these folks many years to make a new home.

Now, what drove those people to do this rather than just walk off and leave it all behind? There wasn't any choice or any other place to go. It would have been nice to have a camera then so people could really get a firsthand knowledge of what war does to the civilian population, including women and kids. The old people had no place to go. They couldn't go to the insurance company and then hire a contractor to rebuild. There was nothing like that for this situation. They were completely on their own trying to salvage their lives and most likely part of their family was gone or missing.

We saw the suffering of the civilians both enemy and allies. When you see that, it is no wonder that you become completely anti-war. The civilians we saw were both French and German. It doesn't make any difference which side you are when you see people suffering. So when you talk about motivation; how were the people able to build up enough to even start on something like that? It's just like I took a picture of it, and can see it now just like a photograph stored right in my mind. It is so vivid. This is just one instance where I can talk about civilians and what suffering I witnessed them going through. There are many more examples I could talk about.

Civilians clearing a roadblock at Ludwigshafen, Germany, as 100th Division infantrymen move in to continue mopping-up operations. March 1945.—U.S. Army

Humanity in War Time

My fellow division member wrote in our newsletter that one time he was going back to the battalion aid station where all the wounded American soldiers were sent. As he walked through an area where there had been a firefight, he heard a moaning noise and here it was a wounded German officer. He went over to him and the man could still talk. Somehow the American soldier rolled him over. The German kept saying, "beutel, beutel." That meant wallet in German. In the wallet was a picture of his family and he asked the American to lay the wallet with the picture right on his chest so he could see his family. The German wanted the photo to be up close to his face. So the American soldier opened the wallet and laid it on the German officer's chest. The German father and husband laid there and looked at his family.

Then the American soldier went back to the aid station to ask the litter bearers to pick up a wounded soldier. The litter bearers got up and went to the wounded soldier as he had requested. They saw the wounded man and said to the American, "That's a Kraut. We are not carrying him back." The American soldier patted the M1 on his shoulder and said, "You are either taking him back or you will take his place." The litter bearers picked him up right away, and the American followed along as they carried the German officer back to the battalion aid station. The medics put him on a cot and started treating him right then.

"By gosh the medics got him patched up," said the guy telling the story. "Later," he said, "I was going back to the medic tent and the medic hollered to me. "Hey, this Kraut wants to talk to you." The American soldier walked over to the German officer who was lying on a cot. The German officer looked up at him and said, "I want to thank you for what you did for me."

That is another instance I heard about. This was impressive and made me wonder, "Why does a guy do this for an enemy soldier?" The question comes up, "Who is my neighbor?" There are many sides to war. It may not be a common occurrence to help our enemies but it did happen several times in my experience. We usually hear hero stories but in this case no one got medals, it is just stories of humanity during war time.

"Adopts" a homeless German boy

One night in Verdun, France I was off duty and went to get something to eat at a place in town. One of the Army guys in there had found a young fifteen- year- old boy running around in town and by himself. The soldier decided he was going to "adopt" this kid. The kid looked like he was German but he spoke both French and German. The American soldier took the boy along with him wherever he went; even in this eating place where drinks were also served. He had cut an Army uniform down to fit the kid and he stayed right with the soldiers all time. Wherever the soldiers went, the young boy followed along. While he hung around with the soldiers, they were trying to teach him to speak some English. Of course he was taught a few words he shouldn't have been learning. He said something and then all of them laughed because he was speaking a few inappropriate words.

One time I asked, "What are you going to do with him when you go back to the states?" "Oh," he said, "I am taking him to the states with me; I am not leaving him here." The soldier was just a young guy about my age around 21 years old. "You know," I said, "It could be a little problem when you get on board the ship with a little German kid. You know you can't just take the kid; he might have a family here. He may find his family some time, we don't know. Do you think the Army will let you do that, just have the kid get on a ship?" With plenty of confidence he told me, "Oh, I am not leaving him here, I will think of something. Somehow or other I am getting him back to the states, I'm keeping him."

He had gotten so attached to the kid that he wasn't going to leave him in France after the war. Just imagine the kid meeting his new folks in the states and talking like the soldiers had taught him with plenty of swear words. I left before finding out what happened with the soldier and the kid so I never found out how everything came out. Maybe he managed somehow to take the kid to the states or the kid had to stay in France. That young soldier was determined to help this young kid after the war. This is another example of the caring and compassion of an American soldier.

"Me want to go back to jail"

After the war was over our MP outfit was stationed in Verdun, France. One boy was all by himself and he was about fourteen or fifteen years old. An MP caught this kid breaking into the warehouse at the camp where the American Army's food was stored. The kid had been in the warehouse just looking for some food because he was hungry. This was an MP unit at the time so he hadn't really picked a good outfit to steal from. Of course he was arrested and put in the prison close by where American soldier prisoners were kept for whatever crimes they had committed.

There weren't any German prisoners of war in this prison. The young boy was put in a cell like the rest of the American prisoners. It was just across the street from the MP headquarters there in Verdun. It was an old French prison that looked like it must have been a dungeon from way back in the medieval times. There was a real high wall around it and a big heavy wooden gate.

The jailer brought this young kid with him over to the mess hall; he never ate with the rest of the prisoners. He was a nice kid and we got used to him as he sat and ate together with all of us. We didn't know if he was German or French because he spoke a little of both. He had no idea where his parents were and how long he'd been running around no one knows. He had gotten separated from his family during the long war. Maybe his family was gone, nobody knew.

This went on for quite a while until one day the jailer thought the kid had served his sentence. "You are free and you can leave," the jailer told him. One night when I was visiting at the jail, the jailer told me, "It wasn't very long after the boy left when one night there was some pounding on the big wooden gate. When I heard the pounding, I went out there to check to see who was at the gate. Here it was the young boy again. The kid said to me, "Me want to go back to jail again."

The kid spoke some English and he wanted to go back to a place where he had something to eat and a place to sleep. So the jailer said, "Well come on in and you can find a cell where you can sleep." He let him stay and come back to the mess hall and eat with us again. He stayed there as long we were there and when we transferred to another place I lost track of the young boy. It was good that some American soldiers had compassion for these homeless kids.

Infantry: First into Town

There are many stories about civilians and what happened in their lives. There could be whole books written about the civilian's conditions and what their lives were like. We saw them standing there in the rubble with their homes gone and no water systems working and no electric power. The infantry were always the first ones into the towns and the civilians were standing in the rubble just staring at us. The civilians hadn't seen any American soldiers before us and now there were a bunch of young teenage soldiers slogging through town with M1s slung over their shoulders. Some just stared at us and some of the civilians talked with us. It didn't seem like we were the ones blamed for all of the destruction around us. The people in the towns knew it was the bombers and artillery that had done that. It wasn't the young infantry guys who destroyed their homes. We didn't go after the civilians or blow up their houses. It seemed like there wasn't really any hate for us.

Of course we gave any rations we could to the kids that were wandering around. We didn't care if they were French or German or anything else. The word must have spread because whenever we got to another town the kids came running up to the soldiers. Maybe we were the first American soldiers to get to their town. I couldn't believe this. It seems like these children would be so afraid of enemy soldiers. It didn't seem like any of them were afraid of us at all. Once the kids found out the American soldiers gave out our food rations they came up real close to us. We didn't carry much food as we just had K rations but we gave the kids what we could.

It seemed like the infantry guys had the most compassion. Later on when the "rear echelon" came in with their big trucks a few were known to loot. Not all of them of course. The infantry couldn't carry anything besides what we needed to get by in the midst of the war. A lot of my impressions of the war came from what went on beyond the military stuff as I saw how the civilians suffered and were left with absolutely nothing. These people had many difficult years of war and were on their own just trying to survive with no place to go and no place to find any food and supplies. We saw many thousands of people like this.

It made quite an impression on me when seeing all of this. No one really prepared us for it. There wasn't a meeting beforehand to get us ready for what we might run into. No American soldiers had been there before so no one knew what to expect. We just went in there as the German Army was leaving in retreat. There was no way to prepare us for what we were going to see. We were all the same with no one helping the other guy to cope with what we saw. The officers had never seen the aftermath of war and didn't know how to talk to the young infantry guys. No matter what rank we were, we all went in there on equal footing. You could never really know about it until it happened.

What happens to the country and civilian population in a war is more than anything you can ever imagine. You can't even begin to convey just how much suffering the civilians went through. There is no real way to describe the sounds, smells and emotions of war. There were wounded civilians all over the place as the infantry went through the towns. It was hard to figure how their injuries could be taken care of as all the hospitals were bombed out. Those suffering couldn't get medical attention.

What about the parents with kids who were wondering just how to take care of all of this? If more people saw this first hand by putting their feet right there and seeing it happen: bang, right there, they'd be mighty careful before even mentioning starting a war. But then there are not many people who ever see anything like what I saw during this war.

Verdie Gilbertson

by Jacob Gilbertson
From a report my grandson Jacob presented
in his 11th Grade History Class 2003

Born on September 7, 1923, Verdie Gilbertson was the third of four sons of Selma and Gerhard Gilbertson to enter into the war. He went in with the thirst for adventure and travel, and came back with many memorable experiences and stories that he could share with his children and grandchildren.

Verdie was young when he decided to enlist in the army, only 19 years old, a year removed from high school. He wanted to be a pilot, and a good way for him to achieve this goal was to join the Army Air Corps. However things didn't play out exactly as Verdie had planned when he got to basic training. At the base you were allowed to choose the branch of the Army that you wanted to go into. After two months of basic training he chose the Army Air Corps in hopes of fulfilling his dream of becoming a pilot. It wasn't soon after his new training began, that his plans were changed yet again, but this time not by his own choosing.

The U.S was beginning to plan the upcoming invasion of Europe, and needed much more ground support than air support, so Verdie's division was now forced to switch to infantry. His dream of being a pilot had to be put on hold.

Once in the infantry, Verdie underwent specialized training as a mortar-man and traveled many different places across the U.S in preparation for the much anticipated European offensive. Fort Campbell

Kentucky, Oklahoma, North Carolina, and New York were a few of the places he was stationed at in order to get ready to go over to Europe.

In this training he underwent many new challenges and experiences including getting hit with one of his own countrymen's bullets on the firing range, a story which he was only too eager to tell me. According to him, he was going through his normal training at the firing range one day and was standing upright when all of the sudden he felt a little pain in his chest as if somebody hit him with a stone. He looked down in his breast pocket where the pain had occurred, and to his surprise found a bullet lying inside of it!

Verdie maintains that it was probably a defective round that had been fired out of someone's gun and ricocheted off of the ground to hit him, but nonetheless counts himself very lucky to have come out of the situation without any harm.

With the rest of his training gone by without further incident, and after much anticipation, Verdie boarded a ship from New York in October 1944 to go over to France. It was only about three months after D-Day and troops were still being sent over to ensure the advancement of the Allied forces.

After a two- week- long sea voyage, Verdie and the other members of 100th Infantry Division, 399th Regiment landed on the shores of Marseilles, France and prepared for their advance through France and north on up to Germany, where they stayed until the end of the war.

Verdie doesn't like to talk much about the fighting he encountered during his term of duty but, from what we can gather from past reports and news of where he was, the battles and exchanges were heated and resulted in many fatalities. It was war, after all. But no, Verdie likes to talk more about the many towns he went through, the new people he met, and the new culture he was able to experience from being over in a new place. He thinks more about the good things and experiences during the war rather than dwelling on any bad ones he might have had.

You ask him to tell you a story about the war and he laughs. He will tell you about the rations he had. He didn't think the food was so bad but one time a starved dog wouldn't take some from the soldiers. Or he will tell you about how the guys in his company were like a family, and looked out for each other. It's a lot more interesting listening to those types of stories, than hearing some old guy talk about a battle you haven't even heard of, and that he will get upset about.

During his time over in Europe, Verdie went through many important towns and landmarks on his regiment's advance through France and Germany. They went through the Vosges Mountains of France as well as the French towns of LaSalle, Lyons, and Lorenz. On their way they also passed the Maginot Line which had been originally built by the French in World War 1 for protection from Germany. In Germany is where they spent most of their time and went through many towns including Manheim, Tintertalb, and Heisenberg.

The 100ᵗʰ Division also passed the German defense against all countries to the West (now useless) which was called the Siegfried Line. Verdie's regiment remained in Germany until the war was finally over.

After the war was over it was still a long time before Verdie was able to go back home. There was a shortage of ships available for the voyage back so Verdie and the other members of his company stayed in Europe and worked as Military Police for almost another year. The army seemed to think that the infantry would be good for this job and they didn't disappoint.

Finally, after almost a year and a half in Europe, Verdie and his regiment were allowed to return home which made many of them very grateful. Once back, Verdie tried to adjust to a civilian life but he said it was kind of strange and hard getting used to, after being away for so long. To try and take his mind off of some of his memories of the war, he finally fulfilled his dream of becoming a pilot and even purchased a plane of his own.

He describes his plane as being kind of like his therapist after the war. Verdie also worked on his family farm for a while, and worked for the Northwestern Bell Telephone Company upon his return. Along with the work he performed, Verdie also received many medals for his service once he got back including the Bronze Star, Combat Infantry Badge, and the American Defense Medal. Don't ask Grandpa to talk about these medals though because he is very modest.

All in all Grandpa says he had a pretty positive experience while in the Army, but looking back on it he says he wouldn't have served in the military again if given the chance. He says then that he was young and adventurous, but now he is older and wiser and knows better.

CHAPTER NINETEEN

The sons of Gerhard and Selma Gilbertson

They served their country in the military during War II

Verdie, Curtis, Roy and Earl Gilbertson

PFC Verdie Gilbertson
PFC Verdie Gilbertson
US Army
100th Division
399th Regiment
2nd Battalion
Company F
4th Platoon
France and Germany
Combat Infantry Badge, Bronze Star Medal, Three
battle stars, Presidential Unit Citations

THE UNITED STATES OF AMERICA

TO ALL WHO SHALL SEE THESE PRESENTS, GREETING: THIS IS TO CERTIFY THAT THE PRESIDENT
OF THE UNITED STATES OF AMERICA AUTHORIZED BY EXECUTIVE ORDER, 24 AUGUST 1962 HAS AWARDED

THE BRONZE STAR MEDAL

TO PRIVATE FIRST CLASS VERDIE R. GILBERTSON, UNITED STATES ARMY

FOR meritorious achievement in ground combat against the armed enemy
during World War II in the European African Middle Eastern
Theater of Operations.

GIVEN UNDER MY HAND IN THE CITY OF WASHINGTON
THIS 21st DAY OF May 19 91

THE ADJUTANT GENERAL   SECRETARY OF THE ARMY

My Bronze Star Medal Certificate

Cpl. Roy Gilbertson
Cpl. Roy Gilbertson
US Marine Corps

Second Marine Division

2nd Tank Battalion
3rd Platoon
Tank Commander (flame thrower)
Saipan, Tinian, Okinawa
Bronze Star Medal, 3 Battle Stars, 2 Presidential Unit Citations

Together... in Peace and War...
Montevideo American December 22, 1944

Cousins Share Marine Careers

By Tech Sgt. Pete Zurlinden Marine Corps combat correspondent Somewhere in the Pacific (Delayed)

Two Montevideo, Minnesota Marines-cousins in fact- who enlisted together to help defeat the Axis and see the world too, have never been separated in almost three years. Privates First Class Calmer Ellingson 26, and Roy Gilbertson 29, both of Route 1 Montevideo, were sworn in as Marines on January 24, 1942, have service serial numbers in sequence and have been stationed together in Alaska, Bremerton, Washington, the Hawaiian Islands and with the famed Second Marine Division.

During the past summer the pair fought together at Saipan and Tinian, in the Marianas Islands taking on the Japs as Ellingson puts it, "Just about like we used to take on the Montevideo boys in neighborhood scraps when we were grade school kids- side-by-side."

Back in Montevideo the boys grew up on their parent's farms. At Pearl Harbor time they decided to enter service together selecting the Marine Corps because a leatherneck career appealed most to their imaginations.

"We asked the recruiting sergeant if we could stick together," said Gilbertson. "His reply was to the effect that we just might land in the same recruit platoon at San Diego-but after that, well anything might split us up- and probably would.

Roy Gilbertson and Calmer Ellingson somewhere in the Pacific

Sgt. Earl Gilbertson
Sgt. Earl Gilbertson
US Army
96th Infantry Division
382th Regiment
Company H
Saipan, Okinawa

Heavy Weapons Company with 81mm mortars and heavy 30 Caliber Machine Guns

Earl was a machine gun squad leader

Mishap Reunited Gilbertson Boys
Montevideo American May 18th, 1945

A misfortune which turned into a bit of good luck sent Army Sgt. Earl wounded in action in Okinawa to the island on which his brother, Marine corporal Roy Gilbertson was stationed. Needless to say the joy which the brothers experienced overshadowed the discomfort Earl suffered from the slight wound. The incident also brought about Earl's meeting with Calmer Ellingson a neighbor back home.

Mr. and Mrs. Gerhard Gilbertson of Route 5, Montevideo last week learned of the meeting of their two sons in a letter which came to them from Roy. Portions of the letter follow:

Dear Mom and Dad,

I have a very pleasant surprise for you. I saw Earl today. Yes, I spent the afternoon with him. He is in the hospital but take my word for it he is getting along fine and will be as good as new shortly. He received shrapnel in his neck and hips. One piece in the neck and four pieces in the left hip but it isn't serious. He said his neck was a little stiff but otherwise he wouldn't even know he was hit.

We had supper together and strolled around outside for more than an hour. Earl said he had to get some exercise so he can keep his appetite sharp. We sat outside in the shade all afternoon and talked and talked some more. It was a thrill to see him and I believe he was as happy as I was. Cal was with me.

I received his message about one o'clock and it didn't take me a shake of a lamb's tail to get there. He had tried all morning to get the message through but they couldn't locate me until noon. He was expecting me but he didn't notice us when we walked in as he was sitting on his bunk facing the other way. Well we walked right up behind and I said, "How are you getting along Earl?" He said, "Roy and Calmer." We were both so excited I guess that neither one of us spoke for a second, then we both spoke at once. "Gee it's sure nice to see you again." Makes a person feel sort of funny you know when we hadn't see each other for so long.

Love,
Roy

Earl's Purple Heart Medal

Cpl. Curtis Gilbertson
Cpl. Curtis Gilbertson
1st Marine Air Wing
VMO # 6

Tsingtao, China

The 1ˢᵗ Marine Aircraft Wing had planes and men at airfields in China at Tsingtao, Tientsin, and Peiping.

A letter to my brother Curtis

Hi "Leatherneck,"   *Sunday Nov 11, 1945*   *Rheims, France*

Well how do you like the Marines? I sure was surprised to hear you had enlisted. I didn't know it before you had left. I sure hope you like it. It will be lot of good experience for you and you'll get to a quite a bit of the world too. I suppose boot camp training is pretty rugged but you'll get used to it. It takes about 3 or 4 months to get used to military life.

I am glad Roy and Calmer could visit you. I can imagine you had plenty to talk about. I had a letter from Mom and she said Roy was in Minneapolis.

I'm an MP now. I don't exactly care to be an MP but I don't have any choice you know. I'm on duty six hours every other day so it isn't hard work. I don't have to stand any formation, no reveille, retreat or inspections. I can sleep as late as I want to when I'm off duty and I sure take advantage of it. I live in a tent but it has wooden walls and we have a stove and radio so it isn't so bad. This town is plenty rough. There has been quite a few murders and knifings and plenty of fights and drunks.

We had a parade today for Armistice Day you know. This outfit can't parade worth a darn. It hasn't had any practice and the infantry is the only outfit that can parade. I was glad to get out of the infantry but when it comes to parading the infantry sure had this outfit beat.

A year ago tomorrow is a day I'll never forget. That was the first time we attacked the Krauts. We got them off the hill and when we got up there our own artillery started shelling us and then the Kraut artillery started in too. We hadn't even dug in but it didn't take long to get a hole dug.

I got paid today. I'm getting $17 more a month now. The French government is paying us some sort of bonus. I'm getting $91 a month now. I am still getting my Combat Infantry pay.

Well I'll have to go for now. I have to be on duty at 12:00 tonite. Write soon

So long,
Bro. Verdie

Curtis standing by an F 4U Corsair fighter. He was stationed in Tsingtao, China in 1947 while the Chinese Communists and Chinese Nationalists were fighting.

The Home Front while the boys were off to war

My parents and the people at Mandt Church said so many prayers for us back home and that helped all four of Gerhard and Selma's boys make it through the war years. My dad always said that when the war is over. "I am going to ring the church bell until it almost falls off." The minute it was announced on the news the war was over in Germany Dad hurried up to the church and rang it a long time. Even after the war had ended in Germany, the war went on for Roy and Earl in the Pacific so the celebration was not so long.

Then when my dad got the official news that Japan had surrendered in August of 1945, he was right up at the church again ringing the bell and he rang it even longer this time because now all four of their sons could come home. Our parents had a very strong faith and a great belief in the power of prayer. I am very grateful for that. You can just imagine the celebration and relief of all the families when the war ended. It wasn't just knowing that we had won the war, but more that the fighting was over and our boys were out of danger now. At the time it was a bigger relief for our parents than it was for us. Their long worry and anxiety was over. Many times I told them not to worry but I doubt that they were relaxed and worry free.

In addition to the war, our parents had gone through many years of the Depression and the drought which had meant many years of stress and uncertainty even before us boys went off to fight overseas. Our parents had done their best to keep the farm going and have enough food to feed our big family; then as soon as life straightened out some and we started getting crops and a little money, World War II started. So from 1930 to 1946 there were sixteen years of one thing after the other. It seemed like all of it just kept on and on.

CHAPTER TWENTY

Nice comments to a world war two vet

A man who was a young boy during the war said to me when he saw I was a World War Two vet "Thank you for letting me grow up". It was at the state capital in St. Paul in 2008. My daughter Kay took me down there for a ceremony honoring WW II veterans. This was the first time after the war that I remember ever being thanked for my service in the Army. Each veteran got a medal with a red, white, and blue ribbon. The woman who put the medal on my neck gave me a big hug and said to me, "Thank you for serving our country." It was great to be remembered and I am sure grateful for this after all these years. It is very nice that even people who were born after WW II appreciate our service.

In 2009 a Mexican- American man was carrying out my groceries at Bill's Supermarket store in Montevideo. When he spotted my World War Two veteran's license plate, he shook my hand and said, "Thank you for serving *our* country.

My World War Two veteran's license plate

A Special Trip to Washington, DC

By Judy Swenson
Courtesy of Montevideo American News
May 26, 2011

Speaking about his recent Honor Flight trip to Washington, D.C., in April, Verdi Gilbertson said in an exuberant Norwegian lilt, "It was just amazing! I couldn't believe the reception we got at all these places. I thought World War II had kind of faded back ... you know ..."

Gilbertson was having his morning coffee with a booth full of companions at Valentino's restaurant when this reporter caught up with him. His enthusiastic laughter and lighthearted banter were contagious. When he finally put down his latest gadget, an electronic notebook, Gilbertson described his trip, with jubilation. "Well, we went on this trip and I couldn't believe it.

"At the airport when we left from Sioux Falls there was a whole line up there, military people and kids. "In Baltimore, when the plane taxied in, a fire truck was out on the runway blowing a stream (of water) over the top of the airplane. They said it was kind of like a salute. "And then, when we got off the airplane in Baltimore, the same thing. There was a big reception with people from the Navy, the Army and the Marines, even a two-star general," laughed Verdi.

"We stayed at the Westin Hotel — talk about luxurious! I can't believe how they treated us. I never expected that. One of my favorite parts was when all these elementary school kids showed up with their little artwork. I got a whole pile of them. Then they wanted to take pictures with us and shake our hands. You'd think we were some kind of hero or something. They studied it (WWII) in school and they were so congenial. That's one of the big things that the young kids learn about it. To them, it's history. So we were maybe like historical figures ... kind of like antiques," he said, with a hearty laugh.

*At the World War II Memorial with a card one of the school kids gave to me.
It says, "You're Heroes, You're my Hero, Thank You for your service."*

He said another highlight was being able to have his family with him. "It was like a family reunion!" Verdi was accompanied by his two sons, Greg and Keith, two grandsons, Matthew and Eric, as well as Matthew's girlfriend *(now his wife)*, Amanda, and her mother Chon Hwa. "That was really nice. I was glad that they could come. Then of course you meet so many guys that I didn't know before to visit with and talk with. Of course, we didn't have a lot of time. It was only two days and we were so busy."

Keith, Eric, Matthew, Verdie, Greg and Amanda at the
World War II Memorial in Washington, DC.

"We had a (heroes) banquet at the Westin Hotel in Arlington, where we stayed overnight. "Oh, talk about fancy," he quipped. "The waiters were dressed up just real formal with ties and stuff. Cloth napkins and three forks here (gesturing toward the left of his coffee cup) and one up here."

"I learned from a long time ago, you always start from the left side," he said, teasing. "So you'd better not make a mistake or you'd be in trouble. "The highlight was the World War II Memorial. We went to the Navy Memorial, the Marine Memorial and the Korean War Memorial and we drove by the Capitol and the White House. "I thought maybe Obama would be out on the porch up there waving, but we didn't see him. He's too busy, you know. He was in Florida at the space launch, which they didn't do. It's the last one, you know. So the only high ranking dignitary was Senator Dole at the memorial. It would have been fun to shake his hand, but there were so many people lined up. He left just before we got close enough to him. He's a World War II vet. He was wounded and he can't use his right arm."

"When I was overseas I was in the infantry. So my job was on a mortar." Gilbertson trained in Kentucky, North Carolina, Texas, Oklahoma and New York before being sent overseas as an infantryman.

"We backpacked across France and Germany," he said. While a few war stories were shared on the *Honor Flight* journey, Gilbertson said they don't talk about them much at home. "Nobody believes them anymore anyway," he said with a laugh.

CHAPTER TWENTY ONE

Closing Thoughts

I am thankful for 92 years with a good family,
good friends and good health.
There is always something new to think about and to accomplish.
We are happy to have published three books
for our whole family to enjoy.
Takk for alt
Thanks for everything
Du fa lave sa vare
I wish that you live well
Det er slik det var
That's the way it was

Some original handwritten letters

My mother's first letter when I was in combat

Montevideo Minn
Nov 3rd 1944

Dear Vurdis.

Were we ever glad to hear from you again today. and that you had landed safely means so much for you and all of us too.

We were thinking you maybe would land in England But understand you went to france instead. Sure was nice you didn't get seasick on the way as that must be pretty tough to be sick on a ship like that.

How many days were you on the water maybe you can't tell us that. but it is strange to step of the ship on the other side of the Big Water But our prayers are and we know yours are too that God keeps his protecting hand over you & bring you safely across coming back home again It going to be a great wonderful day when all our loved once return and there is peace all over the world again. It cant come too soon.

We were so happy to hear from Earl again on Wed. after waiting for six long weeks to hear from him He cant say were he is. et. But that he is allright is the main thing.

We are worried that he is in Phillysine Islands someplace. and that is a pretty place right now. We had a letter from Roy today too. He is still on

Saiyers and was allright" which means so much Russell & Arthur has been home on a few days leave. He left again on Tuesday so imagine he is soon back to camp again by this time.

His in a camp named Shoemaker close to San Francisco he expects to get shipped out anytime the way he talked. imagine he will go to S. pacific then

Milo Pederson lift today you know he enlisted in the Navy a while ago and has been home on a 24 hour call.

Roy said he was waiting to hear from you again. So if you have time you better write him soon. I havent met Phyllis since you was home yet dont spose she goes to Monte very often either.

We have been having real nice Indian summer here for a long time now. But think its due for a cold spell now as its blowing from the N. west tonite and is pretty cold out. But we havent had any snow yet. Hope we dont have any either for at least another month.

Say Birdie if there is anything you want us to send you you have to request it as we cant send any packages except x mas packages without a request from you.

We will be glad to send anything you want just let us know.

Glad you got mail already we were wondering about that. Say Birdie i know you would like to get the Monte americans but you have to request that too So you better do that soon and we will subscribe for you than you get it more regular.

Curtis is working for Alvin & Lowell picking corn. They still have about 2 weeks left yet.

Curtis is still taking flying lessons don't know how many hours he has he will have to write and tell you about that i guess.

The plane has been out here a couple times its kind of interesting to watch them too.

Hope you have good eats where you are and hope you get a nice Thanksgiving dinner too.

Wish i could send you pheasents & such like i did last year at this time. But i spose thats out of the question now.

Hope and pray you boys are all back when next Thanksgiving comes around then its going to be real Thanksgiving day.

May God grant it to us very soon.

Hope this finds you feeling fine and hope to hear from you soon again.

We are all the same as ever. am enclosing a picture of all the boys that were home on furlough at the same time, sent a one to Ellington. They all look real good.

So long then Verdie
& God Bless you

Greetings from all
Love Mother.

My mother's first letter after we arrived in France. We still have it because I wrote her a letter on the back of this one. This is a very precious letter.

Dear Mom;   Fri. Dec. 15

I'm in a house again right now. There is a fire going in the stove so I'm nice & comfortable. I got a letter from Mildred & I from Caryl the _____ a bit of snow by now. I spose you've had a few snowstorms too. I bet you're glad that you've got the new road.

Well, only 10 more shopping days 'till Christmas. I bet everything is plenty scarce & hard to get. That's what everybody is saying. We had church services the other day and we sang some Christmas carols. It made me homesick. I imagine you will have the program in church pretty soon now. It won't seem much like Christmas here but we feel the real meaning of Christmas so much anyway and that is the main thing. I wish I could get hold of a few Christmas cards to send at least. I got only 3 sent.

Have you heard from Carl lately? I spose you hear from Roy quite often.

I expect the war over here should be over soon now. That will be a wonderful day. The Japs are going back plenty steady too.

It's only a little over 2 weeks left of 44 too. I hope & pray that 45 will get the world settled down to peace again.

Say, would you send me the addresses of some of the boys over here that I know? Maybe I could run across some of them. I met another fellow I went to radio school with back in the states.

How are Abner & Sam coming along now? Greet them from me will you?

Hope, I have to close again now. I'll write again as soon as I can. So long for now. God Bless you all.

Love, Verdie

Wednesday
Jan. 3, 1945 evening

Dear Dad,
Happy New Year to you all! I'm a little
late as usual but you know what
a doughboy is like. How did you
celebrate New Years? I imagine things
were pretty quiet. New Year sure came in
with a bang here. I saw the new year
in too. I think we all celebrated by saying
a prayer to God that this year will be
a peaceful year.

I received your letter the other day &
today I got Moms mailed Dec. 23. Thanks
a million. And I got a very nice box
from Styl today with plenty of stationery
& candy. I was so glad to get it.

Oh I have to tell you. I got the combat
infantryman's badge the other day. I'm
kinda proud of that. To get it you have
to see action under small arms fire
like rifles & machine guns, and also artillery
fire. I feel that I've earned it too 'cause
I've been on the front lines for 63 days
now. I didn't do anything heroic to get it tho.
I also got a $10 a month raise with it so I
get $74.80 a month now. The badge is something
us infantrymen get when we've seen action.
Maybe you've seen pictures of them. It has
a silver rifle on a blue background
with a wreath around it. I'm planning
to send it to either you folks or Styl to
keep for me. I never get a chance to dress
up over here so I don't think it's any use
to keep it over here.

I'm glad to hear that you're all okay.
I'm just fine. We've got it pretty nice now so
don't worry a bit about me. I get a chance

to stay in a building once in awhile & that really helps. I've gotten so many good clothes too now. I've got a fur lined overcoat & wool lined pants. I've also got shoes that look just like those hunting pacs. I'm really waiting for those gloves & socks you sent tho. I realize how hard it is to get rubber gloves so don't worry about that. It isn't raining now so I don't suffer any.

Well, we had a white New Years anyway, not much tho. Have you had any more snow? I heard that it was 18° below in Minn. now so I imagine its been kinda cold.

_____ I'm in the 7th Army so you know about where I am.

Can you send me Dan's address? If I know what outfit his in I might be able to run into him sometime.

I haven't heard from Carl yet. I'm waiting to hear from him. I imagine he's seen plenty.

I sure hope that you & Mr. Brown get a chance to go fishing together. Say, I was going to ask you how you two get along in politics?

There's a couple of cows in one of these barns in this village so I was kinda figuring on going out & milking tonite. I'm hungry for milk. I think the farmer moved out today. I think he milked tonite so I'll have to wait awhile till some more milk has come in he sa. I spose I'll get kicked but its worth the chance.

I have one more letter (of course) to write tonite so I better close now. I'll tell you next time whether I got the milk or not. So long & may God bless you all. Goodnite.

Love,
Verdie

Tell Shep Hi

Printed in the United States
By Bookmasters